Money is tighter than ever these days, but the federal government still has millions of dollars in funding that goes unused because the public is unaware of its availability and how to go about obtaining it. *Free Dollars from the Federal Government* gives you all the facts you need to identify the programs for which you are eligible, together with easy-to-follow, step-by-step instructions on applying for your grant.

Includes a directory of over 1,000 grant programs in areas like:

- Arts and literature
- Business development
- Education
- Health care
- Scientific research

Also features a special section on federal grants administered through state agencies.

ARCO
Free Dollars
from the
Federal Government

Laurie Blum

Prentice Hall
New York • London • Toronto • Sydney • Tokyo • Singapore

First Edition

Prentice Hall General Reference
15 Columbus Circle
New York, NY 10023

An Arco Book

Arco, Prentice Hall and colophons are
registered trademarks of Simon & Schuster, Inc.

Manufactured in the United States of America

1 2 3 4 5 6 7 8 9 10

ISBN 0-13-327396-2

I would like briefly but sincerely to thank Fori Kay, my wonderful editor Barbara Gilson, and of course, Peri Winkler.

Table of Contents

Introduction ix

How to Use This Book x

Glossary of Terms xii

Programs by Field of Interest/Activity 1

    Arts and Literature   Humanities
    Business Development   Medical Research
    Education   Scholarships
    Environment   Science Research
    Health Care   Social Services

Regional Programs 157

    Arts and Literature   Health Care
    Business Development   Medical Research
    Education   Science Research
    Environment   Social Services

Fiscal Sponsorship 221

How to Write a Proposal 223

    Successful Proposal Sample

Alphabetical Index to Grants 227

Regional Index 243

Index of Grants by Field of Interest 248

Bibliography 271

INTRODUCTION

This book represents a continuation and extension of my earlier books on nonprofit funding.

Nonprofit funding is money given to individuals, as well as to nonprofit organizations which have filed for and successfully achieved a 501(c)(3) tax-exempt status with the Internal Revenue Service (i.e., orchestras, hospitals, museums, medical research societies, social service agencies), by foundations (such as Rockefeller), corporations, government agencies, and individual donors.

In the past I have concentrated primarily on private sources of funding (i.e., foundations, corporations and individuals). This book is a much-needed addition to my other free money books as it is a directory to government sources of funds available to individuals.

Although philanthropy of all kinds has existed since colonial times, broad-based government funding flowered during the 1960's and 1970's, fueled by the social consciousness and economic surplus of both the Kennedy and Johnson administrations. During these years it was assumed that "responsibility-taking" government funding could provide for basic societal needs (feeding the hungry, building low-income housing, underwriting the arts), and a myriad of programs were set up for both the individual and nonprofit organizations.

Under President Reagan, this direction was dramatically reversed through enactment of the 1981 Budget Reconciliation Act. In one fell swoop, this piece of legislation severely cut the overall amount of federal monies available and effectively killed the broad spectrum of federal funding programs established by the two previous administrations.

Fortunately, in 1982 and 1983, the consensus of support for this funding shift crumbled, and the public clamored for the reinstatement of a broad base of socially responsive federal funding programs. Over the last ten years, the growth in federal funds available through an ever-increasing number of programs is witness to our government's response to this expressed need of its voting constituencies. Though our economy is in a dangerous inflationary state, our stock market unstable, and the reality of a recession here for the present, billions of dollars are currently available for individuals from agencies at the various levels of government: federal, state, county, and city.

According to the Catalog of Federal Domestic Assistance, over $735 million and nearly 1,200 federal assistance programs (administered by 52 federal agencies) were available in 1990. Approximately 71% of these monies and programs offer eligibility to individuals and nonprofits through direct payments (including entitlements such as veterans benefits, social security, etc.), direct loans, project grants, and "other." Although these figures do not directly reflect the exact number of grant dollars and programs available specifically to nonprofits and individuals, they are an indication of the millions of dollars provided through the thousands of funding programs existing at the federal level.

The level of support available for specific programs in any year varies with the national, international, and local political climate. Factors that influence appropriations at any level of government include the state of the economy, the political party in office, the popularity with both the media and the public of a specific cause (i.e., the environment), the strength of competing demands (such as other more pressing social issues; i.e., homelessness, AIDS funding), and demographics. The primary advantage of government support is that government grants and contracts are frequently larger than those awarded by private foundations or corporations; in fact, in many instances a government grant or contract alone is large enough to finance an entire project.

By far the largest category of individual grants is for scholarships, then fellowships, and finally grants for independent projects or research and for work related to doctoral dissertations. However, do not despair. You as an individual can get a grant if you have a project or idea that will contribute demonstrably to some recognized social or artistic purpose—provided you are able to present that idea or project effectively to an appropriate funder. This book will show you how.

HOW TO USE THIS BOOK

Organization of This Book

Substantial funding is available for both individuals and nonprofit organizations from agencies at the various levels of government: the federal government, state governments, counties, and cities.

Because the nature of many of the government publications and other reference guides makes accessing this information nearly impossible, I have written this book as an easy-to-use directory, listing over 1,000 grant programs in eleven general areas. Available grants are organized by the field of interest or professional activity to which they belong: arts and literature; business development; education; the environment; health care; the humanities; medical research; scholarships; scientific research; and social services.

Within each field of interest are various subcategories. To illustrate, under "Arts and Literature" are listed such subcategories as design, film, and video; under "Business Development"—health care, minority development, science, medicine; under "Education"— adult, arts, literature, bilingual; under "Environment"—agriculture, business development; under "Health Care"—AIDS, children, the disabled; under "Humanities"—education, international understanding, libraries, museums; under "Medical Research"—business development, children, the environment; under "Scholarships"—arts and literature, health professions, humanities; under "Science Research"—business development, energy, environment; and, under "Social Services"—the aged, business development, children.

Check these ten general grant "subject" areas and related subcategories to see which grants apply to you. Remember, regardless of what type of project or enterprise you want to undertake, there should be a government funding source that's right for you.

The largest part of the book is the section containing the listings of federal government grants. I have included a section on fiscal sponsorship (these grants are marked with asterisks), showing how to associate your project with a nonprofit organization. A number of government funding programs will not fund individuals directly but require the funds to be distributed through nonprofit organizations. I'll explain how you can acquire a nonprofit sponsor, thereby increasing your potential for funding.

I've also included an important section: *How to Write a Proposal*. Unlike private funders, government agencies almost always use a printed application form. Detailed instructions are usually provided and there is little room for free-form creative writing. However, from my own experience writing many successful proposals for government grants, I have found a number of rules that must be adhered to in order to produce a successful proposal. The chapter *How to Write a Proposal* not only outlines what should be involved in a grant proposal, but also includes an example of a successful proposal.

The bibliography lists government source books, private foundation source books, and some books on how to go about seeking government grants which I thought the reader would find helpful.

The Entry

Name of Program: Each entry lists at the top of each grant the name of the grant program. This is very important in any communication you will have with the government agency. Be sure to get the exact name of the program, as government agencies often have many programs.

Amount Awarded: The range of grant monies given appears opposite the program name. The listed dollar amount gives the range of money awarded. Often the range is enormous (e.g., $7,000 to $290,000), because in many cases money is awarded to individuals as well as to nonprofit organizations. If you are applying as an individual and are a first–time grant seeker, keep your grant request modest.

Granting Agency name, address, phone number: Underneath the name of the grant program, I have listed the name of the administering government agency as well as the address and phone number. Be sure to call and verify the correct address. By the time this book is published, some of the information contained here will have changed. No reference book can be as up-to-date as the reader (or author) would like. Names, addresses, dollar amounts, telephone numbers, and other data are always in flux. However, most of the information will not have changed.

Field of Interest: I have included this heading to allow the reader to see at a glance if it applies to him.

Average Amount Given: When available, this is a range of the most often awarded monies (i.e., of $6,967,105 given for 196 grants, the highest award was for $250,000, the lowest was for $150, and the average was between $20,000 and $60,000).

Purpose: Describes what the program was instituted to accomplish and what the grant is to be used for. I have tried to make this description as succinct, yet as comprehensive, as possible.

Who May Apply: Describes the types of applications eligible for funding: individuals, nonprofit organizations, or state and local governments. Often funding is given in all three areas. If you are applying as an individual, be sure to check this section carefully to make sure you are eligible.

Requirements: Conditions that the applicant must possess or follow in order to qualify for the grant. These can include geographic restrictions, ethnicity, institutional affiliation, level of educational achievement, or the need to raise an equal amount of money to "match" the government money if you receive the grant from nongovernment sources.

Contact: Whom you should address your application to. Many times there is no specific person to write c/o; if there is, be sure to call and verify that the person is still with the agency.

Application Information: Will often state that an application form is required. If this is so, under no circumstances will an application be considered unless it is properly filled out on the required form.

Initial Approach: A vital step in the success of your application. More often than not it is listed as letter or phone. Write or call the federal agencies and/or programs that offer grants in your field of interest to get a copy of their guidelines and a grant application. In cases where the contact's name is not listed, begin your letter "To Whom It May Concern." If you call, just request the guidelines; do not cross-examine the person who answers the phone!

GLOSSARY

Conferences and seminars: A grant to cover the expenses of hosting or holding a conference.

Consulting services: Professional staff support provided to a nonprofit to consult on a project of mutual interest or to evaluate services (not a cash grant).

Continuing support: A grant that is renewed on a regular basis or extended over several years' time.

Emergency funds: A one-time grant to cover immediate short-term funding needs.

Equipment: A grant to purchase equipment, furnishings, or other materials.

Exchange programs: Usually refers to funds for educational exchange programs for foreign students.

Fellowships: Funds awarded to educational institutions to support fellowship programs which are then paid directly to individuals (generally for postgraduate academic work).

Fiscal Adoption: Occurs when an individual aligns with a nonprofit sponsor whose mission is similar to that for which the individual is seeking grant monies. Such an adoption allows the individual to apply through a sponsor to programs or agencies that will only fund nonprofit organizations with tax-exempt status.

Fiscal sponsorship: When a nonprofit organization "adopts" an individual grant seeker, allowing him or her to apply through the organization for a grant—the stated goals and purposes of which are in keeping with the mission of the nonprofit sponsor.

Foundation: A privately endowed, nonprofit institution established to award monies to individual and organizational grant seekers within the foundation's field of interest; e.g., arts, social services, education, etc.

General purposes: A grant made to further the general purpose of work of an organization, rather than for a specific project; also called unrestricted grants or funds.

Grant: A financial award made directly to an individual or non-profit organization; includes aid to the needy. (See also "Fellowships," "Scholarships," and "Student aid.")

Internships: Usually indicates funds awarded to an institution or organization to support an internship program rather than a grant to an individual.

Land acquisition: A grant to purchase real estate property.

Loans: Temporary award of funds which usually must be repaid. (See also "Student loans.")

Matching funds: A grant which is made to match funds provided by another donor.

Nonprofit: An organization with a tax-exempt status from the Internal Revenue Service whose function it is to provide nonprofit services to the general community or to a particular group according to a stated mission or area of interest.

Operating budgets: A grant to cover the day-to-day personnel, administrative, and other expenses for an existing program or organization.

Professorships: Indicates a grant to an educational institution to endow a professorship or chair.

Publications: A grant to fund reports or other publications issued by a nonprofit, usually resulting from research or conferences.

Renovation projects: Grants for renovating, remodeling, or rehabilitating property/buildings.

Research: Refers to funds awarded to institutions to cover costs of investigations and clinical trials. (Research grants for individuals are usually referred to as fellowships.)

Scholarships: Usually indicates a grant to an educational institution or organization to support a scholarship program, mainly for students at the undergraduate level. (See also "Student aid.")

Seed money: A grant to start a new project or organization. Seed grants may cover salaries and other operating expenses of a new project. Also known as "start-up funds."

Special projects: Grants to support specific projects or programs (as opposed to general purpose grants).

Student aid: Assistance awarded directly to individuals in the form of educational grants or scholarships. (See also "Scholarships.")

Student loans: Assistance awarded directly to individuals in the form of educational loans.

Technical assistance: Operational or management assistance given to nonprofit organizations; may include fundraising assistance, budgeting and financial planning, program planning, legal advice, marketing, and other aids to management.

ARTS AND LITERATURE

Dance Project Grants $9,450,000

National Endowment for the Arts
1100 Pennsylvania Ave., NW
Washington, DC 20506
(202) 682-5435

Field of Interest: Arts and Literature – Dance
Average Amount Given: $45,000
Purpose: To support professional choreographers and individuals who present or serve dance.
Who May Apply: Individuals.
Requirements: None.
Contact: Dance Program.
Application Information: Application required.
Initial Approach: Letter or phone.

---

*Dance Project Grants $2,000–$400,000

National Endowment for the Arts
1100 Pennsylvania Ave., NW
Washington, DC 20506
(202) 682-5435

Field of Interest: Arts and Literature – Dance
Average Amount Given: N/A
Purpose: To support professional dance companies or organizations.
Who May Apply: Nonprofit organizations.
Requirements: None.
Contact: Dance Program.
Application Information: Application required.
Initial Approach: Letter or phone.

Design Arts Project Grants $4,150,000

National Endowment for the Arts
1100 Pennsylvania Ave., NW
Washington, DC 20506
(202) 682-5437

Field of Interest: Arts and Literature – Design
Average Amount Given: $15,000
Purpose: To promote excellence in architecture, landscape architecture, urban design, historic preservation, planning, interior design, graphic design, industrial design and fashion design.
Who May Apply: Individuals.
Requirements: None.
Contact: Director, Design Arts Program.
Application Information: Application required.
Initial Approach: Letter or phone.

---

*Design Arts Project Grants $4,150,000

National Endowment for the Arts
1100 Pennsylvania Ave., NW
Washington, DC 20506
(202) 682-5437

Field of Interest: Arts and Literature – Design
Average Amount Given: $50,000
Purpose: To award excellence in architecture, landscape architecture, urban design, historic preservation, planning, interior design, graphic design, industrial design and fashion design.
Who May Apply: Nonprofit organizations.
Requirements: None.
Contact: Director, Design Arts Program.
Application Information: Application required.
Initial Approach: Letter or phone.

---

*Indicates grants for which fiscal sponsorship is required.

***Film, Radio and Television
Project Grants** $3,000–$500,000

National Endowment for the Arts
1100 Pennsylvania Ave., NW
Washington, DC 20506
(202) 682-5452

Field of Interest: Arts and Literature – Film and Video
Average Amount Given: N/A
Purpose: To fund, exhibit, and disseminate media arts projects.
Who May Apply: Nonprofit organizations.
Requirements: 50% matching funding required.
Contact: Director.
Application Information: Application required.
Initial Approach: Letter or phone.

**Film, Radio and Television
Project Grants** $4,500–$25,000

National Endowment for the Arts
1100 Pennsylvania Ave., NW
Washington, DC 20506
(202) 682-5452

Field of Interest: Arts and Literature – Film and Video
Average Amount Given: N/A
Purpose: To support high-quality individual film, television, video, and radio projects.
Who May Apply: Individuals.
Requirements: None.
Contact: Laura Welsh.
Application Information: Application required.
Initial Approach: Letter or phone.

*Folk Arts Project Grants

National Endowment for the Arts
1100 Pennsylvania Ave., NW
Washington, DC 20506
(202) 682-5449

Field of Interest: Arts and Literature – Folk Arts
Average Amount Given: $50,000
Purpose: To foster and make publicly available traditional American folk arts.
Who May Apply: Nonprofit organizations.
Requirements: At least 50% matching funding required.
Contact: Director.
Application Information: Application required.
Initial Approach: Letter or phone.

Folk Arts Project Grants

National Endowment for the Arts
1100 Pennsylvania Ave., NW
Washington, DC 20506
(202) 682-5449

Field of Interest: Arts and Literature – Folk Arts
Average Amount Given: $5,000
Purpose: To foster and make publicly available traditional American folk arts.
Who May Apply: Individuals.
Requirements: None.
Contact: Director.
Application Information: Application required.
Initial Approach: Letter or phone.

Literature Project Grants $10,000–$20,000

National Endowment for the Arts
1100 Pennsylvania Ave., NW
Washington, DC 20506
(202) 682-5451

Field of Interest: Arts and Literature – Literature
Average Amount Given: N/A
Purpose: To aid creative writers of fiction and non-fiction, poets, and translators.
Who May Apply: Individuals.
Requirements: None.
Contact: Director, Literature Program.
Application Information: Application required.
Initial Approach: Letter or phone.

*Literature Project Grants $1,000–$175,000

National Endowment for the Arts
1100 Pennsylvania Ave., NW
Washington, DC 20506
(202) 682-5451

Field of Interest: Arts and Literature – Literature
Average Amount Given: N/A
Purpose: For residencies, reading series, and support for non-commercial literary magazines and small presses, literary service organizations, and literary centers.
Who May Apply: Nonprofit organizations.
Requirements: None.
Contact: Director, Literature Program.
Application Information: Application required.
Initial Approach: Letter or phone.

*Expansion Arts Project Grants $5,000–$50,000

National Endowment for the Arts
1100 Pennsylvania Ave., NW
Washington, DC 20506
(202) 682-5443

Field of Interest: Arts and Literature – Minority Development
Average Amount Given: N/A
Purpose: To support minority, inner-city, rural, or tribal arts.
Who May Apply: Nonprofit organizations.
Requirements: 50% matching funding required.
Contact: E'Vonne C. Rorie.
Application Information: Application required.
Initial Approach: Letter or phone.

Music Project Grants $2,000–$35,000

National Endowment for the Arts
1100 Pennsylvania Ave., NW
Washington, DC 20506
(202) 682-5445

Field of Interest: Arts and Literature – Music
Average Amount Given: N/A
Purpose: To assist talented individuals in the field of music.
Who May Apply: Individuals.
Requirements: None.
Contact: Director.
Application Information: Application required.
Initial Approach: Letter or phone.

*Music Project Grants $3,000–$290,000

National Endowment for the Arts
1100 Pennsylvania Ave., NW
Washington, DC 20506
(202) 682-5445

Field of Interest: Arts and Literature – Music
Average Amount Given: N/A
Purpose: To support a wide range of musical organizations, including performing groups, support organizations, festival organizations and others.
Who May Apply: Nonprofit organizations.
Requirements: 50% matching funding required.
Contact: Director.
Application Information: Application required.
Initial Approach: Letter or phone.

**Opera and Musical Theater
Project Grants** $5,000–$300,000

National Endowment for the Arts
1100 Pennsylvania Ave., NW
Washington, DC 20506
(202) 682-5447

Field of Interest: Arts and Literature – Opera
Average Amount Given: N/A
Purpose: To support excellence in the performance and creation of opera and musical theater.
Who May Apply: Individuals.
Requirements: At least 50% matching funding required.
Contact: Director.
Application Information: Application required.
Initial Approach: Letter or phone.

***Opera and Musical Theater
Project Grants** $5,000–$300,000

National Endowment for the Arts
1100 Pennsylvania Ave., NW
Washington, DC 20506
(202) 682-5447

Field of Interest: Arts and Literature – Opera
Average Amount Given: N/A
Purpose: To support excellence in the creation and performance of opera and musical theater.
Who May Apply: Professional nonprofit organizations.
Requirements: At least 50% matching funding required.
Contact: Director.
Application Information: Application required.
Initial Approach: Letter or phone.

Theater Project Grants $5,000–$37,000

National Endowment for the Arts
1100 Pennsylvania Ave., NW
Washington, DC 20506
(202) 682-5425

Field of Interest: Arts and Literature – Theater
Average Amount Given: N/A
Purpose: To support theater artists and professional theater presenters.
Who May Apply: Individuals.
Requirements: None.
Contact: Director.
Application Information: Application required.
Initial Approach: Letter or phone.

*Theater Project Grants $5,000–$300,000

National Endowment for the Arts
1100 Pennsylvania Ave., NW
Washington, DC 20506
(202) 682-5451

Field of Interest: Arts and Literature – Theater
Average Amount Given: N/A
Purpose: To support professional theater companies, theater training institutions, and festivals.
Who May Apply: Nonprofit organizations.
Requirements: 50% matching funding required.
Contact: Director.
Application Information: Application required.
Initial Approach: Letter or phone.

Visual Arts Project Grants $5,000–$15,000

National Endowment for the Arts
1100 Pennsylvania Ave., NW
Washington, DC 20506
(202) 682-5425

Field of Interest: Arts and Literature – Visual Arts
Average Amount Given: N/A
Purpose: To assist sculptors, photographers, crafts artists, print makers, book makers, video artists, performance artists, conceptual artists, and artists working in new genres.
Who May Apply: Individuals.
Requirements: None.
Contact: Director.
Application Information: Application required.
Initial Approach: Letter or phone.

---

*Visual Arts Project Grants $2,000–$75,000

National Endowment for the Arts
1100 Pennsylvania Ave., NW
Washington, DC 20506
(202) 682-5425

Field of Interest: Arts and Literature – Visual Arts
Average Amount Given: N/A
Purpose: To support institutions devoted to the development of the visual arts in America.
Who May Apply: Nonprofit organizations.
Requirements: 50% matching funding required.
Contact: Director.
Application Information: Application required.
Initial Approach: Letter or phone.

---

*Challenge Grants in the Arts $50,000–$100,000

National Endowment for the Arts
1100 Pennsylvania Ave., NW
Washington, DC 20506
(202) 682-5436

Field of Interest: Arts and Literature – General
Average Amount Given: N/A
Purpose: To support, on a one-time basis, projects designed to have lasting impact and enhance U.S. excellence in the arts.
Who May Apply: Nonprofit organizations.
Requirements: 50% matching funding required.
Contact: Director.
Application Information: Application required.
Initial Approach: Letter or phone.

*Inter-Arts Project Grants   **$5,000–$50,000**

National Endowment for the Arts
1100 Pennsylvania Ave., NW
Washington, DC 20506
(202) 682-5444

Field of Interest: Arts and Literature – General
Average Amount Given: $15,000
Purpose: To support arts projects which have potential national or regional impact.
Who May Apply: Nonprofit organizations.
Requirements: 50% matching funding required.
Contact: Director.
Application Information: Application required.
Initial Approach: Letter or phone.

BUSINESS DEVELOPMENT

Small Business Innovation Research $40,000–$294,000

National Institute of Mental Health
Parklawn Bldg., 5600 Fishers Lane
Rockville, MD 20857
(301) 443-3107

Field of Interest: Business Development – Health Care
Average Amount Given: $48,600
Purpose: To use small businesses to meet alcohol, drug, mental-health research, and developmental needs.
Who May Apply: Small businesses.
Requirements: None.
Contact: James Moynihan.
Application Information: Application required.
Initial Approach: Letter or phone.

*Appalachian Community Development Project Grants $18,000–$750,000

Appalachian Regional Commission
1666 Connecticut Ave., NW
Washington, DC 20235
(202) 673-7874

Field of Interest: Business Development – Minority and Disadvantaged
Average Amount Given: $180,000
Purpose: To create jobs and private sector involvement in the needs of Appalachia, including water and sewer systems and developing industrial sites.
Who May Apply: Private nonprofit entities.
Requirements: None.
Contact: Executive Director.
Application Information: Application required.
Initial Approach: Letter or phone.

Appalachian Housing Project Development Grants $200,000–$750,00

Appalachian Regional Commission
1666 Connecticut Ave., NW
Washington, DC 20235
(202) 673-7874

Field of Interest: Business Development – Minority and Disadvantaged
Average Amount Given: $60,000
Purpose: To stimulate jobs and private sector investment through low and moderate housing construction and rehabilitation.
Who May Apply: Private nonprofit and some profit entities.
Requirements: Variable.
Contact: Executive Director.
Application Information: Application required.
Initial Approach: Letter or phone.

Appalachian Local Access Roads $5,600–$8,200,000

Appalachian Regional Commission
1666 Connecticut Ave., NW
Washington, DC 20235
(202) 673-7874

Field of Interest: Business Development – Minority and Disadvantaged
Average Amount Given: $488,000
Purpose: To improve industrial and residential access in Appalachia.
Who May Apply: Private groups within Appalachia.
Requirements: 20% of matching costs must be provided by the state.
Contact: Executive Director.
Application Information: Application required.
Initial Approach: Letter or phone.

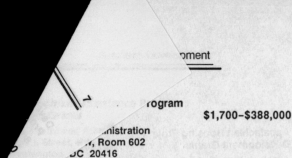

...rogram   **$1,700–$388,000**

...nistration
...v, Room 602
...DC 20416
...6407

... of Interest: Business Development – Minority and Disadvan-
..aged
Average Amount Given: $78,620
Purpose: To provide management and technical assistance to busi-
nesses which are economically or socially disadvantaged or located in
areas with high concentrations of unemployment.
Who May Apply: Individuals, public or private organizations, and
educational institutions.
Requirements: None.
Contact: Associate Administrator.
Application Information: Application required.
Initial Approach: Letter or phone.

Human Resource Programs   **$1,000,000**

Urban Mass Transportation Administration, Department of
Transportation
400 Seventh Street, SW
Washington, DC 20590
(202) 366-4018

Field of Interest: Business Development – Minority and Disadvan-
taged
Average Amount Given: N/A
Purpose: To develop jobs, especially for minorities and females, in
public transportation.
Who May Apply: Nonprofit and educational entities and some for
profit entities.
Requirements: Variable.
Contact: Director of Civil Rights.
Application Information: Application required.
Initial Approach: Letter or phone.

**Minority Business
Development Centers**   **$165,000–$622,000**

Office of Program Development, Room 5096
Department of Commerce
14th and Constitution Ave., NW
Washington, DC 20230

Field of Interest: Business Development – Minority and Disadvan-
taged
Average Amount Given: $212,000
Purpose: To develop services to minority firms and individuals.
Who May Apply: Individuals and corporations.
Requirements: None.
Contact: Georgina Sanchez.
Application Information: Application required.
Initial Approach: Letter.

**Research and Evaluation
Project Grant**   **$11,300–$200,000**

Department of Commerce
14th and Constitution Ave., NW
Washington, DC 20230
(202) 377-4085

Field of Interest: Business Development – Minority and Disadvan-
taged
Average Amount Given: $72,000
Purpose: To determine the causes of unemployment and underde-
velopment in the U.S. and to develop solutions to these conditions.
Who May Apply: Individuals, small businesses and corporations, and
public and private organizations.
Requirements: Pre-application coordination necessary.
Contact: David H. Geddes.
Application Information: Application required.
Initial Approach: Letter or phone.

Small Business Innovation Research Project Grant $43,600–$230,000

Office of Grants and Program Systems
Department of Agriculture
14th and Independence Ave., SW
Washington, DC 20250
(202) 447-7002

Field of Interest: Business Development – Minority and Disadvantaged
Average Amount Given: $100,000
Purpose: To stimulate and to enourage minority participation in technological innovation.
Who May Apply: Small businesses.
Requirements: The business cannot be dominant in the field of research.
Contact: Coordinator, Competitive Research Grants.
Application Information: Application required.
Initial Approach: Letter or phone.

Women's Business Ownership Assistance Project Grants $185,000–$1,000,000

Small Business Administration
1441 L Street, NW
Room 602
Washington, DC 20416
(202) 653-8000

Field of Interest: Business Development – Minority and Disadvantaged
Average Amount Given: $408,407
Purpose: To promote the legitimate interests of small businesses owned by women and to remove the discriminatory barriers faced by women in accessing capital and other issues of production.
Who May Apply: Qualified profit or nonprofit entities.
Requirements: None.
Contact: Bill Truitt.
Application Information: Application required.
Initial Approach: Letter or phone.

Aging Research Small Business Innovation Research Grants $50,000–$500,000

National Institutes of Health, PHS
Bethesda, MD 20892
(301) 496-1472

Field of Interest: Business Development – Science and Medicine
Average Amount Given: N/A
Purpose: To establish the technical merit and feasibility of a proposed research method that may lead to a commercial product or process.
Who May Apply: Educational or research institutions and the individuals associated with them, as well as small businesses.
Requirements: None.
Contact: Carol Tippery.
Application Information: Application required.
Initial Approach: Letter or phone.

Aging Research Small Instrumentation Grants $6,000–$50,000

National Institutes of Health, PHS
Bethesda, MD 20892
(301) 496-1472

Field of Interest: Business Development – Science and Medicine
Average Amount Given: N/A
Purpose: To develop small instrumentation to support research in this area.
Who May Apply: Educational or research institutions and the individuals associated with them, as well as small businesses.
Requirements: None.
Contact: Carol Tippery.
Application Information: Application required.
Initial Approach: Letter or phone.

Allergy, Immunology, and Transplantation Research Small Business Innovation Research Grants $50,000–$500,000

National Institutes of Health, PHS
Bethesda, MD 20892
(301) 496-7075

Field of Interest: Medical Research – Business Development
Average Amount Given: N/A
Purpose: To establish the technical merit and feasibility of a proposed research method that may lead to a commercial product or process.
Who May Apply: Educational or research institutions and the individuals associated with them, as well as small businesses.
Requirements: None.
Contact: Gary Thompson.
Application Information: Application required.
Initial Approach: Letter or phone.

Allergy, Immunology, and Transplantation Research Small Instrumentation Grants $6,000–$50,000

National Institutes of Health, PHS
Bethesda, MD 20892
(301) 496-7075

Field of Interest: Business Development – Science and Medicine
Average Amount Given: N/A
Purpose: To develop small instrumentation to support research in this area.
Who May Apply: Educational or research institutions and the individuals associated with them, as well as small businesses.
Requirements: None.
Contact: Gary Thompson.
Application Information: Application required.
Initial Approach: Letter or phone.

Anterior Segment Diseases Research Small Business Innovation Research Grants $50,000–$500,000

National Institutes of Health, PHS
Bethesda, MD 20892
(301) 496-5884

Field of Interest: Business Development – Science and Medicine
Average Amount Given: N/A
Purpose: To establish the technical merit and feasibility of a proposed research method that may lead to a commercial product or process.
Who May Apply: Educational or research institutions and the individuals associated with them, as well as small businesses.
Requirements: None.
Contact: Carolyn Grimes.
Application Information: Application required.
Initial Approach: Letter or phone.

Anterior Segment Diseases Research Small Instrumentation Grants $6,000–$50,000

National Institutes of Health, PHS
Bethesda, MD 20892
(301) 496-5884

Field of Interest: Business Development – Science and Medicine
Average Amount Given: N/A
Purpose: To develop small instrumentation to support research in this area.
Who May Apply: Educational or research institutions and the individuals associated with them, as well as small businesses.
Requirements: None.
Contact: Carolyn Grimes.
Application Information: Application required.
Initial Approach: Letter or phone.

**Arthritis, Musculoskeletal, and Skin Diseases
Research Small Business Innovation
Research Grants**   **$50,000–$500,000**

National Institutes of Health, PHS
Bethesda, MD 20892
(301) 496-7495

Field of Interest: Business Development – Science and Medicine
Average Amount Given: N/A
Purpose: To establish the technical merit and feasibility of a proposed research method that may lead to a commercial product or process.
Who May Apply: Educational or research institutions and the individuals associated with them, as well as small businesses.
Requirements: None.
Contact: Diane Watson.
Application Information: Application required.
Initial Approach: Letter or phone.

**Arthritis, Musculoskeletal, and Skin Diseases
Research Small Instrumentation
Grants**   **$6,000–$50,000**

National Institutes of Health, PHS
Bethesda, MD 20892
(301) 496-7495

Field of Interest: Business Development – Science and Medicine
Average Amount Given: N/A
Purpose: To develop small instrumentation to support research in this area.
Who May Apply: Educational or research institutions and the individuals associated with them, as well as small businesses.
Requirements: None.
Contact: Diane Watson.
Application Information: Application required.
Initial Approach: Letter or phone.

**Biophysics Research Small Business Innovation
Research Grant**   **$50,000–$500,000**

National Institutes of Health, PHS
Bethesda, MD 20892
(301) 496-7463

Field of Interest: Business Development – Science and Medicine
Average Amount Given: N/A
Purpose: To apply physics and engineering principles to the study of biomedical problems and to develop new technologies to deal with these problems.
Who May Apply: Individuals associated with research or educational institutions or small businesses.
Requirements: None.
Contact: Dr. Marvin Cassman, Director.
Application Information: Application required.
Initial Approach: Letter or phone.

**Biophysics Small Instrumentation
Grant**   **$6,000–$50,000**

National Institutes of Health, PHS
Bethesda, MD 20892
(301) 496-7463

Field of Interest: Business Development – Science and Medicine
Average Amount Given: N/A
Purpose: To apply physics and engineering principles to the study of biomedical problems and to develop new technologies to deal with these problems.
Who May Apply: Individuals associated with research or educational institutions or small businesses.
Requirements: None.
Contact: Dr. Marvin Cassman, Director.
Application Information: Application required.
Initial Approach: Letter or phone.

Blood Diseases Research – Small Business Innovation Research Grants $50,000–$500,000

National Institutes of Health, PHS
Bethesda, MD 20892
(301) 496-7255

Field of Interest: Business Development – Science and Medicine
Average Amount Given: N/A
Purpose: To establish the technical merit and feasibility of a proposed research method that may lead to a commercial product or process.
Who May Apply: Educational or research institutions and the individuals associated with them, as well as small businesses.
Requirements: None.
Contact: Lois Hinde.
Application Information: Application required.
Initial Approach: Letter or phone.

Blood Diseases Research – Small Instrumentation Grants $6,000–$50,000

National Institutes of Health, PHS
Bethesda, MD 20892
(301) 496-7255

Field of Interest: Business Development – Science and Medicine
Average Amount Given: N/A
Purpose: To develop small instrumentation to support research in this area.
Who May Apply: Educational or research institutions and the individuals associated with them, as well as small businesses.
Requirements: None.
Contact: Lois Hinde.
Application Information: Application required.
Initial Approach: Letter or phone.

Cancer Biology – Small Business Innovation Research Grants   Budgeted at $100,000

National Institutes of Health, PHS
Department of Health and Human Services
Bethesda, MD 20892
(301) 496-7753

Field of Interest: Business Development – Science and Medicine
Average Amount Given: N/A
Purpose: To stimulate technological innovation and to use small businesses to meet research and development needs.
Who May Apply: Small businesses and the individuals associated with them.
Requirements: None.
Contact: Leo Buscher.
Application Information: Application required.
Initial Approach: Letter or phone.

Cancer Biology Research – Small Instrumentation Program $6,000–$50,000

National Institutes of Health, PHS
Department of Health and Human Services
Bethesda, MD 20892
(301) 496-7753

Field of Interest: Business Development – Science and Medicine
Average Amount Given: N/A
Purpose: To develop small instrumentation to support research in this area.
Who May Apply: Small businesses and the individuals associated with them.
Requirements: None.
Contact: Leo Buscher.
Application Information: Application required.
Initial Approach: Letter or phone.

**Cancer Cause and Prevention – Small Business
Innovation Research Grants   Budgeted at $228,000**
National Institutes of Health, PHS
Department of Health and Human Services
Bethesda, MD 20892
(301) 496-7753

Field of Interest: Business Development – Science and Medicine
Average Amount Given: N/A
Purpose: To stimulate technological innovation and to use small
businesses to meet research and development needs.
Who May Apply: Small businesses and the individuals associated
with them.
Requirements: None.
Contact: Leo Buscher.
Application Information: Application required.
Initial Approach: Letter or phone.

**Cancer Centers Support –
Small Instrumentation Program $6,000–$50,000**
National Institutes of Health, PHS
Department of Health and Human Services
Bethesda, MD 20892
(301) 496-7753

Field of Interest: Business Development – Science and Medicine
Average Amount Given: N/A
Purpose: To develop small instrumentation to support research in
this area.
Who May Apply: Small businesses and the individuals associated
with them.
Requirements: None.
Contact: Leo Buscher.
Application Information: Application required.
Initial Approach: Letter or phone.

**Cancer Control –
Methods, Development, and Testing $37,700–$790,000**
National Institutes of Health, PHS
Department of Health and Human Services
Bethesda, MD 20892
(301) 496-7753

Field of Interest: Medical Research – Business Development
Average Amount Given: $244,000
Purpose: To reduce cancer incidence and morbidity through re-
search on interventions and their impact on defined populations.
Who May Apply: Academic institutions, nonprofit or profit entities,
and the individuals associated with them.
Requirements: None.
Contact: Leo Buscher.
Application Information: Application required.
Initial Approach: Letter or phone.

**Cancer Control –
Small Instrumentation Program $6,000–$50,000**
National Institutes of Health, PHS
Department of Health and Human Services
Bethesda, MD 20892
(301) 496-7753

Field of Interest: Business Development – Science and Medicine
Average Amount Given: N/A
Purpose: To develop small instrumentation to support research in
this area.
Who May Apply: Small businesses and the individuals associated
with them.
Requirements: None.
Contact: Leo Buscher.
Application Information: Application required.
Initial Approach: Letter or phone.

Cancer Detection and Diagnosis – Small Business Innovation Research Grants $2,914,000

National Institutes of Health, PHS
Department of Health and Human Services
Bethesda, MD 20892
(301) 496-7753

Field of Interest: Business Development – Science and Medicine
Average Amount Given: N/A
Purpose: To stimulate technological innovation and to use small businesses to meet research and development needs.
Who May Apply: Small businesses and the individuals associated with them.
Requirements: None.
Contact: Leo Buscher.
Application Information: Application required.
Initial Approach: Letter or phone.

Cancer Detection and Diagnosis – Small Instrumentation Program $6,000–$50,000

National Institutes of Health, PHS
Department of Health and Human Services
Bethesda, MD 20892
(301) 496-7753

Field of Interest: Business Development – Science and Medicine
Average Amount Given: N/A
Purpose: To develop small instrumentation to support research in this area.
Who May Apply: Small businesses and the individuals associated with them.
Requirements: None.
Contact: Leo Buscher.
Application Information: Application required.
Initial Approach: Letter or phone.

Cancer Treatment Research – Small Business Innovation Research Grants $5,400,000

National Institutes of Health, PHS
Department of Health and Human Services
Bethesda, MD 20892
(301) 496-7753

Field of Interest: Business Development – Science and Medicine
Average Amount Given: N/A
Purpose: To stimulate technological innovation and to use small businesses to meet research and development needs.
Who May Apply: Small businesses and the individuals associated with them.
Requirements: None.
Contact: Leo Buscher.
Application Information: Application required.
Initial Approach: Letter or phone.

Cancer Treatment Research – Small Instrumentation Program $6,000–$50,000

National Institutes of Health, PHS
Department of Health and Human Services
Bethesda, MD 20892
(301) 496-7753

Field of Interest: Business Development – Science and Medicine
Average Amount Given: N/A
Purpose: To develop small instrumentation to support research in this area.
Who May Apply: Small businesses and the individuals associated with them.
Requirements: None.
Contact: Leo Buscher.
Application Information: Application required.
Initial Approach: Letter or phone.

Cellular and Molecular Basis for Disease Research
Small Business Innovation
Research Grants   **$50,000–$500,000**
National Institutes of Health, PHS
Bethesda, MD 20892
(301) 496-7746

Field of Interest: Business Development – Science and Medicine
Average Amount Given: N/A
Purpose: To establish the technical merit and feasibility of a proposed research method that may lead to a commercial product or process.
Who May Apply: Educational or research institutions and the individuals associated with them, as well as small businesses.
Requirements: None.
Contact: Evelin Carlin.
Application Information: Application required.
Initial Approach: Letter or phone.

Cellular and Molecular Basis for Disease Research
Small Instrumentation Grants   **$6,000–$50,000**
National Institutes of Health, PHS
Bethesda, MD 20892
(301) 496-7746

Field of Interest: Business Development – Science and Medicine
Medical Research – Business Development
Average Amount Given: N/A
Purpose: To develop small instrumentation to support research in this area.
Who May Apply: Educational or research institutions and the individuals associated with them, as well as small businesses.
Requirements: None.
Contact: Evelin Carlin.
Application Information: Application required.
Initial Approach: Letter or phone.

Diabetes, Endocrinology, and Metabolism Research
Small Business Innovation
Research Grants   **$50,000–$500,000**
National Institutes of Health, PHS
Bethesda, MD 20892
(301) 496-7793

Field of Interest: Business Development – Science and Medicine
Average Amount Given: N/A
Purpose: To establish the technical merit and feasibility of a proposed research method that may lead to a commercial product or process.
Who May Apply: Educational or research institutions and the individuals associated with them, as well as small businesses.
Requirements: None.
Contact: John Garthune.
Application Information: Application required.
Initial Approach: Letter or phone.

Diabetes, Endocrinology, and Metabolism Research
Small Instrumentation Grants   **$6,000–$50,000**
National Institutes of Health, PHS
Bethesda, MD 20892
(301) 496-7793

Field of Interest: Business Development – Science and Medicine
Average Amount Given: N/A
Purpose: To develop small instrumentation to support research in this area.
Who May Apply: Educational or research institutions and the individuals associated with them, as well as small businesses.
Requirements: None.
Contact: John Garthune.
Application Information: Application required.
Initial Approach: Letter or phone.

Digestive Diseases and Nutrition Research Small Business Innovation
Research Grants $50,000–$500,000

National Institutes of Health, PHS
Bethesda, MD 20892
(301) 496-7793

Field of Interest: Business Development – Science and Medicine
Medical Research – Business Development
Average Amount Given: N/A
Purpose: To establish the technical merit and feasibility of a proposed research method that may lead to a commercial product or process.
Who May Apply: Educational or research institutions and the individuals associated with them, as well as small businesses.
Requirements: None.
Contact: John Garthune.
Application Information: Application required.
Initial Approach: Letter or phone.

Digestive Diseases and Nutrition Research
Small Instrumentation Grants $6,000–$50,000

National Institutes of Health, PHS
Bethesda, MD 20892
(301) 496-7793

Field of Interest: Business Development – Science and Medicine
Average Amount Given: N/A
Purpose: To develop small instrumentation to support research in this area.
Who May Apply: Educational or research institutions and the individuals associated with them, as well as small businesses.
Requirements: None.
Contact: John Garthune.
Application Information: Application required.
Initial Approach: Letter or phone.

Genetics Research Small Business Innovation
Research Grants $50,000–$500,000

National Institutes of Health, PHS
Bethesda, MD 20892
(301) 496-7746

Field of Interest: Business Development – Science and Medicine
Average Amount Given: N/A
Purpose: To establish the technical merit and feasibility of a proposed research method that may lead to a commercial product or process.
Who May Apply: Educational or research institutions and the individuals associated with them, as well as small businesses.
Requirements: None.
Contact: Evelin Carlin.
Application Information: Application required.
Initial Approach: Letter or phone.

Genetics Research Small Instrumentation
Grants $6,000–$50,000

National Institutes of Health, PHS
Bethesda, MD 20892
(301) 496-7746

Field of Interest: Business Development – Science and Medicine
Average Amount Given: N/A
Purpose: To develop small instrumentation to support research in this area.
Who May Apply: Educational or research institutions and the individuals associated with them, as well as small businesses.
Requirements: None.
Contact: Evelin Carlin.
Application Information: Application required.
Initial Approach: Letter or phone.

Heart and Vascular Diseases Research
Small Business Innovation
Research Grants $50,000–$500,000

National Institutes of Health, PHS
Bethesda, MD 20892
(301) 496-7255

Field of Interest: Business Development – Science and Medicine
Average Amount Given: N/A
Purpose: To establish the technical merit and feasibility of a proposed research method that may lead to a commercial product or process.
Who May Apply: Educational or research institutions and the individuals associated with them, as well as small businesses.
Requirements: None.
Contact: Lois Hinde.
Application Information: Application required.
Initial Approach: Letter or phone.

Heart and Vascular Diseases Research Small
Instrumentation Grants $6,000–$50,000

National Institutes of Health, PHS
Bethesda, MD 20892
(301) 496-7255

Field of Interest: Business Development – Science and Medicine
Average Amount Given: N/A
Purpose: To develop small instrumentation to support research in this area.
Who May Apply: Educational or research institutions and the individuals associated with them, as well as small businesses.
Requirements: None.
Contact: Lois Hinde.
Application Information: Application required.
Initial Approach: Letter or phone.

Kidney Diseases, Urology, and Hematology Research
Small Business Innovation
Research Grants $50,000–$500,000

National Institutes of Health, PHS
Bethesda, MD 20892
(301) 496-7793

Field of Interest: Business Development – Science and Medicine
Average Amount Given: N/A
Purpose: To establish the technical merit and feasibility of a proposed research method that may lead to a commercial product or process.
Who May Apply: Educational or research institutions and the individuals associated with them, as well as small businesses.
Requirements: None.
Contact: John Garthune.
Application Information: Application required.
Initial Approach: Letter or phone.

Kidney Diseases, Urology, and Hematology Research
Small Instrumentation Grants $6,000–$50,000

National Institutes of Health, PHS
Bethesda, MD 20892
(301) 496-7793

Field of Interest: Business Development – Science and Medicine
Average Amount Given: N/A
Purpose: To develop small instrumentation to support research in this area.
Who May Apply: Educational or research institutions and the individuals associated with them, as well as small businesses.
Requirements: None.
Contact: John Garthune.
Application Information: Application required.
Initial Approach: Letter or phone.

**Lung Diseases Research Small Business Innovation
Research Grants $50,000–$500,000**
National Institutes of Health, PHS
Bethesda, MD 20892
(301) 496-7255

Field of Interest: Business Development – Science and Medicine
Average Amount Given: N/A
Purpose: To establish the technical merit and feasibility of a proposed research method that may lead to a commercial product or process.
Who May Apply: Educational or research institutions and the individuals associated with them, as well as small businesses.
Requirements: None.
Contact: Lois Hinde.
Application Information: Application required.
Initial Approach: Letter or phone.

**Lung Diseases Research Small Instrumentation
Grants $6,000–$50,000**
National Institutes of Health, PHS
Bethesda, MD 20892
(301) 496-7255

Field of Interest: Business Development – Science and Medicine
Average Amount Given: N/A
Purpose: To develop small instrumentation to support research in this area.
Who May Apply: Educational or research institutions and the individuals associated with them, as well as small businesses.
Requirements: None.
Contact: Lois Hinde.
Application Information: Application required.
Initial Approach: Letter or phone.

**Microbiology and Infectious Diseases Research
Small Business Innovation
Research Grants $50,000–$500,000**
National Institutes of Health, PHS
Bethesda, MD 20892
(301) 496-7255

Field of Interest: Business Development – Science and Medicine
Medical Research – Business Development
Average Amount Given: N/A
Purpose: To establish the technical merit and feasibility of a proposed research method that may lead to a commercial product or process.
Who May Apply: Educational or research institutions and the individuals associated with them, as well as small businesses.
Requirements: None.
Contact: Gary Thompson.
Application Information: Application required.
Initial Approach: Letter or phone.

**Microbiology and Infectious Diseases Research
Small Instrumentation Grants $6,000–$50,000**
National Institutes of Health, PHS
Bethesda, MD 20892
(301) 496-7075

Field of Interest: Business Development – Science and Medicine
Average Amount Given: N/A
Purpose: To develop small instrumentation to support research in this area.
Who May Apply: Educational or research institutions and the individuals associated with them, as well as small businesses.
Requirements: None.
Contact: Gary Thompson.
Application Information: Application required.
Initial Approach: Letter or phone.

**Neurological Disorders Biological Research
Small Business Innovation
Research Grants**   **$50,000–$500,000**

National Institutes of Health, PHS
Bethesda, MD 20892
(301) 496-9231

Field of Interest: Business Development – Science and Medicine
Average Amount Given: N/A
Purpose: To establish the technical merit and feasibility of a proposed research method that may lead to a commercial product or process.
Who May Apply: Educational or research institutions and the individuals associated with them, as well as small businesses.
Requirements: None.
Contact: Mary Whitehead.
Application Information: Application required.
Initial Approach: Letter or phone.

**Neurological Disorders Biological Research
Small Instrumentation Grants**   **$6,000–$50,000**

National Institutes of Health, PHS
Bethesda, MD 20892
(301) 496-9231

Field of Interest: Business Development – Science and Medicine
Average Amount Given: N/A
Purpose: To develop small instrumentation to support research in this area.
Who May Apply: Educational or research institutions and the individuals associated with them, as well as small businesses.
Requirements: None.
Contact: Mary Whitehead.
Application Information: Application required.
Initial Approach: Letter or phone.

**Neurological Disorders Clinical Research
Small Business Innovation
Research Grants**   **$50,000–$500,000**

National Institutes of Health, PHS
Bethesda, MD 20892
(301) 496-9231

Field of Interest: Business Development – Science and Medicine
Average Amount Given: N/A
Purpose: To establish the technical merit and feasibility of a proposed research method that may lead to a commercial product or process.
Who May Apply: Educational or research institutions and the individuals associated with them, as well as small businesses.
Requirements: None.
Contact: Mary Whitehead.
Application Information: Application required.
Initial Approach: Letter or phone.

**Neurological Disorders Clinical Research Small
Instrumentation Grants**   **$6,000–$50,000**

National Institutes of Health, PHS
Bethesda, MD 20892
(301) 496-9231

Field of Interest: Business Development – Science and Medicine
Average Amount Given: N/A
Purpose: To develop small instrumentation to support research in this area.
Who May Apply: Educational or research institutions and the individuals associated with them, as well as small businesses.
Requirements: None.
Contact: Mary Whitehead.
Application Information: Application required.
Initial Approach: Letter or phone.

**Pharmacological Sciences Research
Small Business Innovation
Research Grants**   **$50,000–$500,000**

National Institutes of Health, PHS
Bethesda, MD 20892
(301) 496-7746

Field of Interest: Business Development – Science and Medicine
Average Amount Given: N/A
Purpose: To establish the technical merit and feasibility of a proposed research method that may lead to a commercial product or process.
Who May Apply: Educational or research institutions and the individuals associated with them, as well as small businesses.
Requirements: None.
Contact: Evelin Carlin.
Application Information: Application required.
Initial Approach: Letter or phone.

**Pharmacological Sciences Research Small
Instrumentation Grants**   **$6,000–$50,000**

National Institutes of Health, PHS
Bethesda, MD 20892
(301) 496-7746

Field of Interest: Business Development – Science and Medicine
Average Amount Given: N/A
Purpose: To develop small instrumentation to support research in this area.
Who May Apply: Educational or research institutions and the individuals associated with them, as well as small businesses.
Requirements: None.
Contact: Evelin Carlin.
Application Information: Application required.
Initial Approach: Letter or phone.

**Physiological Sciences Small Business Innovation
Research Grant**   **$50,000 –$500,000**

National Institutes of Health, PHS
Bethesda, MD 20892
(301) 496-7463

Field of Interest: Business Development – Science and Medicine
Average Amount Given: N/A
Purpose: To apply physics and engineering principles to the study of biomedical problems and to develop new technologies to deal with these problems.
Who May Apply: Individuals associated with research or educational institutions or small businesses.
Requirements: None.
Contact: Dr. Marvin Cassman, Director.
Application Information: Application required.
Initial Approach: Letter or phone.

**Physiological Sciences
Small Instrumentation Grant**   **$6,000–$50,000**

National Institutes of Health, PHS
Bethesda, MD 20892
(301) 496-7463

Field of Interest: Business Development – Science and Medicine
Average Amount Given: N/A
Purpose: To apply physics and engineering principles to the study of biomedical problems and to develop new technologies to deal with these problems.
Who May Apply: Individuals associated with research or educational institutions or small businesses.
Requirements: None.
Contact: Dr. Marvin Cassman, Director.
Application Information: Application required.
Initial Approach: Letter or phone.

Population Research Small Business Innovation Research Grants $50,000–$500,000

National Institutes of Health, PHS
Bethesda, MD 20892
(301) 496-5001

Field of Interest: Business Development – Science and Medicine
Average Amount Given: N/A
Purpose: To establish the technical merit and feasibility of a proposed research method that may lead to a commercial product or process.
Who May Apply: Educational or research institutions and the individuals associated with them, as well as small businesses.
Requirements: None.
Contact: Donald Clark.
Application Information: Application required.
Initial Approach: Letter or phone.

Population Research Small Instrumentation Grants $6,000–$50,000

National Institutes of Health, PHS
Bethesda, MD 20892
(301) 496-5001

Field of Interest: Business Development – Science and Medicine
Average Amount Given: N/A
Purpose: To develop small instrumentation to support research in this area.
Who May Apply: Educational or research institutions and the individuals associated with them, as well as small businesses.
Requirements: None.
Contact: Donald Clark.
Application Information: Application required.
Initial Approach: Letter or phone.

Research for Mothers and Children Small Business Innovation Research Grants $50,000–$500,000

National Institutes of Health, PHS
Bethesda, MD 20892
(301) 496-5001

Field of Interest: Business Development – Science and Medicine
Average Amount Given: N/A
Purpose: To establish the technical merit and feasibility of a proposed research method that may lead to a commercial product or process.
Who May Apply: Educational or research institutions and the individuals associated with them, as well as small businesses.
Requirements: None.
Contact: Donald Clark.
Application Information: Application required.
Initial Approach: Letter or phone.

Research for Mothers and Children Small Instrumentation Grants $6,000–$50,000

National Institutes of Health, PHS
Bethesda, MD 20892
(301) 496-5001

Field of Interest: Business Development – Science and Medicine
Average Amount Given: N/A
Purpose: To develop small instrumentation to support research in this area.
Who May Apply: Educational or research institutions and the individuals associated with them, as well as small businesses.
Requirements: None.
Contact: Donald Clark.
Application Information: Application required.
Initial Approach: Letter or phone.

Retinal and Choroidal Diseases Research Small Business Innovation
Research Grants $50,000–$500,000

National Institutes of Health, PHS
Bethesda, MD 20892
(301) 496-5884

Field of Interest: Business Development – Science and Medicine
Average Amount Given: N/A
Purpose: To establish the technical merit and feasibility of a proposed research method that may lead to a commercial product or process.
Who May Apply: Educational or research institutions and the individuals associated with them, as well as small businesses.
Requirements: None.
Contact: Carolyn Grimes.
Application Information: Application required.
Initial Approach: Letter or phone.

Retinal and Choroidal Diseases Research Small
Instrumentation Grants $6,000–$50,000

National Institutes of Health, PHS
Bethesda, MD 20892
(301) 496-5884

Field of Interest: Business Development – Science and Medicine
Average Amount Given: N/A
Purpose: To develop small instrumentation to support research in this area.
Who May Apply: Educational or research institutions and the individuals associated with them, as well as small businesses.
Requirements: None.
Contact: Carolyn Grimes.
Application Information: Application required.
Initial Approach: Letter or phone.

Strabismus, Amblyopia, and Visual Processing Research
Small Instrumentation Grants $6,000–$50,000

National Institutes of Health, PHS
Bethesda, MD 20892
(301) 496-5884

Field of Interest: Business Development – Science and Medicine
Average Amount Given: N/A
Purpose: To develop small instrumentation to support research in this area.
Who May Apply: Educational or research institutions and the individuals associated with them, as well as small businesses.
Requirements: None.
Contact: Carolyn Grimes.
Application Information: Application required.
Initial Approach: Letter or phone.

Advanced Technology Program
Project Grants $9,400,000

Advanced Technology Program
National Institute of Standards and Technology
Gaithersburg, MD 20899
(301) 975-4500

Field of Interest: Business Development
Average Amount Given: N/A
Purpose: To assist U.S. business in rapid commercialization of new technologies and discoveries; and to refine manufacturing processes to improve U.S. industry competitiveness.
Who May Apply: U.S. businesses, research and development ventures, and independent research organizations.
Requirements: None.
Contact: George Uriano, Acting Director.
Application Information: Application required.
Initial Approach: Letter or phone.

Capital Construction Fund $295,000

Office of Maritime Labor and Training
Maritime Administration, Department of Transportation
400 Seventh Street, SW
Washington, DC 20590
(202) 366-0364

Field of Interest: Business Development
Average Amount Given: N/A
Purpose: To provide replacement or additional vessels for operation in the Great Lakes, U.S., foreign or non-contiguous domestic trades.
Who May Apply: Individuals owning at least one eligible vessel and having a program for building or reconstructing more.
Requirements: Individuals must be U.S. citizens.
Contact: Associate Administrator for Maritime Aids.
Application Information: Application required.
Initial Approach: Letter or phone.

Construction Reserve Fund $70,000

Maritime Administration
Department of Transportation
400 Seventh Street, SW
Washington, DC 20590
(202) 366-0364

Field of Interest: Business Development
Average Amount Given: N/A
Purpose: To promote the construction and reconstruction or acquisition of merchant vessels.
Who May Apply: Any individual who owns, in whole or in part, a vessel operating in U.S. domestic or foreign commerce or in fisheries.
Requirements: Individual must be a U.S. citizen.
Contact: Associate Administrator for Maritime Aids.
Application Information: Application required.
Initial Approach: Letter or phone.

Development and Promotion of Ports and Intermodal Transportation $800,000

Office of Port and Intermodal Development
Maritime Administration, Department of Transportation
400 Seventh Street, SW
Washington, DC 20590
(202) 366-4357

Field of Interest: Business Development
Average Amount Given: N/A
Purpose: To develop and utilize U.S. port facilities and to provide technical information to government agencies.
Who May Apply: Individual private terminal operators.
Requirements: 50% cost sharing required.
Contact: John Pisani.
Application Information: Application required.
Initial Approach: Letter or phone.

Labor and Management Cooperation Project Grants $37,000–$100,000

Grant Programs
Labor and Management Conciliation Service
2100 K Street, NW
Washington, DC 20427

Field of Interest: Business Development
Average Amount Given: Variable.
Purpose: To establish joint labor-management committees at the worksite and industry-wide to improve these relationships, economic development, and productivity.
Who May Apply: Private, nonprofit labor-management committees and private companies applying jointly with such nonprofits.
Requirements: 10% matching cash required.
Contact: Director.
Application Information: Application required.
Initial Approach: Letter.

Maritime Operations Differential
Subsidies $7,500–$10,000 per day

Maritime Administration
Department of Transportation
400 Seventh Street, SW
Washington, DC 20590
(202) 366-0364

Field of Interest: Business Development
Average Amount Given: $8,500 per day
Purpose: To subsidize vessels to be used in foreign service and for-
eign commerce for the U.S.
Who May Apply: Qualified individuals.
Requirements: Individuals must be U.S. citizens.
Contact: Associate Administrator for Maritime Aids.
Application Information: Application required.
Initial Approach: Letter or phone.

Service Corps of Retired Executives (SCORE) Project
Grants   Budgeted at $1,400,000

Small Business Administration
1441 L Street, NW
Room 602
Washington, DC 20416
(202) 653-2369

Field of Interest: Business Development
Average Amount Given: N/A
Purpose: To utilize the management experience of retired and active
business executives to counsel and train potential and existing small
businesses.
Who May Apply: All small business men and women.
Requirements: None.
Contact: SCORE Director.
Application Information: Application required.
Initial Approach: Letter or phone.

Trade Adjustment Assistance
Project Grant $5,000–$500,000

Office of Trade Adjustment Assistance
Department of Commerce
14th and Constitution Ave., NW
Washington, DC 20230
(202) 377-3373

Field of Interest: Business Development
Average Amount Given: N/A
Purpose: To provide trade adjustment assistance to businesses ad-
versely affected by increased imports.
Who May Apply: U.S. businesses.
Requirements: Businesses must be financially at risk because of for-
eign imports.
Contact: Daniel F. Harrington.
Application Information: Application required.
Initial Approach: Letter or phone.

Veterans Entrepreneurial Training
Assistance $45,000–$91,500

Small Business Administration
1441 L Street, NW
Room 602
Washington, DC 20416
(202) 653-8220

Field of Interest: Business Development
Average Amount Given: $71,000
Purpose: To provide technical and managerial assistance to veterans
operating or starting new businesses.
Who May Apply: Qualified nonprofit volunteer organizations and
veterans.
Requirements: None.
Contact: Greg Diercks.
Application Information: Application required.
Initial Approach: Letter or phone.

EDUCATION

Educational Opportunity Centers $123,000–$631,000

Department of Education
400 Maryland Ave., SW
Washington, DC 20202
(202) 732-4804

Field of Interest: Education – Adult
Average Amount Given: $290,000
Purpose: To provide information on financial and academic assistance to qualified adults and to help them apply to colleges and universities.
Who May Apply: Institutions of higher education, public and private entities, and individuals associated with them.
Requirements: None.
Contact: Goldia Hodgdon.
Application Information: Application required.
Initial Approach: Letter or phone.

English Literacy Program $1,200–$953,000

Department of Education
400 Maryland Ave., SW
Washington, DC 20202
(202) 732-2365

Field of Interest: Education – Adult
Average Amount Given: $78,000
Purpose: To establish literacy projects for limited-English-speaking individuals.
Who May Apply: Public and private, profit, and nonprofit entities.
Requirements: None.
Contact: Laura Karl.
Application Information: Application required.
Initial Approach: Letter or phone.

Even Start Local Education Project Grants $62,300–$504,000

Department of Education
400 Maryland Ave., SW
Washington, DC 20202
(202) 732-4682

Field of Interest: Education – Adult
Average Amount Given: $200,000
Purpose: To provide family-centered education projects and literacy education for parents of elementary school children.
Who May Apply: Schools and local educational associations and parents.
Requirements: 10% matching funding required in first year.
Contact: Mary Jean Le Tendre.
Application Information: Application required.
Initial Approach: Letter or phone.

National Adult Education Research $100,000–$300,000

Department of Education
400 Maryland Ave., SW
Washington, DC 20202
(202) 732-2362

Field of Interest: Education – Adult
Average Amount Given: $200,000
Purpose: To support research which contributes to the improvement of adult education.
Who May Apply: Individuals and public or private agencies.
Requirements: None.
Contact: Richard F. DiCola.
Application Information: Application required.
Initial Approach: Letter or phone.

Workplace Literacy Project Grants $50,000–$400,000

Department of Education
400 Maryland Ave., SW
Washington, DC 20202
(202) 732-2269

Field of Interest: Education – Adult
Average Amount Given: $200,000
Purpose: To establish workplace literacy partnerships to provide adult literacy skills services and activities.
Who May Apply: Business, industry, or labor organizations teamed with educational institutions or community-based organizations.
Requirements: 30% matching funding required.
Contact: Nancy Brooks.
Application Information: Application required.
Initial Approach: Letter or phone.

Arts in Education Project Grants $5,000–$50,000

National Endowment for the Arts
1100 Pennsylvania Ave., NW
Washington, DC 20506
(202) 682-5797

Field of Interest: Education – Arts
Average Amount Given: $25,000
Purpose: To establish the arts as basic in education and curriculum, for career development of arts professionals and instructors, and for facilities and operational support.
Who May Apply: Nonprofit organizations.
Requirements: 50% matching funding required.
Contact: Director, Arts in Education Program.
Application Information: Application required.
Initial Approach: Letter or phone.

Bilingual Education $5,000–$1,800,000

Department of Education
330 C Street, SW
Washington, DC 20202
(202) 732-5700

Field of Interest: Education – Bilingual
Average Amount Given: $125,000
Purpose: To develop and carry out programs of bilingual education in preschools, elementary, and secondary schools.
Who May Apply: Private nonprofit and for-profit entities.
Requirements: None.
Contact: Office of Bilingual Education and Minority Languages Affairs.
Application Information: Application required.
Initial Approach: Letter or phone.

Bilingual Education Support Services $75,000–$1,200,000

Office of Bilingual and Minority Languages Affairs
330 C Street, SW
Washington, DC 20202
(202) 732-5706

Field of Interest: Education – Bilingual
Average Amount Given: $200,000
Purpose: To collect data and form clearinghouses for information on bilingual education.
Who May Apply: Private, for-profit organizations.
Requirements: None.
Contact: Carmen Simich-Dudgeon.
Application Information: Application required.
Initial Approach: Letter or phone.

Bilingual Education Training Grants $70,000–$210,000
Office of Bilingual and Minority Languages Affairs
330 C Street, SW
Washington, DC 20202
(202) 732-5722

Field of Interest: Education – Bilingual
Average Amount Given: $125,000
Purpose: To support training for personnel involved in bilingual education.
Who May Apply: Public and private, profit or nonprofit entities.
Requirements: None.
Contact: Dr. John S. Ovard.
Application Information: Application required.
Initial Approach: Letter or phone.

Business and International Education $45,000–$110,000
Department of Education
400 Maryland Ave., SW
Washington, DC 20202
(202) 732-3302

Field of Interest: Education – Business
Average Amount Given: $16,000
Purpose: To improve international business curricula in colleges and universities.
Who May Apply: Accredited educational institutions and the individuals associated with them.
Requirements: None.
Contact: Susanna C. Easton.
Application Information: Application required.
Initial Approach: Letter or phone.

Centers for International Business Education $250,000–$350,000
Department of Education
400 Maryland Ave., SW
Washington, DC 20202
(202) 732-3302

Field of Interest: Education – Business
Average Amount Given: $300,000
Purpose: To promote improved international business strategies, instruction in foreign languages, and international trade.
Who May Apply: Public and private nonprofit entities.
Requirements: 10% matching funding required.
Contact: Susanna C. Easton.
Application Information: Application required.
Initial Approach: Letter or phone.

Educational Partnerships $100,000–$400,000
Department of Education
555 New Jersey Ave., NW
Washington, DC 20208
(202) 357-6116

Field of Interest: Education – Business Development
Average Amount Given: $200,000
Purpose: To encourage alliances between the public schools and the private sector to encourage career awareness on both sides.
Who May Apply: Partnerships of business and industry coupled with local schools.
Requirements: 10% matching funding required.
Contact: Director.
Application Information: Application required.
Initial Approach: Letter or phone.

Clearinghouses for the Handicapped
Project Grants $237,000–$615,000

Special Education and Rehabilitative Services
Department of Education
400 Maryland Ave., SW
Washington, DC 20202
(202) 732-1109

Field of Interest: Education – Disabled
Average Amount Given: $378,000
Purpose: To provide technical assistance to professionals and others interested in special education.
Who May Apply: Public and private, profit and nonprofit entities.
Requirements: None.
Contact: Nancy Safer.
Application Information: Application required.
Initial Approach: Letter or phone.

Early Education Program for the
Handicapped $50,000–$180,000

Special Education and Rehabilitative Services
Department of Education
400 Maryland Ave., SW
Washington, DC 20202
(202) 732-1109

Field of Interest: Education – Disabled
Average Amount Given: $100,000
Purpose: To support effective approaches to preschool and early childhood education for handicapped children.
Who May Apply: Public and private, profit or nonprofit entities.
Requirements: None.
Contact: Nancy Safer.
Application Information: Application required.
Initial Approach: Letter or phone.

*Educational Program for
Severely Handicapped Children $43,200–$189,000

Department of Education
400 Maryland Ave., SW
Washington, DC 20202
(202) 732-1109

Field of Interest: Education – Disabled
Average Amount Given: $116,000
Purpose: To improve innovative educational and training services for severely handicapped children and youth.
Who May Apply: Public and private nonprofit entities.
Requirements: None.
Contact: Nancy Safer.
Application Information: Application required.
Initial Approach: Letter or phone.

*Handicapped Regional
Resource Centers $100,000–$800,000

Special Education and Rehabilitative Services
Department of Education
400 Maryland Ave., SW
Washington, DC 20202
(202) 732-1025

Field of Interest: Education – Disabled
Average Amount Given: $480,000
Purpose: To establish regional resource centers which provide advice and technical services to educators.
Who May Apply: Public and private nonprofit agencies and educational institutions.
Requirements: None.
Contact: William Tyrell.
Application Information: Application required.
Initial Approach: Letter or phone.

Handicapped Special Studies $50,000–$200,000

Department of Education
400 Maryland Ave., SW
Washington, DC 20202
(202) 732-1106

Field of Interest: Education – Disabled
Average Amount Given: $78,000
Purpose: To assess the effectiveness of the Education of the Handicapped Act.
Who May Apply: Individuals and public or private, profit or nonprofit entities.
Requirements: None.
Contact: Marty Kaufman.
Application Information: Application required.
Initial Approach: Letter or phone.

Media Materials for the Handicapped $2,400–$4,650,000

Special Education and Rehabilitative Services
Department of Education
400 Maryland Ave., SW
Washington, DC 20202
(202) 732-1109

Field of Interest: Education – Disabled
Average Amount Given: $200,000
Purpose: To maintain a free loan service of captioned films for the deaf and instructional media for the handicapped, as well as grants for media research to train teachers and parents of the handicapped.
Who May Apply: Public and private entities.
Requirements: None.
Contact: Nancy Safer.
Application Information: Application required.
Initial Approach: Letter or phone.

*National Institute on Disability and Rehabilitation Research Project Grants $10,000–$750,000

Department of Education
400 Maryland Ave., SW
Washington, DC 20202
(202) 732-4532

Field of Interest: Education – Disabled
Average Amount Given: $500,000
Purpose: To support research that will improve the lives of handicapped people.
Who May Apply: Public and private nonprofit entities.
Requirements: None.
Contact: Ramon Garcia.
Application Information: Application required.
Initial Approach: Letter or phone.

*Postsecondary Education for the Handicapped $48,500–$176,000

Department of Education
400 Maryland Ave., SW
Washington, DC 20202
(202) 732-1109

Field of Interest: Education – Disabled
Average Amount Given: $130,000
Purpose: To develop model programs of vocational, adult education for deaf and handicapped persons.
Who May Apply: Public and private nonprofit entities.
Requirements: None.
Contact: Nancy Safer.
Application Information: Application required.
Initial Approach: Letter or phone.

*Rehabilitation Service Projects $70,000–$150,000

Department of Education
400 Maryland Ave., SW
Washington, DC 20202
(202) 732-1347

Field of Interest: Education – Disabled
Average Amount Given: $120,000
Purpose: To improve services to the mentally and physically handicapped above those offered by the states.
Who May Apply: Public and private nonprofits entities.
Requirements: None.
Contact: Dr. Thomas Finch.
Application Information: Application required.
Initial Approach: Letter or phone.

*Research in Education
for the Handicapped $4,000–$500,000

Special Education and Rehabilitative Services
Department of Education
400 Maryland Ave., SW
Washington, DC 20202
(202) 732-1107

Field of Interest: Education – Disabled
Average Amount Given: $105,000
Purpose: To improve the education of handicapped children through research and development projects in model programs.
Who May Apply: Public and private educational and nonprofit institutions and organizations.
Requirements: None.
Contact: Dr. Marty Kaufman.
Application Information: Application required.
Initial Approach: Letter or phone.

*Secondary Education and
Transitional Services for
Handicapped Youth $50,000–$200,000

Department of Education
400 Maryland Ave., SW
Washington, DC 20202
(202) 732-1109

Field of Interest: Education – Disabled
Average Amount Given: $120,000
Purpose: To coordinate education and training for handicapped youth and to ease their way into high school.
Who May Apply: Public and private nonprofit entities.
Requirements: None.
Contact: Nancy Safer.
Application Information: Application required.
Initial Approach: Letter or phone.

*Services for Deaf–Blind Children
and Youth $16,000–$940,000

Special Education and Rehabilitative Services
Department of Education
400 Maryland Ave., SW
Washington, DC 20202
(202) 732-1109

Field of Interest: Education – Disabled
Average Amount Given: $157,000
Purpose: To improve services to deaf–blind children and youth.
Who May Apply: Public or private nonprofit entities.
Requirements: None.
Contact: Nancy Safer.
Application Information: Application required.
Initial Approach: Letter or phone.

Technology Assistance for Disabled Individuals Demonstration Grants

Department of Education
330 C Street, SW
Washington, DC 20202
(202) 732-5066

Field of Interest: Education – Disabled
Average Amount Given: N/A
Purpose: To support model delivery systems, technological devices, and services for disabled individuals.
Who May Apply: Profit and nonprofit entities.
Requirements: None.
Contact: Carol Cohen.
Application Information: Application required.
Initial Approach: Letter or phone.

*Technology, Educational Media, and Materials for the Handicapped $60,000–$300,000

Department of Education
400 Maryland Ave., SW
Washington, DC 20202
(202) 732-1106

Field of Interest: Education – Disabled
Average Amount Given: $120,000
Purpose: To advance the use of new technology, media, and materials in the education of handicapped students.
Who May Apply: Public and private nonprofit entities.
Requirements: None.
Contact: Marty Kaufman.
Application Information: Application required.
Initial Approach: Letter or phone.

Training Interpreters for Deaf Individuals $64,000–$115,000

Department of Education
400 Maryland Ave., SW
Washington, DC 20202
(202) 732-1401

Field of Interest: Education – Disabled
Average Amount Given: $85,000
Purpose: To increase the numbers and improve the skills of manual and oral interpreters who provide services to deaf individuals.
Who May Apply: Public and private nonprofit entities and the individuals associated with them.
Requirements: None.
Contact: Charlotte Cauffield.
Application Information: Application required.
Initial Approach: Letter or phone.

Jacob K. Javits Gifted and Talented Students Project Grants $210,000–$300,000

Programs for the Improvement of Practice
Department of Education
555 New Jersey Ave., NW
Washington, DC 20202
(202) 357-6187

Field of Interest: Education – Gifted
Average Amount Given: $270,000
Purpose: To develop programs in elementary and secondary schools designed to meet the needs of gifted and talented students.
Who May Apply: Public and private agencies of all types.
Requirements: None.
Contact: L. Ann Benjamin.
Application Information: Application required.
Initial Approach: Letter or phone.

***Fund for the Improvement of
Postsecondary Education** $5,000–$150,000

Department of Education
7th and D Streets, SW
Washington, DC 20202
(202) 732-5750

Field of Interest: Education – Higher
Average Amount Given: $68,000
Purpose: To improve access to and the quality of post-secondary education.
Who May Apply: All providers of post-secondary education.
Requirements: None.
Contact: Constance Cook.
Application Information: Application required.
Initial Approach: Letter or phone.

**Law School Clinical Experience
Program** $30,000–$100,000

Department of Education
400 Maryland Ave., SW
Washington, DC 20202
(202) 732-4395

Field of Interest: Education – Higher
Average Amount Given: $74,000
Purpose: To expand law school programs to include new areas of clinical experience and implement new teaching techniques.
Who May Apply: Accredited law schools.
Requirements: 50% matching funding required.
Contact: Charles H. Miller.
Application Information: Application required.
Initial Approach: Letter or phone.

Upward Bound $90,800–$512,000

Office of Postsecondary Education
Department of Education
400 Maryland Ave., SW
Washington, DC 20202
(202) 732-4804

Field of Interest: Education – Higher
Average Amount Given: $196,000
Purpose: To increase academic performance in disadvantaged students so they may attend college.
Who May Apply: Educational institutions, public and private entities, and individuals associated with them.
Requirements: None.
Contact: Goldia Hodgden.
Application Information: Application required.
Initial Approach: Letter or phone.

Fulbright–Hays Seminars Abroad $766,000 plus
                                       3,200,000 rupees

International Studies Branch
Department of Education
ROB-3, 7th and D Streets, SW
Washington, DC 20202
(202) 732-3292

Field of Interest: Education – International Understanding
Average Amount Given: Variable.
Purpose: To increase international understanding through short-term study seminars attended by U.S. educators.
Who May Apply: Full-time, experienced U.S. teachers or administrators.
Requirements: None.
Contact: Ms. Lunching Chao.
Application Information: Application required.
Initial Approach: Letter or phone.

International Research and Studies $ 28,000–$159,000

Division of Advanced Training and Research
Department of Education
ROB-3, 7th and D Streets, SW
Washington, DC 20202
(202) 732-3297

Field of Interest: Education – International Understanding
Average Amount Given: $62,100
Purpose: To improve foreign language and area studies training through research and development of specialized instructional materials.
Who May Apply: Individuals, and public or private entities of all types.
Requirements: None.
Contact: Jose L. Martinez.
Application Information: Application required.
Initial Approach: Letter or phone.

National Resource Centers for Language and International Studies $70,000–$175,000

Department of Education
ROB-3, 7th and D Streets, SW
Washington, DC 20202
(202) 732-3298

Field of Interest: Education – International Understanding
Average Amount Given: N/A
Purpose: To promote instruction in modern foreign languages and international studies.
Who May Apply: Accredited U.S. colleges and universities and individuals associated with them.
Requirements: None.
Contact: Advanced Training and Research Branch.
Application Information: Application required.
Initial Approach: Letter or phone.

Demonstration Centers for the Retraining of Displaced Workers $500,000

Department of Education
400 Maryland Ave., SW
Washington, DC 20202
(202) 732-2364

Field of Interest: Education – Job Retraining and Development
Average Amount Given: $212,000
Purpose: To establish demonstration centers focusing on vocational retraining for displaced workers.
Who May Apply: Any public or private entity.
Requirements: None.
Contact: Paul Geib.
Application Information: Application required.
Initial Approach: Letter or phone.

Mid-Career Teacher Training $80,000–$98,700

Department of Education
555 New Jersey Ave., NW
Washington, DC 20208
(202) 357-6203

Field of Interest: Education – Job Retraining and Development
Average Amount Given: $82,200
Purpose: To create and maintain university programs which will train ex-teachers for other careers.
Who May Apply: Accredited educational institutions and the individuals associated with them.
Requirements: None.
Contact: Douglas Alexander.
Application Information: Application required.
Initial Approach: Letter or phone.

*Desegregation Assistance, Civil Rights Training, and Advisory Services   **$500,000–$1,000,000**

Office of Elementary and Secondary Education
Department of Education
400 Maryland Ave., SW
Washington, DC 20202-6438
(202) 732-4360

Field of Interest: Education – Minority Development
Average Amount Given: $820,000
Purpose: To provide training services to school districts to cope with educational problems occasioned by race, sex, and national origin desegregation.
Who May Apply: Private nonprofit agencies.
Requirements: None.
Contact: Sylvia Wright, Division of Discretionary Grants.
Application Information: Application required.
Initial Approach: Letter or phone.

Follow–Through Project Grants   **$67,000–$230,000**

Department of Education
400 Maryland Ave., SW
Washington, DC 20202-6132
(202) 732-4682

Field of Interest: Education – Minority Development
Average Amount Given: $103,000
Purpose: To follow through with the Head Start Program through the primary grades.
Who May Apply: Public and private nonprofits and educational institutions.
Requirements: 20% matching funding required.
Contact: Mary Jean Le Tendre.
Application Information: Application required.
Initial Approach: Letter or phone.

---

*Migrant Education High School Equivalency Program   **$7,800,000**

Department of Education
400 Maryland Ave., SW
Washington, DC 20202
(202) 732-4742

Field of Interest: Education – Minority Development
Average Amount Given: N/A
Purpose: To assist students who are migrant workers or in the families of migrant workers in obtaining their high school diplomas.
Who May Apply: Private nonprofit entities.
Requirements: None.
Contact: William L. Stormer.
Application Information: Application required.
Initial Approach: Letter or phone.

Talent Search   **$70,300–$1,700,000**

Office of Postsecondary Education
Department of Education
400 Maryland Ave., SW
Washington, DC 20202
(202) 732-4804

Field of Interest: Education – Minority Development
Average Amount Given: $147,000
Purpose: To encourage high-potential disadvantaged youth to graduate from high school and attend college, and to publicize the variety of student financial aid.
Who May Apply: Educational institutions, public and private entities, and individuals associated with these entities.
Requirements: None.
Contact: Goldia Hodgden.
Application Information: Application required.
Initial Approach: Letter or phone.

Training and Special Programs for Leadership Personnel $60,000–$170,000

Department of Education
400 Maryland Ave., SW
Washington, DC 20202
(202) 732-4804

Field of Interest: Education – Minority Development
Average Amount Given: $98,000
Purpose: To provide staff and leadership training for individuals employed in Special Programs for Students from Disadvantaged Backgrounds programs.
Who May Apply: Qualified individuals associated with these special programs.
Requirements: None.
Contact: May Weaver.
Application Information: Application required.
Initial Approach: Letter or phone.

Women's Educational Equity Grants $2,000–$547,000

Department of Education
400 Maryland Ave., SW
Washington, DC 20202
(202) 732-4351

Field of Interest: Education – Minority Development
Average Amount Given: $67,000
Purpose: To promote educational equity for women and girls at all levels of education.
Who May Apply: Individuals, student groups, and public or private nonprofit entities.
Requirements: None.
Contact: Alice T. Ford.
Application Information: Application required.
Initial Approach: Letter or phone.

Women's Educational Equity Project Contracts $2,000–$547,000

Department of Education
400 Maryland Ave., SW
Washington, DC 20202
(202) 732-4351

Field of Interest: Education – Minority Development
Average Amount Given: $500,000
Purpose: To promote educational equity for women and girls at all levels of education.
Who May Apply: Individuals, student groups, and public or private nonprofit entities.
Requirements: None.
Contact: Alice T. Ford.
Application Information: Application required.
Initial Approach: Letter or phone.

Materials Development, Research, and Informal Science Education $17,700–$3,000,000

National Science Foundation
1800 G Street, NW
Washington, DC 20550
(202) 357-7452

Field of Interest: Education – Science and Math
Average Amount Given: $220,000
Purpose: To provide new models and material to improve the quality of and renew the nation's pre-college educational system in mathematics, science, and technology.
Who May Apply: Public or private, profit or nonprofit educational entities, and individuals associated with them.
Requirements: None.
Contact: Director.
Application Information: Application required.
Initial Approach: Letter or phone.

Studies and Program Assessment
Project Grants $10,000–$400,000
National Science Foundation
1800 G Street, NW
Washington, DC 20550
(202) 357-7425

Field of Interest: Education – Science and Math
Average Amount Given: $125,000
Purpose: To strengthen science and engineering education in the U.S.
Who May Apply: Public or private, profit or nonprofit entities and individuals associated with them.
Requirements: None.
Contact: Director.
Application Information: Application required.
Initial Approach: Letter or phone.

Teacher Preparation and Enhancement
Project Grants $7,000–$1,100,000
National Science Foundation
1800 G Street, NW
Washington, DC 20550
(202) 357-7073

Field of Interest: Education – Science and Math
Average Amount Given: $185,000
Purpose: To attract talented individuals to elementary, middle, and- high school mathematics and science teaching through incentives, professional self-renewal, and communications networks.
Who May Apply: Public and private, profit or nonprofit entities and qualified individuals at these institutions.
Requirements: None.
Contact: Division of Teacher Preparation and Enhancement.
Application Information: Application required.
Initial Approach: Letter or phone.

Drug-Free Schools and Communities –
Regional Centers $2,500,000–$3,000,000
Department of Education
400 Maryland Ave., SW
Washington, DC 20202
(202) 732-4599

Field of Interest: Education – Substance Abuse
Average Amount Given: N/A
Purpose: To train school teams to strengthen alcohol and drug abuse education.
Who May Apply: Individuals and public or private entities.
Requirements: None.
Contact: Director.
Application Information: Application required.
Initial Approach: Letter or phone.

School Personnel Training $100,000–$200,000
Department of Education
400 Maryland Ave., SW
Washington, DC 20202
(202) 732-4599

Field of Interest: Education – Substance Abuse
Average Amount Given: $120,000
Purpose: To train elementary and secondary school personnel about drug and alcohol abuse education and prevention.
Who May Apply: Public and private school teachers, administrators, counselors, and other professionals.
Requirements: None.
Contact: Allen King.
Application Information: Application required.
Initial Approach: Letter or phone.

Bilingual Vocational Instructor Training $54,600–$436,000

Department of Education
400 Maryland Ave., SW
Washington, DC 20202
(202) 732-2365

Field of Interest: Education – Vocational
Average Amount Given: $225,100
Purpose: To train instructors for bilingual vocational training.
Who May Apply: Public and private nonprofit and for-profit educational institutions.
Requirements: None.
Contact: Laura Karl.
Application Information: Application required.
Initial Approach: Letter or phone.

Bilingual Vocational Materials, Methods, and Techniques $86,200–$266,500

Department of Education
400 Maryland Ave., SW
Washington, DC 20202
(202) 732-2365

Field of Interest: Education – Vocational
Average Amount Given: $176,000
Purpose: To develop instructional materials, methods, and techniques for bilingual vocational education.
Who May Apply: Individuals and public or private, profit or nonprofit entities.
Requirements: None.
Contact: Laura Karl.
Application Information: Application required.
Initial Approach: Letter or phone.

Bilingual Vocational Training $153,000–$350,500

Department of Education
400 Maryland Ave., SW
Washington, DC 20202
(202) 732-2365

Field of Interest: Education – Vocational
Average Amount Given: $257,000
Purpose: To provide English language instruction and occupational skills to the unemployed.
Who May Apply: Public and private, profit or nonprofit entities, as well as educational institutions.
Requirements: None.
Contact: Laura Karl.
Application Information: Application required.
Initial Approach: Letter or phone.

National Vocational Education Research $98,000–$5,600,000

Department of Education
400 Maryland Ave., SW
Washington, DC 20202
(202) 732-2354

Field of Interest: Education – Vocational
Average Amount Given: $200,000
Purpose: To support special research projects in vocational education.
Who May Apply: Individuals and public and private entities.
Requirements: None.
Contact: Glenn Boerrigter.
Application Information: Application required.
Initial Approach: Letter or phone.

*National Vocational Education Research $100,000–$5,000,000

Department of Education
400 Maryland Ave., SW
Washington, DC 20202
(202) 732-2354

Field of Interest: Education – Vocational
Average Amount Given: $2,000,000
Purpose: To develop curriculum at special vocational curriculum centers.
Who May Apply: Nonprofit entities.
Requirements: None.
Contact: Glenn Boerrigter.
Application Information: Application required.
Initial Approach: Letter or phone.

*Rehabilitation Training $10,000–$382,000

Department of Education
400 Maryland Ave., SW
Washington, DC 20202
(202) 732-1400

Field of Interest: Education – Vocational
Average Amount Given: $85,000
Purpose: To improve the skills of vocational rehabilitation personnel.
Who May Apply: Public or private nonprofit entities.
Requirements: None.
Contact: Delores Watkins.
Application Information: Application required.
Initial Approach: Letter or phone.

Vocational Education Cooperative Dropout Prevention Grants $83,000–$500,000

Department of Education
400 Maryland Ave., SW
Washington, DC 20202
(202) 732-2363

Field of Interest: Education – Vocational
Average Amount Given: $425,700
Purpose: To support exemplary cooperative vocational education demonstration projects.
Who May Apply: Public and private entities.
Requirements: 25% matching funding required.
Contact: Kate Holmberg.
Application Information: Application required.
Initial Approach: Letter or phone.

Vocational Education Cooperative Demonstration Technology Grants $83,000–$500,000

Department of Education
400 Maryland Ave., SW
Washington, DC 20202
(202) 732-2362

Field of Interest: Education – Vocational
Average Amount Given: $305,000
Purpose: To support exemplary cooperative vocational education demonstration projects.
Who May Apply: Public and private entities.
Requirements: 25% matching funding required.
Contact: Richard DiCola.
Application Information: Application required.
Initial Approach: Letter or phone.

Cooperative Education Project Grants $8,000–$240,000

Department of Education
400 Maryland Ave., SW
Washington, DC 20202
(202) 732-4397

Field of Interest: Education – General
Average Amount Given: $80,500
Purpose: To plan and carry out cooperative education projects.
Who May Apply: Accredited institutions of higher education, public and private nonprofit entities and individuals associated with them.
Requirements: None.
Contact: Dr. John Bonas.
Application Information: Application required.
Initial Approach: Letter or phone.

*Educational Leadership Development $44,000–$148,000

Department of Education
400 Maryland Ave., SW
Washington, DC 20208
(202) 357-6181

Field of Interest: Education – General
Average Amount Given: $75,000
Purpose: To establish technical assistance centers that develop leadership skills in school administrators.
Who May Apply: Public and private nonprofit entities.
Requirements: Variable.
Contact: Adria White.
Application Information: Application required.
Initial Approach: Letter or phone.

Educational Research and Development $10,000–$1,300,000

Office of Educational Research and Improvement
555 New Jersey Ave., NW
Washington, DC 20208
(202) 357-6079

Field of Interest: Education – General
Average Amount Given: $55,000
Purpose: To solve and illuminate educational problems.
Who May Apply: Individuals, public or private nonprofit entities, and educational institutions.
Requirements: None.
Contact: Jackie Jenkins.
Application Information: Application required.
Initial Approach: Letter or phone.

First Schools and Teachers Project Grants $5,000–$125,000

Department of Education
400 Maryland Ave., SW
Washington, DC 20208
(202) 357-6496

Field of Interest: Education – General
Average Amount Given: $70,000
Purpose: To improve education for elementary and secondary school students and teachers.
Who May Apply: Nonprofit entities and public and private schools.
Requirements: None.
Contact: Richard LaPointe.
Application Information: Application required.
Initial Approach: Letter or phone.

Language Resource Centers
Project Grants $400,000–$800,000

Department of Education
400 Maryland Ave., SW
Washington, DC 20202
(202) 732-3298

Field of Interest: Education – General
Average Amount Given: $400,000
Purpose: To improve the teaching of foreign languages through every available means.
Who May Apply: Accredited higher educational institutions and the individuals associated with them.
Requirements: None.
Contact: John Paul.
Application Information: Application required.
Initial Approach: Letter or phone.

*Law-Related Education $20,000–$400,000

Department of Education
400 Maryland Ave., SW
Washington, DC 20202
(202) 732-4153

Field of Interest: Education – General
Average Amount Given: N/A
Purpose: To support projects at the elementary and secondary levels that would institutionalize law-related education.
Who May Apply: Public or private nonprofit entities.
Requirements: None.
Contact: Frank Robinson, Jr.
Application Information: Application required.
Initial Approach: Letter or phone.

National Diffusion Network
Development Grants $41,200–$87,000

Programs for the Improvement of Practice
OERI
555 New Jersey Ave., NW
Washington, DC 20208
(202) 357-6134

Field of Interest: Education – General
Average Amount Given: $62,700
Purpose: To accelerate the adoption of educational products and practices across the country.
Who May Apply: Individuals and public and private nonprofit agencies.
Requirements: None.
Contact: Lee E. Wickline.
Application Information: Application required.
Initial Approach: Letter or phone.

National Diffusion Network Dissemination
Processes Project Grant $50,000–$125,000

Programs for the Improvement of Practice
OERI
555 New Jersey Ave., NW
Washington, DC 20208
(202) 357-6134

Field of Interest: Education – General
Average Amount Given: $90,000
Purpose: To accelerate the adoption of educational products and practices across the country.
Who May Apply: Individuals and public and private nonprofit agencies.
Requirements: None.
Contact: Lee E. Wickline.
Application Information: Application required.
Initial Approach: Letter or phone.

National Diffusion Network Private School Facilitator Project Grant $150,000–$200,000

Programs for the Improvement of Practice
OERI
555 New Jersey Ave., NW
Washington, DC 20208
(202) 357-6134

Field of Interest: Education – General
Average Amount Given: $175,000
Purpose: To accelerate the adoption of educational products and practices across the country.
Who May Apply: Individuals and public and private nonprofit agencies.
Requirements: None.
Contact: Lee E. Wickline.
Application Information: Application required.
Initial Approach: Letter or phone.

National Diffusion Network State Facilitators Project Grants $23,000–$242,000

Programs for the Improvement of Practice
OERI
555 New Jersey Ave., NW
Washington, DC 20208
(202) 357-6134

Field of Interest: Education – General
Average Amount Given: $96,000
Purpose: To accelerate the adoption of educational products and practices across the country.
Who May Apply: Individuals and public and private nonprofit agencies.
Requirements: None.
Contact: Lee E. Wickline.
Application Information: Application required.
Initial Approach: Letter or phone.

National Program for Mathematics and Science Education $150,000–$500,000

FIRST
Department of Education
Office of Educational Research and Improvement
Washington, DC 20208
(202) 357-6496

Field of Interest: Education – General
Average Amount Given: $300,000
Purpose: To support projects of national significance to improve public and private, elementary and secondary education.
Who May Apply: Nonprofit entities of all types, including television stations, museums, libraries, and professional societies.
Requirements: None.
Contact: Richard LaPointe.
Application Information: Application required.
Initial Approach: Letter or phone.

National School Volunteer Program $50,000–$400,000

Department of Education
555 New Jersey Ave., NW
Washington, DC 20208
(202) 357-6496

Field of Interest: Education – General
Average Amount Given: $100,000
Purpose: To conduct volunteer programs nationally in schools.
Who May Apply: Public and private entities of all types.
Requirements: None.
Contact: Richard LaPointe.
Application Information: Application required.
Initial Approach: Letter or phone.

The Secretary's Fund for Innovation in Education $50,000–$400,000

Department of Education
400 Maryland Ave., SW
Washington, DC 20208
(202) 357-6496

Field of Interest: Education – General
Average Amount Given: $200,000
Purpose: To discover innovative educational approaches at the pre-school, elementary, and secondary levels.
Who May Apply: Public and private organizations and schools.
Requirements: None.
Contact: Richard LaPointe.
Application Information: Application required.
Initial Approach: Letter or phone.

Student Literacy Corps Project Grants $25,000–$100,000

Department of Education
400 Maryland Ave., SW
Washington, DC 20202
(202) 732-4394

Field of Interest: Education – General
Average Amount Given: $45,000
Purpose: To promote student undergraduates as literacy volunteers in their communities.
Who May Apply: Accredited colleges and universities and the students enrolled at these institutions.
Requirements: None.
Contact: Diana Hayman.
Application Information: Application required.
Initial Approach: Letter or phone.

School Dropout Demonstration Assistance $13,000–$120,000

Department of Education
400 Maryland Ave., SW
Washington, DC 20202
(202) 732-4342

Field of Interest: Education – General
Average Amount Given: $77,200
Purpose: To establish community based dropout prevention and re-entry programs.
Who May Apply: Community-based organizations and educational partnerships.
Requirements: 10% matching funding required.
Contact: John R. Feigel.
Application Information: Application required.
Initial Approach: Letter or phone.

Star Schools Program $1,000,000–$10,000,000

Department of Education
400 Maryland Ave., SW
Washington, DC 20208
(202) 357-6200

Field of Interest: Education – General
Average Amount Given: $2,000,000
Purpose: To develop audio and visual facilities and equipment in the national schools.
Who May Apply: Partnerships of educational institutions and business and industry or qualified community groups.
Requirements: 25% matching funding required.
Contact: Frank Withrow.
Application Information: Application required.
Initial Approach: Letter or phone.

ENVIRONMENT

*Agricultural Research Grant $1,000–$10,000

Department of Agriculture
14th and Independence Ave., SW
Washington, DC 20250
(202) 477-3656

Field of Interest: Environment – Agriculture
Average Amount Given: $3,000
Purpose: To create agricultural research discoveries; to evaluate alternative agricultural research; and to provide scientific technical information.
Who May Apply: Nonprofit research organizations and institutions of higher education.
Requirements: None.
Contact: R.C. Muniak.
Application Information: None required.
Initial Approach: Letter.

Animal Damage Control Project Grant $32,000,000

Budget and Accounting Division
Animal and Plant Health Inspection Service
Department of Agriculture
Hyattsville, MD 20782
(301) 436-8351

Field of Interest: Environment – Agriculture
Average Amount Given: N/A
Purpose: To control agricultural damage by nuisance and diseased animal species.
Who May Apply: Individuals, public and private nonprofits, nonprofit colleges and universities.
Requirements: Not to be used for urban rodent control.
Contact: Amos Bailey.
Application Information: Application form required.
Initial Approach: Letter.

Competitive Agricultural Research Grants $3,000–$312,000

Research Grants Office
Department of Agriculture
14th and Independence Ave., SW
Washington, DC 20250
(202) 447-5022

Field of Interest: Environment – Agriculture
Average Amount Given: $112,727
Purpose: To promote basic research in food, agriculture, and related areas.
Who May Apply: Individuals, private organizations or corporations, U.S. colleges, universities, and research institutions.
Requirements: None.
Contact: Chief Scientist, Research Grants Office.
Application Information: Application required.
Initial Approach: Letter or phone.

Cooperative Agreements for Research in Public Lands Management Project Grants $450,000

Bureau of Land Management
Department of the Interior
Washington, DC 20240
(202) 653-9200

Field of Interest: Environment – Agriculture
Average Amount Given: N/A
Purpose: To enhance the management of resources on public lands.
Who May Apply: Individuals, and any public or private, profit or nonprofit entities.
Requirements: Matching funding negotiated.
Contact: Chief, Resources Sciences Staff.
Application Information: Application required.
Initial Approach: Letter or phone.

Special Agricultural Research Grants $25,000–$150,000

Cooperative State Research Service
Department of Agriculture
14th and Independence Ave., SW
Washington, DC 20250
(202) 447-4423

Field of Interest: Environment – Agriculture
Average Amount Given: $85,726
Purpose: To develop promising breakthroughs in food science and agricultural science.
Who May Apply: Land-grant colleges and universities.
Requirements: None.
Contact: Administrator of CSRS.
Application Information: Application required.
Initial Approach: Letter or phone.

Water Bank Program $7–$66/acre in direct payments

Agricultural Stabilization and Conservation Service
Department of Agriculture
PO Box 2415
Washington, DC 20013
(202) 477-6221

Field of Interest: Environment – Agriculture
Average Amount Given: $18 per acre
Purpose: To conserve the nation's surface waters; to preserve wetlands habitats; and to increase waterfowl habitats.
Who May Apply: Individual landowners.
Requirements: None.
Contact: Director of Program; state or county ASCS.
Application Information: Application required.
Initial Approach: Call county ASCS office.

Air Pollution Control Research $20,000–$190,000

Environmental Protection Agency
PM 216
Washington, DC 20460
(202) 382-7473

Field of Interest: Environment – Air
Average Amount Given: $60,000
Purpose: To promote research and development projects relating to the causes, effects, extent, prevention, and control of air pollution.
Who May Apply: Qualified individuals and public or private non-profit entities.
Requirements: 5% matching funding required.
Contact: Director, Research Grants Staff.
Application Information: Application required.
Initial Approach: Letter or phone.

Climate and Atmospheric Research $10,000–$220,000

National Oceanic and Atmospheric Administration
6010 Executive Blvd.
Rockville, MD 20852
(301) 443-8415

Field of Interest: Environment – Air
Average Amount Given: $85,000
Purpose: To develop the capacity to predict weather.
Who May Apply: Individuals, and public and private educational institutions.
Requirements: None.
Contact: Director, Office of Climate Research.
Application Information: Application required.
Initial Approach: Letter or phone.

Intergovernmental Climate Program Grant $1,400,000

National Oceanic and Atmospheric Administration
Department of Commerce
Universal Building
1825 Connecticut Ave. NW, Suite 518
Washington, DC 20235
(202) 673-5360

Field of Interest: Environment – Air
Average Amount Given: $280,000
Purpose: To create regional climate centers providing data to the public and private sectors.
Who May Apply: Qualified individuals and public or private educational institutions.
Requirements: None.
Contact: National Climate Program Office.
Application Information: Application required.
Initial Approach: Letter or phone.

Characterization of Environmental Health Hazards – Small Business Projects $46,700–$1,100,000

Department of Health and Human Services
PO Box 12233
Research Triangle Park, NC 27709
(919) 541-7634

Field of Interest: Environment – Business Development
Average Amount Given: $50,000
Purpose: To identify and measure the biological, chemical, and physical factors in the human environment, with an emphasis on possible human injury.
Who May Apply: Qualified small businesses.
Requirements: None.
Contact: David Mineo, Grants Management Officer.
Application Information: Application required.
Initial Approach: Letter or phone.

Fisheries Research and Development Project Grants $5,000–$1,200,000

National Oceanic and Atmospheric Administration
Department of Commerce Fish and Wildlife Service
1335 East West Highway
Silver Spring, MD 20910
(301) 427-2358

Field of Interest: Environment, Business Development
Average Amount Given: $100,000
Purpose: To develop and strengthen the U.S. fishing industry.
Who May Apply: Individuals, public and private corporations, colleges and universities, and any profit or nonprofit organizations.
Requirements: 20% of the budget must be in matching funds.
Contact: Office of Trade and Industry Services, National Marine Fisheries Service.
Application Information: Application required.
Initial Approach: Letter or phone.

Senior Environmental Employment Program $7,000–$1,400,000

Environmental Protection Agency
RD 0675
401 M Street
Washington, DC 20460
(202) 382-2574

Field of Interest: Environment – Business Development
Average Amount Given: $122,200
Purpose: To use the talents of older Americans to provide technical assistance to Federal, state, and local environmental agencies.
Who May Apply: Private, nonprofit entities and individuals associated with them.
Requirements: 5% matching funding required.
Contact: Director.
Application Information: Application required.
Initial Approach: Letter or phone.

Characterization of Environmental Health Hazards
– New Research $46,700–$1,100,000
Department of Health and Human Services
PO Box 12233
Research Triangle Park, NC 27709
(919) 541-7634

Field of Interest: Environment – Toxics
Average Amount Given: Variable
Purpose: To identify and measure the biological, chemical, and physical factors in the human environment, with an emphasis on possible human injury.
Who May Apply: Educational or medical entities and for-profit organizations.
Requirements: None.
Contact: David Mineo, Grants Management Officer.
Application Information: Application required.
Initial Approach: Letter or phone.

Environmental Toxicology
Project Grants $46,700–$1,100,000
Department of Health and Human Services
PO Box 12233
Research Triangle Park, NC 27709
(919) 541-7634

Field of Interest: Environment – Toxics
Average Amount Given: $40,000
Purpose: To identify and measure the biological, chemical, and physical factors in the human environment, with an emphasis on possible human injury.
Who May Apply: Qualified individuals with at least three years professional experience.
Requirements: None.
Contact: David Mineo, Grants Management Officer.
Application Information: Application required.
Initial Approach: Letter or phone.

Environmental Protection Research
Project Grants $6,000–$1,000,000
Environmental Protection Agency
PM 216
Washington, DC 20460
(202) 382-7473

Field of Interest: Environment – Toxics
Average Amount Given: $246,000
Purpose: To determine the environmental effects and the control requirements of U.S. energy and to develop pollution control techniques.
Who May Apply: Qualified individuals, educational institutions, and public or private nonprofit entities.
Requirements: 5% matching funding required.
Contact: Director, Research Grants Staff.
Application Information: Application required.
Initial Approach: Letter or phone.

Environmental Restoration
Project Grants $100,000–$30,000,000
Department of Energy
1000 Independence Ave., SW
Washington, DC 20585
(202) 586-7705

Field of Interest: Environment – Toxics
Average Amount Given: Variable.
Purpose: To treat or stabilize radioactive wastes and to decontaminate and decommission federal facilities and sites and related duties.
Who May Apply: Public groups.
Requirements: Variable.
Contact: Office of Waste Management.
Application Information: Application required.
Initial Approach: Letter or phone.

NIEHS Superfund Hazardous Substances
Research and Education $557,100–$1,900,000

National Institute of Environmental Health Sciences
National Institutes of Health, PHS
Department of Health and Human Services
PO Box 12233
Research Triangle Park, NC 27709
(919) 541-0797

Field of Interest: Environment – Toxics
Average Amount Given: $1,256,000
Purpose: To link biomedical research about hazardous substances with engineering and ecological research.
Who May Apply: Any accredited public or private educational institution.
Requirements: None.
Contact: Dr. William Suk.
Application Information: Application required.
Initial Approach: Letter or phone.

Pesticides Control Research $75,000–$80,000

Environmental Protection Agency
RD 675
Washington, DC 20460
(202) 382-7473

Field of Interest: Environment – Toxics
Average Amount Given: $77,500
Purpose: To research the human and ecological effects from pesticides, pesticide degradation products, and alternatives to pesticides.
Who May Apply: Individuals, and colleges and universities
Requirements: 5% matching funding required.
Contact: Director, Research Grants Staff.
Application Information: Application required.
Initial Approach: Letter or phone.

Superfund Innovative Technology
Evaluation Program $20,000,000

Environmental Protection Agency
RD 681
Washington, DC 20460
(202) 382-2583

Field of Interest: Environment – Toxics
Average Amount Given: N/A
Purpose: To coordinate research promoting innovative treatment technologies to be used in response to hazardous waste emergencies.
Who May Apply: Individuals and private sector developers.
Requirements: 50% matching funding required, not to exceed $3,000,000.
Contact: Richard Nalesnik, Chief, ORD.
Application Information: Application required.
Initial Approach: Letter or phone.

Superfund Technical Assistance
Grants for Citizens at Priority Sites $5,000,000

Environmental Protection Agency
401 M Street, WH584–E
Washington, DC 20460
(202) 382-2443

Field of Interest: Environment – Toxics
Average Amount Given: $55,000
Purpose: To allow community groups to hire advisors to inform them about potential hazards, and the selection and design of appropriate remedies at sites eligible for cleanup under the Superfund program.
Who May Apply: Any group of individuals threatened or affected by actual health or economic injury from a Superfund facility.
Requirements: 20% matching funding required.
Contact: Office of Emergency and Remedial Response.
Application Information: Application required.
Initial Approach: Letter or phone.

Toxic Substances Research $20,000–$275,000

Environmental Protection Agency
PM 216
401 M Street
Washington, DC 20460
(202) 382-7473

Field of Interest: Environment – Toxics
Average Amount Given: $147,000
Purpose: To coordinate research projects relating to the effects, extent, prevention, and control of toxic chemical substances or mixtures.
Who May Apply: Individuals, universities, and colleges.
Requirements: 5% matching funding required.
Contact: Director, Research Grants Staff.
Application Information: Application required.
Initial Approach: Letter or phone.

Toxic Substances Research
Project Grants $20,000–$275,000

Environmental Protection Agency
PM 216
Washington, DC 20460
(202) 382-7473

Field of Interest: Environment – Toxics
Average Amount Given: $114,000
Purpose: To coordinate research on the effects, extent, and prevention of toxic chemicals in the environment.
Who May Apply: Individuals, universities, and colleges.
Requirements: 5% matching funding required.
Contact: Director, Research Grants Staff.
Application Information: Application required.
Initial Approach: Letter or phone.

Anadromous Fish Conservation $6,000–$632,000

Division of Fish and Wildlife Management Assistance
Fish and Wildlife Service
Department of the Interior
Washington, DC 20240
(703) 358-1718

Field of Interest: Environment – Water
Average Amount Given: $74,700
Purpose: To conserve, develop, and enhance the nation's anadromous fish.
Who May Apply: Qualified individuals and nonprofit entities.
Requirements: For some projects, the federal government will reimburse 50% of expenses; others are funded.
Contact: Stephen H. Taub.
Application Information: Application required.
Initial Approach: Letter or phone.

Anadromous and Great Lake Fisheries
Conservation Project Grant $2,000–$450,000

National Oceanic and Atmospheric Administration
Department of Commerce Fish and Wildlife Service
1335 East West Highway
Silver Spring, MD 20910
(301) 427-2334

Field of Interest: Environment – Water
Average Amount Given: $45,000
Purpose: To conserve and develop the nation's anadromous fish, including those in the Great Lakes and Lake Champlain; to control the sea lamprey; and to enhance striped bass stocks.
Who May Apply: Individuals and organizations.
Requirements: None.
Contact: Director, Office of Fisheries Conservation.
Application Information: Application required.
Initial Approach: Letter or phone.

National Estuary Program
Project Grants $10,000–$800,000
Office of Marine and Estuarine Protection
Environmental Protection Agency
Washington, DC 20460
(202) 382-7102

Field of Interest: Environment – Water
Average Amount Given: $100,000
Purpose: To protect and restore coastal resources in estuaries of national significance.
Who May Apply: Qualified individuals and public or private nonprofit entities.
Requirements: None.
Contact: Michelle Hiller, Director.
Application Information: Application required.
Initial Approach: Letter or phone.

National Water Resources
Research Program $50,000–$175,000
Geological Survey
Department of the Interior
MS 424 National Center
Reston, VA 22092
(703) 648-6811

Field of Interest: Environment – Water
Average Amount Given: $122,000
Purpose: To support needed research into any aspect of water resource related problems.
Who May Apply: Individuals, educational institutions, and private foundations and firms.
Requirements: 50% matching funding required.
Contact: Melvin Lew.
Application Information: Application required.
Initial Approach: Letter or phone.

Safe Drinking Water Research and Demonstration
Project Grant $25,000–$230,000
Environmental Protection Agency
RD 675
Washington, DC 20460
(202) 382-7473

Field of Interest: Environment – Water
Average Amount Given: $27,500
Purpose: To research the causes, effects, and prevention of physical and mental diseases resulting from contaminated drinking water.
Who May Apply: Qualified individuals, public or private nonprofits, and educational institutions.
Requirements: 5% matching funding required.
Contact: Director, Research Grants Staff.
Application Information: Application required.
Initial Approach: Letter or phone.

Sea Grant Support $45,000–$2,250,000
National Sea Grant College Program
National Oceanic and Atmospheric Administration
6010 Executive Blvd.
Rockville, MD 20852

Field of Interest: Environment – Water
Average Amount Given: $775,000
Purpose: To establish and operate marine resources research.
Who May Apply: Individuals, public or private corporations, colleges, and universities.
Requirements: 1/3 of budget must be privately funded.
Contact: Director, National Sea Grant College Program.
Application Information: Application required.
Initial Approach: Letter.

Undersea Research
Project Grant $10,000–$2,000,000

National Oceanic and Atmospheric Administration
6010 Executive Blvd.
Rockville, MD 20852
(301) 443-8391

Field of Interest: Environment – Water
Average Amount Given: $700,000
Purpose: To conduct research supporting NOAA and national science goals.
Who May Apply: Individuals and public and private educational institutions.
Requirements: None.
Contact: Director, Office of Undersea Research.
Application Information: Application required.
Initial Approach: Letter or phone.

Water Pollution Control Research and Development
Project Grants $27,000–$200,000

Environmental Protection Agency
PM 216
Washington, DC 20460
(202) 382-7473

Field of Interest: Environment – Water
Average Amount Given: $100,000
Purpose: To coordinate and accelerate research projects relating to the causes, effects, and prevention of water pollution.
Who May Apply: Qualified individuals, public or private nonprofit entities, educational institutions, and occasionally, profit organizations.
Requirements: 5% matching funding required.
Contact: Director, Research Grants Staff.
Application Information: Application required.
Initial Approach: Letter or phone.

Biofuels and Municipal Waste Technology Project
Grants $500,000

Department of Energy
1000 Independence Ave., SW
Washington, DC 20585
(202) 586-8021

Field of Interest: Environment – Waste Management
Average Amount Given: Variable.
Purpose: To stimulate research on the conversion of solid waste into feedstock products.
Who May Apply: Businesses, private nonprofit organizations, and educational institutions.
Requirements: None.
Contact: Nicholas Lailas.
Application Information: Application required.
Initial Approach: Letter or phone.

Solid Waste Disposal Research
Project Grants $7,000–$323,000

Environmental Protection Agency
RD 675
Washington, DC 20460
(202) 382-7473

Field of Interest: Environment – Waste Management
Average Amount Given: $165,000
Purpose: To coordinate research in the areas of collection, storage, and utilization of solid waste.
Who May Apply: Qualified individuals and public or private nonprofits as well as educational institutions.
Requirements: 5% matching funding required.
Contact: Director, Research Grants Staff.
Application Information: Application required.
Initial Approach: Letter or phone.

***Solid Waste Management Assistance
Project Grants**   **$5,000–$170,000**

Environmental Protection Agency
PM 216
Washington, DC 20460
(202) 382-4682

Field of Interest: Environment – Waste Management
Average Amount Given: $80,000
Purpose: To integrate solid waste generation and management is-
sues at the local, regional, and national levels.
Who May Apply: Public and private nonprofit entities.
Requirements: 5% matching funding required.
Contact: Director, Research Grants Staff.
Application Information: Application required.
Initial Approach: Letter or phone.

HEALTH CARE

AIDS Activity Project Grant $20,000–$2,750,000

Procurement and Grants Office
Centers for Disease Control, Public Health Service
Department of Health and Human Services
255 E. Paces Ferry Road, NE
Atlanta, GA 30305
(404) 842-6640

Field of Interest: Health Care – AIDS
Average Amount Given: $300,000
Purpose: To develop and implement research and education regarding AIDS.
Who May Apply: Minority businesses, small businesses, public and private organizations, and educational institutions.
Requirements: None.
Contact: Edwin Lin Dixon.
Application Information: Application required.
Initial Approach: Letter or phone.

AIDS Education and Training Centers $267,600–$1,540,000

Department of Health and Human Services, Room 4C05
5600 Fishers Lane
Rockville, MD 20857
(301) 443-6190

Field of Interest: Health Care – AIDS
Average Amount Given: N/A
Purpose: To provide education and training to primary care providers in the treatment of AIDS.
Who May Apply: Academic health sciences schools and schools of medicine and osteopathy.
Requirements: None.
Contact: Dr. Marilyn Gaston, Director.
Application Information: Application required.
Initial Approach: Letter or phone.

Health Services Delivery to Persons with AIDS Demonstration Grants $830,000–$2,900,000

Division of HIV Services
Department of Health and Human Services, Room 9A–05
Parklawn Bldg.
5600 Fishers Lane
Rockville, MD 20857
(301) 443-0652

Field of Interest: Health Care – AIDS
Average Amount Given: $1,320,400
Purpose: To improve medical and social services for AIDS patients and carriers in urban areas.
Who May Apply: All public and private entities.
Requirements: None.
Contact: June Horner.
Application Information: Application required.
Initial Approach: Letter or phone.

Health Services Research and Development Grants $18,000–$900,000

Department of Health and Human Services, Room 18A–10
5600 Fishers Lane
Rockville, MD 20857
(301) 443-4033

Field of Interest: Health Care – AIDS
Average Amount Given: $140,000
Purpose: To create better understanding of the process of health care delivery services, with an emphasis on AIDS issues.
Who May Apply: Individuals, public or nonprofit private agencies, and public or private educational institutions.
Requirements: None.
Contact: Ralph Sloat.
Application Information: Application required.
Initial Approach: Letter or phone.

Integrated Community–Based Primary Care and Drug Abuse Treatment Services Project Grant   **$100,000–$1,000,000**

Department of Health and Human Services, Room 7A-20
5600 Fishers Lane
Rockville, MD 20857
(301) 443-8134

Field of Interest: Health Care – AIDS
Average Amount Given: N/A
Purpose: To combat the spread of HIV and AIDS by joining primary care drug abuse treatment and case management delivery systems.
Who May Apply: Private and public, for-profit and nonprofit entities.
Requirements: None.
Contact: Joan Holloway.
Application Information: Application required.
Initial Approach: Letter or phone.

---

*Long–Term Care Facilities Project Grant   **$100,000 minimum**

Health Resources and Services Administration, PHS
Department of Health and Human Services, Room 11A-10
5600 Fishers Lane
Rockville, MD 20857
(301) 443-0271

Field of Interest: Health Care – AIDS
Average Amount Given: N/A
Purpose: To renovate, expand, repair, equip, or modernize non-acute care long-term facilities for AIDS patients.
Who May Apply: Public or nonprofit entities.
Requirements: 20% matching funding required.
Contact: Katharine Buckner.
Application Information: Application required.
Initial Approach: Letter or phone.

Minority AIDS Education Prevention Grants   **$20,000–$75,000**

Department of Health and Human Services, Room 118F
Hubert H. Humphrey Bldg.
200 Independence Ave., SW
Washington, DC 20201
(202) 245-0020

Field of Interest: Health Care – AIDS
Average Amount Given: N/A
Purpose: To develop innovative strategies against AIDS through community organizations.
Who May Apply: Private nonprofit and for-profit minority community-based organizations and national minority organizations.
Requirements: None.
Contact: Georgia Buggs, RN, MPH.
Application Information: Application required.
Initial Approach: Letter or phone.

Minority Community Health Demonstration Projects – AIDS   **$130,000–$200,000**

Office of Minority Health
Department of Health and Human Services, PHS
200 Independence Ave., SW, Room 118F
Washington, DC 20201
(202) 245-0020

Field of Interest: Health Care – AIDS
Average Amount Given: $183,000
Purpose: To demonstrate that local communities can have an effective impact on disease risk factors and related health problems of minority groups.
Who May Apply: Public and private, profit or nonprofit entities.
Requirements: None.
Contact: Betty Lee Hawks.
Application Information: Application required.
Initial Approach: Letter or phone.

*Non-Acute Care Intermediate Facilities
Project Grant $100,000 minimum

Health Resources and Services Administration, PHS
Department of Health and Human Services, Room 11A-10
5600 Fishers Lane
Rockville, MD 20857
(301) 443-0271

Field of Interest: Health Care – AIDS
Average Amount Given: N/A
Purpose: To renovate, expand, repair, equip, or modernize non-acute-care, intermediate facilities for AIDS patients.
Who May Apply: Public or nonprofit entities.
Requirements: 20% matching funds required.
Contact: Katharine Buckner.
Application Information: Application required.
Initial Approach: Letter or phone.

*Sexually Transmitted Diseases
Research Grants $34,500–$311,000

Centers for Disease Control, PHS
Department of Health and Human Services
1600 Clifton Rd., NE
Atlanta, GA 30333
(404) 639-2552

Field of Interest: Health Care – AIDS
Average Amount Given: $185,200
Purpose: To develop, improve, apply, and evaluate methods for the control of sexually transmitted diseases through research and education.
Who May Apply: Any public or private entity.
Requirements: None.
Contact: Dr. Willard Cates, Jr.
Application Information: Application required.
Initial Approach: Letter or phone.

Adolescent Family Life Research
Grants $56,000–$150,000

Department of Health and Human Services, Room 736E
Hubert Humphrey Bldg.
200 Independence Ave., SW
Washington, DC 20201
(202) 245-0146

Field of Interest: Health Care – Children
Average Amount Given: $111,000
Purpose: To research the causes of and to create solutions to adolescent pregnancy and attendant issues.
Who May Apply: Educational institutions and private nonprofit organizations.
Requirements: None.
Contact: Eugenia Eckard.
Application Information: Application required.
Initial Approach: Letter or phone.

Maternal Child and Health Federal Consolidated
Programs Project Grant $50,000–$1,000,000

Department of Health and Human Services, Room 9-11
Parklawn Bldg.
5600 Fishers Lane
Rockville, MD 20857
(301) 443-1440

Field of Interest: Health Care – Children
Average Amount Given: $174,000
Purpose: For special projects, training and research, and genetic disease testing.
Who May Apply: Educational institutions and any private or public entity.
Requirements: None.
Contact: Dr. Vince L. Hutchins.
Application Information: Application required.
Initial Approach: Letter.

Minority Community Health Demonstration Projects – Infant Mortality   **$130,000–$200,000**

Office of Minority Health
Department of Health and Human Services, PHS
200 Independence Ave., SW, Room 118F
Washington, DC 20201
(202) 245-0020

Field of Interest: Health Care – Children
Purpose: To demonstrate that local communities can have an effective impact on disease risk factors and related health problems of minority groups.
Who May Apply: Public and private, profit or nonprofit entities.
Requirements: None.
Contact: Betty Lee Hawks.
Application Information: Application required.
Initial Approach: Letter or phone.

Pediatric AIDS Health Care Demonstration Program   **$140,000–$730,000**

Department of Health and Human Services, Room 9-48
5600 Fishers Lane
Rockville, MD 20857
(301) 443-2350

Field of Interest: Health Care – Children, AIDS
Average Amount Given: $360,000
Purpose: To create innovative models for the treatment of pediatric AIDS and to coordinate services for at-risk, child-bearing women.
Who May Apply: All public and private entities, profit and nonprofit.
Requirements: None.
Contact: Dr. John Hutchings.
Application Information: Application required.
Initial Approach: Letter or phone.

*Appalachian Health Programs   **$12,000–$500,000**

Appalachian Regional Commission
1666 Connecticut Ave., NW
Washington, DC 20235
(202) 673-7874

Field of Interest: Health Care – Disadvantaged
Average Amount Given: $121,000
Purpose: To make health care accessible, to reduce infant mortality, and to recruit needed manpower in Appalachia.
Who may Apply: Nonprofit organizations.
Requirements: None.
Contact: Executive Director.
Application Information: Application required.
Initial Approach: Letter or phone.

Community Demonstration Grant Projects for Alcohol and Drug Abuse–Treatment of Homeless Individuals   **$378,000–$683,000**

Department of Health and Human Services, Room 16C-02
5600 Fishers Lane
Rockville, MD 20857
(301) 443-0786

Field of Interest: Health Care – Disadvantaged
Average Amount Given: $571,600
Purpose: To provide and evaluate successful, community-based, drug-and-alcohol abuse treatment centers.
Who May Apply: Public and private nonprofit institutions.
Requirements: None.
Contact: Barbara Lubran.
Application Information: Application required.
Initial Approach: Letter or phone.

Health Services
in the Pacific Basin $ 50,000–$300,000

Department of Health and Human Services, Room 7A-55
5600 Fishers Lane
Rockville, MD 20857
(301) 443-8134

Field of Interest: Health Care – Disadvantaged
Average Amount Given: $180,000
Purpose: To develop projects to improve health services in the Asian Pacific Islands.
Who May Apply: For-profit and nonprofit organizations and private entities.
Requirements: None.
Contact: Howard C. Lerner.
Application Information: Application required.
Initial Approach: Letter or phone.

Indian Health Service Health Promotion
and Disease Prevention
Demonstration Projects $ 236,800–$288,000

Department of Health and Human Services, Room 6A-55
5600 Fishers Lane
Rockville, MD 20857
(301) 443-4644

Field of Interest: Health Care – Disadvantaged
Average Amount Given: $262,460
Purpose: To develop cost-effective means to improve Indian health.
Who May Apply: Schools of medicine and osteopathy and qualified individuals within these schools.
Requirements: None.
Contact: Dr. W. Craig Vanderwagen.
Application Information: Application required.
Initial Approach: Letter or phone.

Migrant Health Centers Grants $30,000–$1,300,000

Department of Health and Human Services, Room 7A-55
5600 Fishers Lane
Rockville, MD 20857
(301) 443-1153

Field of Interest: Health Care – Disadvantaged
Average Amount Given: $300,000
Purpose: To develop and operate migrant worker health centers.
Who May Apply: Public or nonprofit private entities.
Requirements: None.
Contact: Sonia M. Leon Reig.
Application Information: Application required.
Initial Approach: Letter or phone.

Project Grants for Health Services
to the Homeless $62,000–$2,000,000

Department of Health and Human Services, Room 4C-25
5600 Fishers Lane
Rockville, MD 20857
(301) 443-6190

Field of Interest: Health Care – Disadvantaged
Average Amount Given: $285,000
Purpose: To deliver primary health services and substance abuse services to homeless individuals.
Who May Apply: Nonprofit private and public organizations.
Requirements: Matching funding required.
Contact: Joan Holloway, Director.
Application Information: Application required.
Initial Approach: Letter or phone.

Rural Health Resource Centers $188,800–$279,900

Department of Health and Human Services, Room 14-22
5600 Fishers Lane
Rockville, MD 20857
(301) 443-0835

Field of Interest: Health Care – Disadvantaged
Average Amount Given: $237,176
Purpose: To develop rural health research centers.
Who May Apply: All public and private, profit and nonprofit entities.
Requirements: None.
Contact: Arlene Granderson.
Application Information: Application required.
Initial Approach: Letter or phone.

**Developmental Disability Projects
of National Significance** $50,000–$200,000

Office of Human Development Services
Department of Health and Human Services
Washington, DC 20201
(202) 245-1961

Field of Interest: Health Care – Disabilities
Average Amount Given: N/A
Purpose: To increase the independence, productivity, and integration into the community of persons with developmental disabilities in projects of national significance.
Who May Apply: Any public or private nonprofit agency.
Requirements: Matching funding required.
Contact: Raymond Sanchez.
Application Information: Application required.
Initial Approach: Letter or phone.

**Disabilities Prevention
Project Grants** $206,200–$348,900

Center for Environmental Health and Injury Control
Centers for Disease Control
Department of Health and Human Services
1600 Clifton Road, NE
Atlanta, GA 30333

Field of Interest: Health Care – Disabilities
Average Amount Given: $275,000
Purpose: To provide national focus on the prevention of disabilities.
Who May Apply: Public and private nonprofit entities.
Requirements: None.
Contact: Joseph B. Smith.
Application Information: Application required.
Initial Approach: Letter.

**Applied Methods in Surveillance
Projects** $75,000–$200,000

Centers for Disease Control, PHS
Department of Health and Human Services
255 E. Paces Ferry Road, NE
Atlanta, GA 30305
(404) 842-6630

Field of Interest: Health Care – Prevention
Average Amount Given: $150,000
Purpose: To support injury control research and demonstration grants.
Who May Apply: Profit and nonprofit entities.
Requirements: None.
Contact: Henry Cassell.
Application Information: Application required.
Initial Approach: Letter or phone.

Community-Based Injury Control Projects $200,000–$300,000

Centers for Disease Control, PHS
Department of Health and Human Services
255 E. Paces Ferry Road, NE
Atlanta, GA 30305
(404) 842-6630

Field of Interest: Health Care – Prevention
Average Amount Given: $260,000
Purpose: To support injury control research and demonstration grants.
Who May Apply: Profit and nonprofit entities.
Requirements: None.
Contact: Henry Cassell.
Application Information: Application required.
Initial Approach: Letter or phone.

Injury Prevention and Control Research Projects $300,000–$500,000

Centers for Disease Control, PHS
Department of Health and Human Services
255 E. Paces Ferry Road, NE
Atlanta, GA 30305
(404) 842-6630

Field of Interest: Health Care – Prevention
Average Amount Given: $400,000
Purpose: To support injury control research and demonstration grants.
Who May Apply: Profit and nonprofit entities.
Requirements: None.
Contact: Henry Cassell.
Application Information: Application required.
Initial Approach: Letter or phone.

Injury Prevention Research Centers $60,000–$225,000

Centers for Disease Control, PHS
Department of Health and Human Services
255 E. Paces Ferry Road, NE
Atlanta, GA 30305
(404) 842-6630

Field of Interest: Health Care – Prevention
Average Amount Given: $150,000
Purpose: To support injury control research and demonstration grants.
Who May Apply: Profit and nonprofit entities.
Requirements: None.
Contact: Henry Cassell.
Application Information: Application required.
Initial Approach: Letter or phone.

Minority Community Health Demonstration Projects – Cancer $130,000–$200,000

Office of Minority Health
Department of Health and Human Services, PHS
200 Independence Ave., SW, Room 118F
Washington, DC 20201
(202) 245-0020

Field of Interest: Health Care – Prevention
Average Amount Given: $190,000
Purpose: To demonstrate that local communities can have an effective impact on disease risk factors and related health problems of minority groups.
Who May Apply: Public and private, profit or nonprofit entities.
Requirements: None.
Contact: Betty Lee Hawks.
Application Information: Application required.
Initial Approach: Letter or phone.

Minority Community Health Demonstration Projects – Cardiovascular Disease and Stroke $130,000–$200,000

Office of Minority Health
Department of Health and Human Services, PHS
200 Independence Ave., SW, Room 118F
Washington, DC 20201
(202) 245-0020

Field of Interest: Health Care – Prevention
Average Amount Given: $200,000
Purpose: To demonstrate that local communities can have an effective impact on disease risk factors and health problems of minority groups.
Who May Apply: Public and private, profit or nonprofit entities.
Requirements: None.
Contact: Betty Lee Hawks.
Application Information: Application required.
Initial Approach: Letter or phone.

Minority Community Health Demonstration Projects – Diabetes $130,000–$200,000

Office of Minority Health
Department of Health and Human Services, PHS
200 Independence Ave., SW, Room 118F
Washington, DC 20201
(202) 245-0020

Field of Interest: Health Care – Prevention
Average Amount Given: $100,000
Purpose: To demonstrate that local communities can have an effective impact on disease risk factors and related health problems of minority groups.
Who May Apply: Public and private, profit or nonprofit entities.
Requirements: None.
Contact: Betty Lee Hawks.
Application Information: Application required.

Minority Community Health Demonstration Projects – Homicide, Suicide, and Injury $130,000–$200,000

Office of Minority Health
Department of Health and Human Services, PHS
200 Independence Ave., SW, Room 118F
Washington, DC 20201
(202) 245-0020

Field of Interest: Health Care – Prevention
Average Amount Given: $130,000
Purpose: To demonstrate that local communities can have an effective impact on disease risk factors and related health problems of minority groups.
Who May Apply: Public and private, profit or nonprofit entities.
Requirements: None.
Contact: Betty Lee Hawks.
Application Information: Application required.
Initial Approach: Letter or phone.

Occupational Safety and Health Research Project Grants $10,000–$250,000

Centers for Disease Control, PHS
Department of Health and Human Services
1600 Clifton Road, NE, MS D30
Atlanta, GA 30333
(404) 639-3343

Field of Interest: Health Care – Prevention
Average Amount Given: $85,000
Purpose: To create effective solutions for occupational safety and health problems.
Who May Apply: Public and private for-profit and nonprofit entities.
Requirements: None.
Contact: Dr. Roy M. Fleming.
Application Information: Application required.
Initial Approach: Letter or phone.

Occupational Safety and Health Training Grants $10,000–$800,000

Centers for Disease Control, PHS
Department of Health and Human Services
4676 Columbia Parkway
Cincinnati, Ohio 45226
(513) 533-8241

Field of Interest: Health Care – Prevention
Average Amount Given: N/A
Purpose: To develop specialized personnel in the occupational safety and health field.
Who May Apply: Any public or private educational institution involved in graduate training.
Requirements: None.
Contact: John Talty.
Application Information: Application required.
Initial Approach: Letter or phone.

Resource and Manpower Development in the Environmental Health Sciences $253,000–$2,231,000

National Institutes of Health, PHS
Department of Health and Human Services
PO Box 12233
Research Triangle Park, NC 27709
(919) 541-7634

Field of Interest: Health Care – Prevention
Average Amount Given: $1,000,000
Purpose: To support multidisciplinary research on environmental health problems in EHS Centers and MFBS Centers.
Who May Apply: Qualified individuals, university-based, nonprofit research institutions, and qualified for-profit entities.
Requirements: None.
Contact: Dr. Christopher Schonwalder, Chief, Scientific Program Branch.
Application Information: Application required.
Initial Approach: Letter or phone.

Alcohol and Drug Abuse Clinical Training Program Grants $4,600,000

Department of Health and Human Services, Room 16-86
5600 Fishers Lane
Rockville, MD 20857
(301) 443-1207

Field of Interest: Health Care – Substance Abuse
Average Amount Given: N/A
Purpose: To provide specialized training in alcohol-related issues to health care professionals.
Who May Apply: Public or private nonprofit entities.
Requirements: None.
Contact: Joseph Weeda.
Application Information: Application required.
Initial Approach: Letter or phone.

Drug Abuse Treatment Waiting List Reduction Grants $20,000–$60,000

Department of Health and Human Services, Room 11-95
5600 Fishers Lane
Rockville, MD 20857
(301) 443-2530

Field of Interest: Health Care – Substance Abuse
Average Amount Given: $25,000
Purpose: To expand the capacity of existing drug abuse treatment centers.
Who May Apply: Qualified public and nonprofit private entities.
Requirements: None.
Contact: James Moynihan.
Application Information: Application required.
Initial Approach: Letter or phone.

Drug and Alcohol Abuse Prevention
Project Grant $25,000–$1,000,000

Demonstration Operations Branch
Department of Health and Human Services
Parklawn Bldg.
5600 Fishers Lane
Rockville, MD 20857(301) 443-0353

Field of Interest: Health Care – Substance Abuse
Average Amount Given: $219,000
Purpose: To support prevention programs which will decrease the incidence of drug and alcohol abuse among high-risk youth.
Who May Apply: Any public or nonprofit private entity.
Requirements: None.
Contact: Dr. Stephen E. Gardner, Chief.
Application Information: Application required.
Initial Approach: Letter or phone.

Minority Community Health Demonstration
Projects – Substance Abuse $130,000–$200,000

Office of Minority Health
Department of Health and Human Services, PHS
200 Independence Ave., SW, Room 118F
Washington, DC 20201
(202) 245-0020

Field of Interest: Health Care – Substance Abuse
Average Amount Given: $150,000
Purpose: To demonstrate that local communities can have an effective impact on disease risk factors and related health problems of minority groups.
Who May Apply: Public and private, profit or nonprofit entities.
Requirements: None.
Contact: Betty Lee Hawks.
Application Information: Application required.
Initial Approach: Letter or phone.

Model Substance Abuse Prevention Projects
for Pregnant and Postpartum Women
and their Infants $30,000,000

Department of Health and Human Services
Rockwall II Bldg.
5600 Fishers Lane
Rockville, MD 20857
(301) 443-4564

Field of Interest: Health Care – Substance Abuse
Average Amount Given: $210,000
Purpose: To coordinate comprehensive health services for low-income, substance-abusing pregnant and postpartum women.
Who May Apply: Any public, private, for-profit, or nonprofit organization may apply.
Requirements: None.
Contact: Dr. Bernard McColgan.
Application Information: Application required.
Initial Approach: Letter or phone.

Substance Abuse Conference Grant $4,000–$50,000

National Clearinghouse for Alcohol and Drug Information
PO Box 2345
Rockville, MD 20857
(301) 468-2600

Field of Interest: Health Care – Substance Abuse
Average Amount Given: $15,000
Purpose: To plan meetings and conferences in an effort to prevent alcohol or other drug abuse.
Who May Apply: Public, private, for-profit, or nonprofit entities.
Requirements: None.
Contact: Kent Auguston.
Application Information: Application required.
Initial Approach: Letter or phone.

*Black Lung Clinics Project Grants $50,000–$250,000

Health Resources and Services Administration, PHS
Department of Health and Human Services, Rm 7A–55
5600 Fishers Lane
Rockville, MD 20857
(301) 443-2260

Field of Interest: Health Care – General
Average Amount Given: N/A
Purpose: To develop high quality, patient–oriented, integrated systems of care with maximum use of existing resources.
Who May Apply: Private nonprofit agencies.
Requirements: None.
Contact: Richard Bohrer, Director.
Application Information: Application required.
Initial Approach: Letter or phone.

**Community Health Centers
Project Grants $25,000–$4,000,000**

Department of Health and Human Services, Room 7A–55
5600 Fishers Lane
Rockville, MD 20857
(301) 443-2260

Field of Interest: Health Care – General
Average Amount Given: $1,200,000
Purpose: To develop and operate community health centers.
Who May Apply: Public or nonprofit private entities.
Requirements: None.
Contact: Richard Bohrer.
Application Information: Application required.
Initial Approach: Letter or phone.

**Family Planning Services
Project Grants $125,000–$8,000,000**

Department of Health and Human Services, Room 736E
Hubert H. Humphrey Bldg.
200 Independence Ave., SW
Washington, DC 20201
(202) 245-0151

Field of Interest: Health Care – General
Average Amount Given: $600,000
Purpose: To provide educational, medical, and social services to individuals to freely plan the spacing of their children.
Who May Apply: Any public or nonprofit private entity.
Requirements: None.
Contact: Nabers Cabaniss.
Application Information: Application required.
Initial Approach: Letter or phone.

**Food and Drug Administration Research
Project Grant $10,000–$425,000**

Food and Drug Administration
Public Health Service
Department of Health and Human Services, HFA – 520,
Room 3–20
Parklawn Bldg.
5600 Fishers LaneRockville, MD 20857

Field of Interest: Health Care – General
Average Amount Given: $65,852
Purpose: To improve research in and education about human and veterinary drugs, poison control, radiation devices, medical diagnostic products, and related issues.
Who May Apply: Educational institutions and small businesses.
Requirements: None.
Contact: Robert L. Robins.
Application Information: Application required.
Initial Approach: Letter.

National Research Service Awards   **$20,000–$33,000**

Department of Health and Human Services, Room 18A–10
5600 Fishers Lane
Rockville, MD 20857
(301) 443-4033

Field of Interest: Health Care – General
Average Amount Given: $28,000
Purpose: To provide pre- and postdoctoral training in health services research.
Who May Apply: Individuals and public and private nonprofit entities.
Requirements: None.
Contact: Ralph Sloat.
Application Information: Application required.
Initial Approach: Letter or phone.

*National Health Promotion   **$50,000–$250,000**

Office of the Assistant Secretary for Health, PHS
Department of Health and Human Services, Room 2132
330 C Street, SW
Washington, DC 20201

Field of Interest: Health Care – General
Average Amount Given: N/A
Purpose: To attract national membership organizations to develop and coordinate programs which promote good health habits.
Who May Apply: Public and private nonprofits.
Requirements: None.
Contact: Deputy Director, Office of Disease Prevention and Health Promotion.
Application Information: Application required.
Initial Approach: Letter.

Nursing Research Project Grants   **$86,336–$755,000**

National Institutes of Health, PHS
Department of Health and Human Services
Building 31, Room B1CO2
Bethesda, MD 20892
(301) 496-0327

Field of Interest: Health Care – General
Average Amount Given: $146,000
Purpose: To support nursing research and research training.
Who May Apply: Qualified individuals and any public or private, profit or nonprofit entity.
Requirements: U.S. citizens or permanent residents only.
Contact: Sally A. Nichols.
Application Information: Application required.
Initial Approach: Letter or phone.

HUMANITIES

*Elementary and Secondary Programs in the Humanities   Up to $170,000

National Endowment for the Humanities
Room 302
Washington, DC 20506
(202) 786-0377

Field of Interest: Humanities – Education
Average Amount Given: N/A
Purpose: To increase the effectiveness of humanities teaching in elementary, middle, and secondary schools through faculty development.
Who May Apply: Public and private nonprofit entities.
Requirements: None.
Contact: Division of State Programs.
Application Information: Application required.
Initial Approach: Letter or phone.

Elementary and Secondary Programs in the Humanities Masterwork Study Grants

National Endowment for the Humanities
Room 302
Washington, DC 20506
(202) 786-0377

Field of Interest: Humanities – Education
Average Amount Given: $20,000
Purpose: To increase the effectiveness of humanities teaching in elementary, middle, and secondary schools through faculty development.
Who May Apply: Qualified individuals.
Requirements: None.
Contact: Division of State Programs.
Application Information: Application required.
Initial Approach: Letter or phone.

*Higher Education in the Humanities $7,000,000

National Endowment for the Humanities
Room 302
Washington, DC 20506
(202) 786-0380

Field of Interest: Humanities – Education
Average Amount Given: Variable
Purpose: To assist higher education to improve the teaching of the humanities.
Who May Apply: Public and private nonprofit entities.
Requirements: None.
Contact: Division of Higher Education.
Application Information: Application required.
Initial Approach: Letter or phone.

NEH/Reader's Digest Teacher-Scholar Program $1,500,000

National Endowment for the Humanities
Room 302
Washington, DC 20506
(202) 786-0377

Field of Interest: Humanities – Education
Average Amount Given: $28,500
Purpose: To increase the effectiveness of humanities training in the nation's schools through a year of full-time study.
Who May Apply: Full-time elementary, middle, or high school teachers with at least three years of experience.
Requirements: None.
Contact: Elementary and Secondary Education in the Humanities.
Application Information: Application required.
Initial Approach: Letter or phone.

*Public Humanities Project Grants   **$15,000–$200,000**
National Endowment for the Humanities
Room 426
Washington, DC 20506
(202) 786-0271

Field of Interest: Humanities – Education
Average Amount Given: $60,000
Purpose: To support humanities projects addressed to out-of-school audiences and drawing upon resources and scholars in the field.
Who may apply: Public and private nonprofit organizations.
Requirements: None.
Contact: Director.
Application Information: Application required.
Initial Approach: Letter or phone.

**International Peace and
Conflict Management**   **$3,000–$200,000**
United States Institute of Peace
1550 M Street, NW, Suite 700
Washington, DC 20005
(202) 457-1700

Field of Interest: Humanities – International Understanding
Average Amount Given: $30,000
Purpose: To support education, research, and training in international peace and conflict management.
Who May Apply: Individuals and nonprofit organizations.
Requirements: None.
Contact: Office of Public Affairs.
Application Information: Application required.
Initial Approach: Letter or phone.

**International Peace and Conflict Management
Articles and Manuscripts**   **$3,000–$100,000**
Commission on the Bicentennial of the U.S. Constitution
1550 M Street, NW, Suite 700
Washington, DC 20005
(202) 457-1700

Field of Interest: Humanities – International Understanding
Average Amount Given: $33,000
Purpose: To support education and training and public information on themes of special interest in the field.
Who May Apply: Individuals and nonprofit institutions.
Requirements: None.
Contact: Office of Public Affairs.
Application Information: Application required.
Initial Approach: Letter or phone.

***International Research Project
Grants**   **$100,000–$700,000**
National Endowment for the Humanities
Room 318
Washington, DC 20506
(202) 786-0204

Field of Interest: Humanities – International Understanding
Average Amount Given: $375,000
Purpose: To foster American understanding of the history, culture, and traditions of other nations.
Who May Apply: Public and private nonprofits.
Requirements: None.
Contact: International Research Division.
Application Information: Application required.
Initial Approach: Letter or phone.

College Library Technology Research and Demonstration Grants $15,000–$125,000

Library Programs
Department of Education
Washington, DC 20208
(202) 357-6902

Field of Interest: Humanities – Libraries and Museums
Average Amount Given: $100,000
Purpose: To encourage resource-sharing among college and university libraries and to develop special projects to meet information processing needs.
Who May Apply: Public and private nonprofit entities.
Requirements: None.
Contact: Linda Loeb, Program Officer.
Application Information: Application required.
Initial Approach: Letter or phone.

College Library Technology Combination Grants $15,000–$125,000

Library Programs
Department of Education
Washington, DC 20208
(202) 357-6902

Field of Interest: Humanities – Libraries and Museums
Average Amount Given: $125,000
Purpose: To encourage resource-sharing among college and university libraries and to develop special projects to meet information processing needs.
Who May Apply: Public and private nonprofit entities.
Requirements: None.
Contact: Linda Loeb, Program Officer.
Application Information: Application required.
Initial Approach: Letter or phone.

College Library Technology Networking Grants $15,000–$125,000

Library Programs
Department of Education
Washington, DC 20208
(202) 357-6902

Field of Interest: Humanities – Libraries and Museums
Average Amount Given: $30,000
Purpose: To encourage resource-sharing among college and university libraries and to develop special projects to meet information processing needs.
Who May Apply: Public and private nonprofit entities.
Requirements: None.
Contact: Linda Loeb, Program Officer.
Application Information: Application required.
Initial Approach: Letter or phone.

College Library Technology Services Grants $15,000–$125,000

Library Programs
Department of Education
Washington, DC 20208
(202) 357-6902

Field of Interest: Humanities – Libraries and Museums
Average Amount Given: $25,000
Purpose: To encourage resource-sharing among college and university libraries and to develop special projects to meet information processing needs.
Who May Apply: Public and private nonprofit entities.
Requirements: None.
Contact: Linda Loeb, Program Officer.
Application Information: Application required.
Initial Approach: Letter or phone.

**Humanities Preservation Project
Grants** $2,800–$2,500,000

National Endowment for the Humanities
Room 802
Washington, DC 20506
(202) 786-0570

Field of Interest: Humanities – Libraries and Museums
Average Amount Given: $301,000
Purpose: To preserve research resources relating to U.S. humanities.
Who May Apply: Individuals and public or private nonprofit entities.
Requirements: None.
Contact: Office of Preservation.
Application Information: Application required.
Initial Approach: Letter or phone.

***Humanities Projects in Libraries
and Archives** $5,000–$300,000

National Endowment for the Humanities
Room 420
Washington, DC 20506
(202) 786-0271

Field of Interest: Humanities – Libraries and Museums
Average Amount Given: N/A
Purpose: To encourage thematic exhibitions, publications, and other library services designed to promote the humanities.
Who May Apply: Public and private nonprofit entities.
Requirements: None.
Contact: Division of General Programs.
Application Information: Application required.
Initial Approach: Letter or phone.

***Humanities Projects in Museums and
Historical Associations** $5,000–$400,000

National Endowment for the Humanities
Room 419
Washington, DC 20506
(202) 786-0284

Field of Interest: Humanities – Libraries and Museums
Average Amount Given: $194,000
Purpose: To assist museums, historical organizations, and other cultural institutions plan effective and imaginative programs to convey and interpret the humanities to the general public.
Who May Apply: Public and private nonprofit entities.
Requirements: None.
Contact: Division of General Programs.
Application Information: Application required.
Initial Approach: Letter or phone.

***Institute of Museum Services
Conservation Projects** $3,200,000

Institute of Museum Services
1100 Pennsylvania Ave., NW
Room 510
Washington, DC 20202
(202) 786-0536

Field of Interest: Humanities – Libraries and Museums
Average Amount Given: $13,100
Purpose: For the conservation of living and non-living collections, research, and training.
Who May Apply: Museums and public or private nonprofits.
Requirements: None.
Contact: Director.
Application Information: Application required.
Initial Approach: Letter or phone.

Library Research and Demonstration
Project Grants $285,000

Office of Educational Research and Improvement
Department of Education
555 New Jersey Ave., NW
Washington, DC 20208
(202) 357-6319

Field of Interest: Humanities – Libraries and Museums
Average Amount Given: N/A
Purpose: To research specialized services intended to improve library and information science practices.
Who May Apply: Public or private entities of all types.
Requirements: None.
Contact: Ray Fry.
Application Information: Application required.
Initial Approach: Letter or phone.

*Museum Project Grants $12,000,000

National Endowment for the Arts
1100 Pennsylvania Ave., NW
Washington, DC 20506
(202) 682-5442

Field of Interest: Humanities – Libraries and Museums
Average Amount Given: Variable
Purpose: To support the essential activities of American museums.
Who May Apply: Nonprofit organizations.
Requirements: 50% matching funding required.
Contact: Director.
Application Information: Application required.
Initial Approach: Letter or phone.

Museum Project Grants   Up to $25,000

National Endowment for the Arts
1100 Pennsylvania Ave., NW
Washington, DC 20506
(202) 682-5442

Field of Interest: Humanities – Libraries and Museums
Average Amount Given: N/A
Purpose: To support the essential activities of American museums.
Who May Apply: Qualified, full-time museum professionals.
Requirements: None.
Contact: Director.
Application Information: Application required.
Initial Approach: Letter or phone.

National Historical Publications and
Records Project Grants $500–$386,000

National Archives and Records Administration
National Archives Building
Washington, DC 20408
(202) 501-5603

Field of Interest: Humanities – Libraries and Museums
Average Amount Given: $41,000
Purpose: To promote a wide range of projects related to the preservation, publication, and use of documentary sources relating to U.S. history.
Who May Apply: Individuals and nonprofit entities, including historical societies, museums, and university presses.
Requirements: Variable.
Contact: Director.
Application Information: Application required.
Initial Approach: Letter or phone.

Reference Materials/Access Project Grants $10,000–$150,000

National Endowment for the Humanities
Room 318
Washington, DC 20506
(202) 786-0358

Field of Interest: Humanities – Libraries and Museums
Average Amount Given: $70,000
Purpose: To fund projects facilitating scholarly access to significant humanities research resources such as libraries and data banks.
Who May Apply: Qualified individuals and public and private nonprofit entities.
Requirements: None.
Contact: Division of Research Programs.
Application Information: Application required.
Initial Approach: Letter or phone.

Reference Materials/Tools Project Grants $28,600–$240,000

National Endowment for the Humanities
Room 318
Washington, DC 20506
(202) 786-0358

Field of Interest: Humanities – Libraries and Museums
Average Amount Given: $91,436
Purpose: To fund projects which create research tools important for scholarly research.
Who May Apply: Individuals and public or private nonprofits.
Requirements: None.
Contact: Division of Research Programs.
Application Information: Application required.
Initial Approach: Letter or phone.

*Strengthening Research Library Resources $64,000–$575,000

Department of Education
Washington, DC 20208
(202) 357-6319

Field of Interest: Humanities – Libraries and Museums
Average Amount Given: $177,300
Purpose: To help research libraries strengthen their collections and to make their collections accessible to researchers.
Who May Apply: Public or private nonprofit entities with major research libraries.
Requirements: None.
Contact: Ray Fry.
Application Information: Application required.
Initial Approach: Letter or phone.

Travel to Collections in the Humanities $300,000

National Endowment for the Humanities
Room 316
Washington, DC 20506
(202) 786-0463

Field of Interest: Humanities – Libraries and Museums
Average Amount Given: $750
Purpose: To enable American scholars to travel to use the research collections of libraries, archives, museums, or other research repositories.
Who May Apply: Individuals.
Requirements: None.
Contact: Division of Fellowships and Seminars.
Application Information: Application required.
Initial Approach: Letter or phone.

*Humanities Projects in Media $4,000–$750,000

National Endowment for the Humanities
Room 420
Washington, DC 20506
(202) 786-0278

Field of Interest: Humanities – Media
Average Amount Given: $137,400
Purpose: To support professional radio and television productions which advance public understanding and appreciation of the humanities by adults and young people.
Who May Apply: Public and private nonprofit organizations.
Requirements: None.
Contact: Division of General Programs.
Application Information: Application required.
Initial Approach: Letter or phone.

Humanities Text and Publications Project Grants $350,000

National Endowment for the Humanities
Room 318
Washington, DC 20506
(202) 786-0207

Field of Interest: Humanities – Publications
Average Amount Given: $7,000
Purpose: To ensure the publication and dissemination of scholarly works in the humanities.
Who May Apply: Commercial and nonprofit scholarly presses and publishing entities.
Requirements: None.
Contact: Division of Research Programs.
Application Information: Application required.
Initial Approach: Letter or phone.

Text/Editions Project Grants $6,250–$180,000

National Endowment for the Humanities
Room 318
Washington, DC 20506
(202) 786-0207

Field of Interest: Humanities – Publications
Average Amount Given: $8,500
Purpose: To fund editions of materials important for scholarly research in the humanities.
Who May Apply: Individuals and public or private nonprofit organizations.
Requirements: None.
Contact: Division of Research Programs.
Application Information: Application required.
Initial Approach: Letter or phone.

Text/Translations Project Grants $3,500–$200,000

National Endowment for the Humanities
Room 318
Washington, DC 20506
(202) 786-0207

Field of Interest: Humanities – Publications
Average Amount Given: $45,000
Purpose: To support translation into English of text and documents that will make major contributions to humanities research.
Who May Apply: Individuals and public or private nonprofits.
Requirements: None.
Contact: Division of Research Programs.
Application Information: Application required.
Initial Approach: Letter or phone.

**Historic Preservation Fund
Grants-in-Aid**   **$72,000–$804,000**

National Park Service
Department of the Interior
Washington, DC 20240
(202) 343-7625

Field of Interest: Humanities – Urban Development
Average Amount Given: $457,000
Purpose: To expand and maintain the National Register of Historic Places and to identify, evaluate, and protect these places.
Who May Apply: Individuals and public and private, profit and non-profit agencies are subcontracted by State Historic Preservation Trusts.
Requirements: 50% matching funding required.
Contact: Director, Cultural Resources.
Application Information: Application required.
Initial Approach: Letter or phone.

***College–Community Forums
on the U.S. Constitution**   **$1,500–$15,000**

Commission on the Bicentennial of the U.S. Constitution
808 17th Street, NW
Washington, DC 20006
(202) 653-7469

Field of Interest: Humanities – General
Average Amount Given: $7,500
Purpose: To engage scholars and citizens in a discussion of constitutional issues and principles.
Who May Apply: Nonprofit entities and educational institutions.
Requirements: None.
Contact: Grant Program Director.
Application Information: Application required.
Initial Approach: Letter or phone.

*Humanities Challenge Grants   **Up to $1,000,000**

National Endowment for the Humanities
Room 429
Washington, DC 20506
(202) 786-0361

Field of Interest: Humanities – General
Average Amount Given: $370,000
Purpose: To increase the financial stability of and to improve the quality of the humanities services of educational and cultural institutions.
Who May Apply: Public and private nonprofit entities.
Requirements: 75% matching funding required.
Contact: Office of Challenge Grants.
Application Information: Application required.
Initial Approach: Letter or phone.

**Humanities Conference
Project Grants**   **$6,000–$40,000**

National Endowment for the Humanities
Room 318
Washington, DC 20506
(202) 786-0210

Field of Interest: Humanities – General
Average Amount Given: $16,000
Purpose: To fund conferences which will allow humanities scholars to discuss and advance issues in the field.
Who May Apply: Individuals and public and private nonprofit entities.
Requirements: None.
Contact: Division of Research Projects.
Application Information: Application required.
Initial Approach: Letter or phone.

**Interpretive Research and Projects
in the Humanities**   **$20,000–$300,000**

National Endowment for the Humanities
Room 318
Washington, DC 20506
(202) 786-0210

Field of Interest: Humanities – General
Average Amount Given: $60,000
Purpose: To advance important and original research in all fields of
the humanities through collaborative, multi-year scholarly projects.
Who May Apply: Qualified individuals and public or private non-
profit entities.
Requirements: None.
Contact: Division of Research Programs.
Application Information: Application required.
Initial Approach: Letter or phone.

**Interpretive Research in the Humanities,
Science and Technology**   **$17,400–$100,000**

National Endowment for the Humanities
Room 318
Washington, DC 20506
(202) 786-0210

Field of Interest: Humanities – General
Average Amount Given: $60,000
Purpose: To support research designed to deepen our understand-
ing of science and technology and its role in our culture.
Who May Apply: Individuals and public and private nonprofit enti-
ties.
Requirements: None.
Contact: Division of Research Programs.
Application Information: Application required.
Initial Approach: Letter or phone.

**Selected Areas of Humanities
Promotion**   **$50,000–$100,000**

National Endowment for the Humanities
Room 318
Washington, DC 20506
(202) 786-0204

Field of Interest: Humanities – General
Average Amount Given: $83,333
Purpose: To support American scholars pursuing humanities re-
search.
Who May Apply: Public and private nonprofit entities.
Requirements: None.
Contact: Division of International Research.
Application Information: Application required.
Initial Approach: Letter or phone.

MEDICAL RESEARCH

Biological Response to Environmental Health Hazards Small Business Project Grants $50,000–$500,000

Department of Health and Human Services
PO Box 12233
Research Triangle Park, NC 27709
(919) 541-7634

Field of Interest: Medical Research – Business Development
Average Amount Given: N/A
Purpose: To understand how chemical agents cause pathological changes in cells and to obtain necessary equipment for this research.
Who May Apply: Small businesses.
Requirements: None.
Contact: David Mineo, Grants Management Officer.
Application Information: Application required.
Initial Approach: Letter or phone.

Research for Mothers and Children $11,000–$1,230,000

National Institutes of Health, PHS, DHHS
Bethesda, MD 20892
(301) 496-1848

Field of Interest: Medical Research – Children
Average Amount Given: $180,000
Purpose: To coordinate and support clinical, biomedical, and behavioral research associated with normal development from conception to maturity, and those factors which may delay or interfere with it.
Who May Apply: Individuals, small businesses, and public and private, profit and nonprofit entities.
Requirements: None.
Contact: Hildegard Topper.
Application Information: Application required.
Initial Approach: Letter or phone.

Biological Response to Environmental Health Hazards Research Grants $53,800–$1,600,000

Department of Health and Human Services
PO Box 12233
Research Triangle Park, NC 27709
(919) 541-7634

Field of Interest: Medical Research – Environment
Average Amount Given: $153,000
Purpose: To understand how chemical agents cause pathological changes in cells.
Who May Apply: Profit or nonprofit medical, educational, or research institutions and the individuals associated with them.
Requirements: None.
Contact: David Mineo, Grants Management Officer.
Application Information: Application required.
Initial Approach: Letter or phone.

Biological Response to Environmental Health Hazards Small Instrumentation Program $5,000–$60,000

Department of Health and Human Services
PO Box 12233
Research Triangle Park, NC 27709
(919) 541-7634

Field of Interest: Medical Research – Environment
Average Amount Given: N/A
Purpose: To understand how chemical agents cause pathological changes in cells and to obtain necessary equipment for this research.
Who May Apply: Profit or nonprofit medical, educational, or research institutions and the individuals associated with them.
Requirements: None.
Contact: David Mineo, Grants Management Officer.
Application Information: Application required.
Initial Approach: Letter or phone.

Aging Research Project Grants $15,800–$1,275,000

National Institutes of Health, PHS
Department of Health and Human Services
Bethesda, MD 20892
(301) 496-4996

Field of Interest: Medical Research – Gerontology
Average Amount Given: $170,000
Purpose: To support biomedical, social, and behavioral research on the aging process and the diseases connected with it.
Who May Apply: Individuals, small businesses, and public and private, profit and nonprofit entities.
Requirements: None.
Contact: Dr. Richard L. Sprott.
Application Information: Application required.
Initial Approach: Letter or phone.

Minority Biomedical Research Support $100,000–$1,500,000

National Institutes of Health, PHS
Department of Health and Human Services
Bethesda, MD 20892
(301) 496-6745

Field of Interest: Medical Research – Minority Development
Average Amount Given: N/A
Purpose: To increase the pool of minorities pursuing biomedical research careers.
Who May Apply: Educational entities with over 50% minority enrollment, and those with a history of encouragement and assistance to minorities; and qualified individuals at these institutions.
Requirements: None.
Contact: Dr. Ciriaco Gonzales.
Application Information: Application required.
Initial Approach: Letter or phone.

Biomedical Research – Minority High School Student Research Apprentice Grants

National Center for Research Resources
National Institutes of Health, PHS
Department of Health and Human Services
Bethesda, MD 20892
(301) 496-6743

Field of Interest: Medical Research – Minority Development
Average Amount Given: $5,000
Purpose: To strengthen U.S. health-related research.
Who May Apply: Accredited academic institutions and individuals associated with them.
Requirements: None.
Contact: Dr. Marjorie Tingle.
Application Information: Application required.
Initial Approach: Letter or phone.

Medical Library Assistance Scientific Publication Grants $12,000–$1,000,000

National Institutes of Health, PHS
Department of Health and Human Services
Bethesda, MD 20892
(301) 496-4221

Field of Interest: Medical Research – Publications
Average Amount Given: $25,000 per year
Purpose: Support of investigations into health knowledge, organization, representation, and utilization.
Who May Apply: Qualified individuals.
Requirements: None.
Contact: Dr. Roger Dahlen.
Application Information: Application required.
Initial Approach: Letter or phone.

Medical Library Assistance Project Grants $12,000–$1,000,000

National Institutes of Health, PHS
Department of Health and Human Services
Bethesda, MD 20892
(301) 496-4221

Field of Interest: Medical Research – Publications
Average Amount Given: $157,000 per year
Purpose: To train professionals, strengthen library and information services, support biomedical publications, and conduct research in information science and in medical information.
Who May Apply: Any qualified public or private nonprofit.
Requirements: None.
Contact: Dr. Roger Dahlen.
Application Information: Application required.
Initial Approach: Letter or phone.

Alcohol Research Center Project Grants $460,000–$1,500,000

Health Resources and Services Administration, PHS
Department of Health and Human Services
5600 Fishers Lane
Rockville, MD 20857
(301) 443-2530

Field of Interest: Medical Research – Substance Abuse
Average Amount Given: $1,260,000
Purpose: To create a national alcohol research center to coordinate the activities of investigators from biomedical, behavioral, and social science disciplines.
Who May Apply: Any public or nonprofit private entity affiliated with a qualified institution.
Requirements: None.
Contact: Dr. Helen Chao, Acting Director.
Application Information: Application required.
Initial Approach: Letter or phone.

Alcohol Research Programs $22,400–$917,600

Department of Health and Human Services, Room 16–86
5600 Fishers Lane
Rockville, MD 20857
(301) 443-4703

Field of Interest: Medical Research – Substance Abuse
Average Amount Given: $164,000
Purpose: To develop a knowledge base which can be applied to alcohol treatment and prevention.
Who May Apply: Pubic and private, profit and nonprofit entities.
Requirements: None.
Contact: Dr. Helen Chao.
Application Information: Application required.
Initial Approach: Letter or phone.

Drug Abuse Research Programs $24,000–$1,500,000

Department of Health and Human Services, Room 8A–54
5600 Fishers Lane
Rockville, MD 20857
(301) 443-6021

Field of Interest: Medical Research – Substance Abuse
Average Amount Given: $215,000
Purpose: To develop new approaches to the medical and social issues regarding drug addiction through traditional research.
Who May Apply: Public and private profit and nonprofit entities.
Requirements: None.
Contact: Dr. Jack Manischewitz.
Application Information: Application required.
Initial Approach: Letter or phone.

Allergy, Immunology, and Transplantation Research $1,500–$870,000

National Institutes of Health, PHS
Department of Health and Human Services
Bethesda, MD 20892
(301) 496-7075

Field of Interest: Medical Research
Average Amount Given: $150,400
Purpose: To improve biomedical research and training in this area, including the development of related technology.
Who May Apply: Individuals, small businesses, and public and private, profit or nonprofit entities.
Requirements: None.
Contact: Gary Thompson.
Application Information: Application required.
Initial Approach: Letter or phone.

Anterior Segment Diseases Research $5,000–$532,000

National Institutes of Health, PHS
Department of Health and Human Services
Bethesda, MD 20892
(301) 496-5884

Field of Interest: Medical Research
Average Amount Given: $154,000
Purpose: For applied research, including prevention and non-surgical treatment, on diseases of the cornea and of the external ocular structures.
Who May Apply: Individuals, small businesses, and any public or private, profit or nonprofit entity.
Requirements: None.
Contact: Dr. Peter Dudley.
Application Information: Application required.
Initial Approach: Letter or phone.

Arthritis, Musculoskeletal, and Skin Diseases Research $10,000–$1,200,000

National Institutes of Health, PHS
Department of Health and Human Services
Bethesda, MD 20892
(301) 496-7495

Field of Interest: Medical Research
Average Amount Given: $177,600
Purpose: To support laboratory research and to provide postdoctoral training for individuals interested in careers in this field.
Who May Apply: Individuals and public and private, profit and nonprofit institutions.
Requirements: None.
Contact: Dr. M. Lockshin.
Application Information: Application required.
Initial Approach: Letter or phone.

Biological Basis Research in the Neurosciences $20,000–$1,000,000

National Institutes of Health, PHS
Department of Health and Human Services
Bethesda, MD 20892
(301) 496-9248

Field of Interest: Medical Research
Average Amount Given: $170,000
Purpose: To support research exploring the fundamental structure and function of the brain; pathological conditions within the brain and nervous system and related issues.
Who May Apply: Qualified individuals, small businesses, and public and private, profit and nonprofit entities.
Requirements: None.
Contact: Dr. John C. Dalton.
Application Information: Application required.
Initial Approach: Letter or phone.

Biological Models and Material Resources
$90,500–$1,000,000

National Center for Research Resources
National Institutes of Health
Public Health Service
Bethesda, MD 20892
(301) 402-0630

Field of Interest: Medical Research
Average Amount Given: $287,000
Purpose: To develop nonmammalian models for biological research.
Who May Apply: For-profit and nonprofit entities.
Requirements: None.
Contact: Dr. Louise Ramm.
Application Information: Application required.
Initial Approach: Letter or phone.

Biological Research Related to Deafness and Communicative Disorders
$72,500–$458,300

Department of Health and Human Services
Federal Bldg., Room 1C-11
Bethesda, MD 20892
(301) 496-1804

Field of Interest: Medical Research
Average Amount Given: $186,000
Purpose: To solve medical problems of deafness and disorders of human communication, including hearing, balance, voice, speech, language, taste, and smell.
Who May Apply: Individuals associated with any public, private, nonprofit or for-profit institution.
Requirements: None.
Contact: Dr. Ralph Naunto.
Application Information: Application required.
Initial Approach: Letter or phone.

Biomedical Research Support Grants
$6,000–$321,000

National Center for Research Resources
National Institutes of Health, PHS
Department of Health and Human Services
Bethesda, MD 20892
(301) 496-6743

Field of Interest: Medical Research – General
Average Amount Given: $88,000
Purpose: To strengthen U.S. health-related research.
Who May Apply: Accredited academic institutions and individuals associated with them.
Requirements: None.
Contact: Dr. Marjorie Tingle.
Application Information: Application required.
Initial Approach: Letter or phone.

Biophysics and Physiological Sciences Project Grants
$19,000–$1,000,000

National Institutes of Health, PHS
Department of Health and Human Services
Bethesda, MD 20892
(301) 496-7463

Field of Interest: Medical Research
Average Amount Given: $163,000
Purpose: To encourage the development of instruments, devices, and methodologies for biological research and to strengthen selected areas of clinical and physiological research.
Who May Apply: Individuals and any public or private, profit or nonprofit entity.
Requirements: None.
Contact: Dr. Marvin Cassman.
Application Information: Application required.
Initial Approach: Letter or phone.

Blood Diseases and Resources
Research $1,000–$2,200,000

National Institutes of Health, PHS
Department of Health and Human Services
Bethesda, MD 20892
(301) 496-4868

Field of Interest: Medical Research
Average Amount Given: $224,500
Purpose: To research prevention, improved diagnosis, and treatment of blood diseases; to improve the safety and availability of blood products; and to develop new scientists for blood disease research.
Who May Apply: Individuals, small businesses, and nonprofit organizations.
Requirements: None.
Contact: Director, Division of Blood Diseases and Resources.
Application Information: Application required.
Initial Approach: Letter or phone.

Cancer Biology Research $2,400–$1,880,000

National Cancer Institute
National Institutes of Health, PHS
Department of Health and Human Services
Bethesda, MD 20892
(301) 496-8636

Field of Interest: Medical Research
Average Amount Given: $201,000
Purpose: To provide fundamental information about the cause of cancer in man.
Who May Apply: Qualified individuals associated with educational institutions, public agencies, and profit or nonprofit entities, including small businesses.
Requirements: None.
Contact: Dr. Faye Austin.
Application Information: Application required.
Initial Approach: Letter or phone.

Cancer Cause and Prevention
Research $2,500–$6,860,000

National Cancer Institute
National Institutes of Health, PHS
Department of Health and Human Services
Bethesda, MD 20892
(301) 496-6745

Field of Interest: Medical Research
Average Amount Given: $250,000
Purpose: To identify the cause of cancer in man.
Who May Apply: Qualified individuals associated with educational institutions, public agencies, and profit or nonprofit entities, including small businesses.
Requirements: None.
Contact: Dr. Richard Adamson.
Application Information: Application required.
Initial Approach: Letter or phone.

Cancer Control $37,800–$791,200

National Cancer Institute
National Institutes of Health, PHS
Department of Health and Human Services
Bethesda, MD 20892
(301) 496-9569

Field of Interest: Medical Research
Average Amount Given: $244,000
Purpose: To reduce cancer incidence, morbidity, and mortality through research on interventions and their impact in defined populations.
Who May Apply: Qualified individuals associated with educational institutions, public agencies, and profit or nonprofit entities.
Requirements: None.
Contact: Dr. Edward Sondik.
Application Information: Application required.
Initial Approach: Letter or phone.

Cancer Control – Controlled Intervention $37,700–$790,000

National Institutes of Health, PHS
Department of Health and Human Services
Bethesda, MD 20892
(301) 496-7753

Field of Interest: Medical Research – General
Average Amount Given: $244,000
Purpose: To reduce cancer incidence and morbidity through research on interventions and their impact on defined populations.
Who May Apply: Academic institutions, nonprofit or profit entities, and the individuals associated with them.
Requirements: None.
Contact: Leo Buscher.
Application Information: Application required.
Initial Approach: Letter or phone.

Cancer Control – Defined Populations Research $37,700–$790,000

National Institutes of Health, PHS
Department of Health and Human Services
Bethesda, MD 20892
(301) 496-7753

Field of Interest: Medical Research – General
Average Amount Given: $244,000
Purpose: To reduce cancer incidence and morbidity through research on interventions and their impact on defined populations.
Who May Apply: Academic institutions, nonprofit or profit entities, and the individuals associated with them.
Requirements: None.
Contact: Leo Buscher.
Application Information: Application required.
Initial Approach: Letter or phone.

Cancer Control – Demonstration and Implementation Grants $37,700–$790,000

National Institutes of Health, PHS
Department of Health and Human Services
Bethesda, MD 20892
(301) 496-7753

Field of Interest: Medical Research – General
Average Amount Given: $244,000
Purpose: To reduce cancer incidence and morbidity through research on interventions and their impact on defined populations.
Who May Apply: Academic institutions, nonprofit or profit entities, and the individuals associated with them.
Requirements: None.
Contact: Leo Buscher.
Application Information: Application required.
Initial Approach: Letter or phone.

Cancer Detection and Diagnosis Research $20,000–$1,500,000

National Cancer Institute
Department of Health and Human Services
Bethesda, MD 20892
(301) 496-7815

Field of Interest: Medical Research
Average Amount Given: $227,000
Purpose: To identify cancer early and precisely enough so that the latest methods of treatment can be applied to the disease.
Who May Apply: Qualified individuals associated with educational institutions, public agencies, and profit or nonprofit entities, including small businesses.
Requirements: None.
Contact: Dr. Faye Austin.
Application Information: Application required.
Initial Approach: Letter or phone.

Cancer Treatment Research $4,850–$4,000,000

National Cancer Institute
Department of Health and Human Services
Bethesda, MD 20892
(301) 496-6711

Field of Interest: Medical Research
Average Amount Given: $265,000
Purpose: To develop the means to cure as many cancer patients as possible and to control the disease in patients who are not cured.
Who May Apply: Qualified individuals associated with educational institutions, public agencies, and profit or nonprofit entities, including small businesses.
Requirements: None.
Contact: Dr. Michael Grever.
Application Information: Application required.
Initial Approach: Letter or phone.

Cellular and Molecular Basis for Disease Research $19,000–$1,400,000

National Institutes of Health, PHS
Department of Health and Human Services
Bethesda, MD 20892
(301) 496-7021

Field of Interest: Medical Research
Average Amount Given: $141,000
Purpose: To research ways to prevent, treat, and cure diseases that result from disturbed or abnormal cell activities, centering on cellular events at the molecular level.
Who May Apply: Individuals, small businesses, and public and private, profit and nonprofit entities.
Requirements: None.
Contact: Dr. Charles Miller.
Application Information: Application required.
Initial Approach: Letter or phone.

Centers for Disease Control – Research Program Grants $317,000,000

Centers for Disease Control, PHS
Department of Health and Human Services
255 E Paces Ferry Road NE
Atlanta, GA 30305
(404) 842-6630

Field of Interest: Medical Research
Average Amount Given: N/A
Purpose: To control and prevent communicable and chronic diseases.
Who May Apply: Qualified individuals and organizations.
Requirements: None.
Contact: Henry Cassell.
Application Information: Application required.
Initial Approach: Letter or phone.

Clinical Research Related to Neurological Disorders $20,000–$3,000,000

National Institutes of Health, PHS
Department of Health and Human Services
Bethesda, MD 20892
(301) 496-9248

Field of Interest: Medical Research
Average Amount Given: $470,000
Purpose: To research solutions to neurological problems, including prevention, diagnosis and treatment, drug development, technical devices, and epidemiological research.
Who May Apply: Qualified individuals, small businesses, and public and private, profit and nonprofit entities.
Requirements: None.
Contact: Dr. John C. Dalton.
Application Information: Application required.
Initial Approach: Letter or phone.

Diabetes, Endocrinology, and Metabolism Research $16,000–$2,000,000

National Institutes of Health, PHS
Department of Health and Human Services
Bethesda, MD 20892
(301) 496-7348

Field of Interest: Medical Research
Average Amount Given: $180,000
Purpose: To support laboratory research and to provide postdoctoral training for individuals interested in careers in this field.
Who May Apply: Individuals and public and private, profit and non-profit institutions.
Requirements: None.
Contact: Dr. E. Johnson.
Application Information: Application required.
Initial Approach: Letter or phone.

Digestive Diseases and Nutrition Research $26,500–$1,400,000

National Institutes of Health, PHS
Department of Health and Human Services
Bethesda, MD 20892
(301) 496-133

Field of Interest: Medical Research
Average Amount Given: $164,000
Purpose: To support laboratory research and to provide postdoctoral training for individuals interested in careers in this field.
Who May Apply: Individuals and public and private, profit and non-profit institutions.
Requirements: None.
Contact: Dr. Jay Hoofnagle.
Application Information: Application required.
Initial Approach: Letter or phone.

Diseases of the Teeth and Supporting Tissue $15,000–$672,000

National Institutes of Health, PHS
Department of Health and Human Services
Bethesda, MD 20892
(301) 496-7437

Field of Interest: Medical Research
Average Amount Given: $120,000
Purpose: For research and equipment related to diseases of the teeth and supporting tissues.
Who May Apply: Qualified scientists associated with institutions.
Requirements: None.
Contact: Dr. Gerassimos G. Roussos.
Application Information: Application required.
Initial Approach: Letter or phone.

Disorders of the Craniofacial Structure and Function and Behavioral Aspects of Dentistry $15,000–$500,000

National Institute of Dental Research
Naitonal Institutes of Health, PHS
Department of Health and Human Services
Bethesda, MD 20892
(301) 496-7807

Field of Interest: Medical Research
Average Amount Given: $114,000
Purpose: For research and equipment related to craniofacial structure and function.
Who May Apply: Qualified scientists associated with institutions.
Requirements: None.
Contact: Dr. John D. Townsley.
Application Information: Application required.
Initial Approach: Letter or phone.

Genetics Research Project
Grants $19,000–$1,500,000

National Institutes of Health, PHS
Department of Health and Human Services
Bethesda, MD 20892
(301) 496-7175

Field of Interest: Medical Research
Average Amount Given: $156,000
Purpose: To research the prevention, therapy, and control of genetic diseases in man.
Who May Apply: Individuals, small businesses, and public and private, profit or nonprofit entities.
Requirements: None.
Contact: Dr. Judith Greenberg.
Application Information: Application required.
Initial Approach: Letter or phone.

Heart and Vascular Diseases
Research $8,000–$3,100,000

National Institutes of Health, PHS
Department of Health and Human Services
Bethesda, MD 20892
(301) 496-2553

Field of Interest: Medical Research
Average Amount Given: $236,500
Purpose: To research prevention, education and control activities related to heart and vascular diseases, and to develop young science investigators in this area.
Who May Apply: Individuals, small businesses, and nonprofit organizations.
Requirements: None.
Contact: Dr. David Robinson.
Application Information: Application required.
Initial Approach: Letter or phone.

Human Genome Research
Project Grant $15,000–$1,500,000

National Institutes of Health, PHS
Department of Health and Human Services
Bethesda, MD 20892
(301) 496-7531

Field of Interest: Medical Research
Average Amount Given: $265,000
Purpose: To map the human genome as a model for the biological sciences.
Who May Apply: Individuals, any public or private, for-profit or nonprofit entities, and any qualified small business.
Requirements: None.
Contact: Dr. Mark Guyer.
Application Information: Application required.
Initial Approach: Letter or phone.

Immunization Research
Project Grants $50,000–$250,000

Center for Preventive Services
Centers for Disease Control
Department of Health and Human Services
1600 Clifton Road, NE
Atlanta, GA 30333 (404) 639-1880

Field of Interest: Medical Research, Health Care
Average Amount Given: $110,000
Purpose: To conduct research and provide public information on vaccine-preventable diseases and conditions.
Who May Apply: Public and private nonprofit entities.
Requirements: None.
Contact: Dr. Walter A. Orenstein.
Application Information: Application required.
Initial Approach: Letter or phone.

Kidney Diseases, Urology, and
Hematology Research $15,000–$1,650,000

National Institutes of Health, PHS
Department of Health and Human Services
Bethesda, MD 20892
(301) 496-6325

Field of Interest: Medical Research
Average Amount Given: $171,000
Purpose: To support laboratory research and to provide postdoctoral training for individuals interested in careers in this field.
Who May Apply: Individuals and public and private, profit and non-profit institutions.
Requirements: None.
Contact: Dr. G. Striker, Director.
Application Information: Application required.
Initial Approach: Letter or phone.

Laboratory Animal Sciences
Project Grants $47,650–$574,000

National Center for Research Resources
National Institutes of Health, PHS
Department of Health and Human Services
Bethesda, MD 20892
(301) 402-0630

Field of Interest: Medical Research
Average Amount Given: $211,000
Purpose: To support research projects using animals effectively in research on human health problems.
Who May Apply: Qualified medical, educational, and health entities.
Requirements: None.
Contact: Dr. Louise Ramm.
Application Information: Application required.
Initial Approach: Letter or phone.

Lung Diseases Research $2,000–$2,100,000

National Institutes of Health, PHS
Department of Health and Human Services
Bethesda, MD 20892
(301) 496-7208

Field of Interest: Medical Research
Average Amount Given: $197,000
Purpose: To use available technology to cure diseases of the lungs and to stimulate technology related to these diseases.
Who May Apply: Individuals, small businesses, and nonprofit organizations.
Requirements: None.
Contact: Director, Division of Lung Diseases.
Application Information: Application required.
Initial Approach: Letter or phone.

Medical Treatment Effectiveness
Research $50,000–$1,000,000

Department of Health and Human Services, Room 18A–10
5600 Fishers Lane
Rockville, MD 20857
(301) 443-4033

Field of Interest: Medical Research
Average Amount Given: $250,000
Purpose: To improve the process of health service and care and to identify, analyze, and minimize sources of adverse outcomes.
Who May Apply: Individuals and public and private, for-profit and nonprofit entities.
Requirements: None.
Contact: Ralph Sloat, Grants Management Officer.
Application Information: Application required.
Initial Approach: Letter or phone.

Microbiology and Infectious Diseases
Research   **$1,000–$1,500,000**

National Institutes of Health, PHS
Department of Health and Human Services
Bethesda, MD 20892
(301) 496-7075

Field of Interest: Medical Research
Average Amount Given: $160,000
Purpose: To support research in this field by controlling disease caused by infectious or parasitic agents, including drug development and epidemiological research and related issues.
Who May Apply: Individuals and public or private nonprofit institutions.
Requirements: None.
Contact: Gary Thompson.
Application Information: Application required.
Initial Approach: Letter or phone.

Pharmacological Sciences
Project Grants   **$19,000–$752,000**

National Institutes of Health, PHS
Department of Health and Human Services
Bethesda, MD 20892
(301) 496-7707

Field of Interest: Medical Research
Average Amount Given: $134,000
Purpose: To research the chemical and molecular processes in therapeutic drugs and to design and synthesize new drugs and related issues.
Who May Apply: Individuals, small businesses, and public and private, profit or nonprofit entities.
Requirements: None.
Contact: Dr. Christine Carrico.
Application Information: Application required.
Initial Approach: Letter or phone.

Physiological Sciences
Project Grants   **Budgeted at $7,000,000**

National Institutes of Health, PHS
Bethesda, MD 20892
(301) 496-7463

Field of Interest: Medical Research – General
Average Amount Given: N/A
Purpose: To apply physics and engineering principles to the study of biomedical problems and to develop new technologies to deal with these problems.
Who May Apply: Individuals associated with research or educational institutions.
Requirements: None.
Contact: Dr. Marvin Cassman, Director.
Application Information: Application required.
Initial Approach: Letter or phone.

Primate Research
Project Grants   **$3,560,000–$5,400,000**

National Center for Research Resources
National Institutes of Health, PHS
Department of Health and Human Services
Bethesda, MD 20892
(301) 402-0630

Field of Interest: Medical Research
Average Amount Given: $5,222,000
Purpose: To support research projects using primates effectively in research on human health problems.
Who May Apply: Qualified medical, educational, and health entities.
Requirements: None.
Contact: Dr. Leo Whitehair.
Application Information: Application required.
Initial Approach: Letter or phone.

**Retinal and Choroidal Diseases
Research**   **$5,000–$2,860,000**
National Institutes of Health, PHS
Department of Health and Human Services
Bethesda, MD 20892
(301) 496-5884

Field of Interest: Medical Research
Average Amount Given: $153,000
Purpose: To research the structure and function of the retina in health and disease and related issues.
Who May Apply: Qualified individuals, small businesses, and any public or private, profit or nonprofit entity.
Requirements: None.
Contact: Peter A. Dudley.
Application Information: Application required.
Initial Approach: Letter or phone.

**Strabismus, Amblyopia, and
Visual Processing**   **$5,000–$349,000**
National Institutes of Health, PHS
Department of Health and Human Services
Bethesda, MD 20892
(301) 496-5301

Field of Interest: Medical Research
Average Amount Given: $127,000
Purpose: To study the central visual pathways from the retina to the brain and the processing of visual information, visual perception, the optical properties of the eye, the functioning of the pupil, and the control of the ocular muscles.
Who May Apply: Individuals, small businesses, and any public or private, profit or nonprofit entity.
Requirements: None.
Contact: Dr. Constance Atwell.
Application Information: Application required.
Initial Approach: Letter or phone.

SCHOLARSHIPS

Arts Administration Fellows Program $200,000

National Endowment for the Arts
1100 Pennsylvania Ave., NW
Washington, DC 20506
(202) 682-5486

Field of Interest: Scholarships – Arts and Literature
Average Amount Given: $4,000
Purpose: To provide 13-week fellowships for professionals in arts management and related fields.
Who May Apply: Individuals.
Requirements: None.
Contact: Director.
Application Information: Application required.
Initial Approach: Letter or phone.

Distinguished Designer Fellowships $4,150,000

National Endowment for the Arts
1100 Pennsylvania Ave., NW
Washington, DC 20506
(202) 682-5437

Field of Interest: Scholarships – Arts and Literature
Average Amount Given: $20,000
Purpose: Awarded for excellence in architecture, landscape architecture, urban design, historic preservation, planning, interior design, graphic design, industrial design, and fashion design.
Who May Apply: Individuals.
Requirements: None.
Contact: Director, Design Arts Program.
Application Information: Application required.
Initial Approach: Letter or phone.

Literature Fellowships $5,000,000

National Endowment for the Arts
1100 Pennsylvania Ave., NW
Washington, DC 20506
(202) 682-5451

Field of Interest: Scholarships – Arts and Literature
Average Amount Given: $40,000
Purpose: Award for creative writers of fiction and non-fiction, poets, and translators.
Who May Apply: Individuals.
Requirements: None.
Contact: Director, Literature Program.
Application Information: Application required.
Initial Approach: Letter or phone.

Advanced Nurse Education $19,400–$334,900

Department of Health and Human Services, Room 5C–26
5600 Fishers Lane
Rockville, MD 20857
(301) 443-6333

Field of Interest: Scholarships – Health Professions
Average Amount Given: N/A
Purpose: To prepare registered nurses at the master's or doctoral level to become teachers and administrators or clinical nurse specialists.
Who May Apply: Qualified individuals at accredited schools of nursing.
Requirements: None.
Contact: Dr. Thomas Phillips.
Application Information: Application required.
Initial Approach: Letter or phone.

Allied Health Project Grants

Department of Health and Human Services, Room 8C-02
5600 Fishers Lane
Rockville, MD 20857
(301) 443-6763

Field of Interest: Scholarships – Health Professions
Average Amount Given: N/A
Purpose: To strengthen allied health training by expanding enrollment in professions of greatest need and to recruit minority and disadvantaged students.
Who May Apply: Public or private nonprofit educational institution or hospital.
Requirements: None.
Contact: Norman Clark.
Application Information: Application required.
Initial Approach: Letter or phone.

Geriatrics Health Professions Training Grant $45,000–$503,000

Health Resources and Services Administration, PHS
Department of Health and Human Services
5600 Fishers Lane
Rockville, MD 20857
(301) 443-6887

Field of Interest: Scholarships – Health Professions
Average Amount Given: $280,000
Purpose: To create regional resource centers focused on multidisciplinary training of health professionals in geriatric care.
Who May Apply: Any accredited health professions school and qualified individuals at these schools.
Requirements: None.
Contact: Donald Blandford.
Application Information: Application required.
Initial Approach: Letter or phone.

Graduate Programs in Health Administration $1,500,000

Health Resources and Services Administration, PHS
Department of Health and Human Services, Rm 8C-09
5600 Fishers Lane
Rockville, MD 20857
(301) 443-6896

Field of Interest: Scholarships – Health Professions
Average Amount Given: $42,200
Purpose: To support accredited graduate educational programs in health and hospital administration and health planning.
Who May Apply: Any public or private nonprofit educational entity and qualified individuals at these institutions.
Requirements: None.
Contact: Ronald B. Merrill.
Application Information: Application required.
Initial Approach: Letter or phone.

Grants for Graduate Training in Family Medicine $17,100–$295,000

Department of Health and Human Services, Room 4C-25
5600 Fishers Lane
Rockville, MD 20857
(301) 443-6190

Field of Interest: Scholarships – Health Professions
Average Amount Given: $110,262
Purpose: To increase the number of physicians practicing family medicine.
Who May Apply: Public and private nonprofit hospitals, health, or educational entities.
Requirements: None.
Contact: Dr. Marilyn Gaston.
Application Information: Application required.
Initial Approach: Letter or phone.

**Grants for Residency Training in
General Internal Medicine and/or
General Pediatrics**   **$58,300–$400,700**

Health Resources and Services Administration, PHS
Department of Health and Human Services
5600 Fishers Lane
Rockville, MD 20857
(301) 443-6880

Field of Interest: Scholarships – Health Professions
Average Amount Given: $172,161
Purpose: To promote the graduate education of physicians who plan to enter general internal practice or pediatrics.
Who May Apply: Any accredited school offering these appropriate degrees and individuals at those schools.
Requirements: None.
Contact: Dr. Marilyn Gaston.
Application Information: Application required.
Initial Approach: Letter or phone.

**Health Administration Graduate
Traineeships**   **$3,700–$36,500**

Health Resources and Services Administration, PHS
Department of Health and Human Services, Rm 8C–09
5600 Fishers Lane
Rockville, MD 20857
(301) 443-6896

Field of Interest: Scholarships – Health Professions
Average Amount Given: $13,000
Purpose: To enroll qualified students in accredited graduate programs in health and hospital administration and health policy analysis and planning.
Who May Apply: Any public or private nonprofit educational entity and qualified individuals at these institutions.
Requirements: None.
Contact: Ronald B. Merrill.
Application Information: Application required.
Initial Approach: Letter or phone.

**Indian Health Service Educational
Loan Repayment**   **$3,000–$75,000**

Indian Health Service
Department of Health and Human Services
12300 Twinbrook Parkway, Suite 100
Rockville, MD 20852
(301) 443-4242

Field of Interest: Scholarships – Health Professions
Maximum Amount Given: $25,000 per year for two years
Purpose: To attract health professionals to the Indian Health Service.
Who May Apply: Individuals who are in the last year of health profession education or who are in practice.
Requirements: None.
Contact: Darrell Pratt.
Application Information: Application required.
Initial Approach: Letter or phone.

**National Health Service Corps Loan
Repayment Project Grant**   **$25,000–$100,000**

Department of Health and Human Services, Room 7–34
5600 Fishers Lane
Rockville, MD 20857
(301) 443-1650

Field of Interest: Scholarships – Health Professions
Average Amount Given: $50,000
Purpose: To assure a supply of trained health professionals for the National Health Service Corps.
Who May Apply: Individuals in last year of health care training or in professional practice.
Requirements: Must be U.S. citizens.
Contact: Dr. Lewis Norris.
Application Information: Application required.
Initial Approach: Letter or phone.

National Health Service Corps Scholarship Program

Department of Health and Human Services, Room 7–16
5600 Fishers Lane
Rockville, MD 20857
(301) 443-1650

Field of Interest: Scholarships – Health Professions
Average Amount Given: $24,500
Purpose: To train medical professionals for the National Health Service Corps to serve in shortage areas of the U.S.
Who May Apply: Individual students in health professions studies at accredited U.S. colleges and universities.
Requirements: Awardees must serve for at least one year in the National Health Service Corps.
Contact: Dr. Norris Lewis.
Application Information: Application required.
Initial Approach: Letter or phone.

Nurse Practitioner and Nurse Midwife Education and Traineeships $3,700–$88,100

Department of Health and Human Services, Room 5C–26
5600 Fishers Lane
Rockville, MD 20857
(301) 443-6333

Field of Interest: Scholarships – Health Professions
Average Amount Given: $6,500 plus tuition and books
Purpose: To educate registered nurses qualified to provide primary health care.
Who May Apply: Qualified individuals and appropriate accredited medical training institutions.
Requirements: None.
Contact: Anastasia Buchanan.
Application Information: Application required.
Initial Approach: Letter or phone.

Nurse Training Improvement Special Project Grants $7,100–$233,000

Department of Health and Human Services, Room 5C–14
5600 Fishers Lane
Rockville, MD 20857
(301) 443-6193

Field of Interest: Scholarships – Health Professions
Average Amount Given: $150,000
Purpose: To improve the quality of nursing education through educating nurses for long-term and specialized practice.
Who May Apply: Public and nonprofit private schools of nursing and qualified individuals at these schools.
Requirements: None
Contact: Dr. Mary Hill.
Application Information: Application required.
Initial Approach: Letter or phone.

*Physician's Assistant Training Program Grants $1,200,000

Health Resources and Services Administration, PHS
Department of Health and Human Services
5600 Fishers Lane
Rockville, MD 20857
(301) 443-6880

Field of Interest: Scholarships – Health Professions
Average Amount Given: $12,000 per year
Purpose: To plan, develop, and operate physician's assistant programs.
Who May Apply: Public or nonprofit private health or educational entities.
Requirements: None.
Contact: Dr. Marilyn Gaston.
Application Information: Application required.
Initial Approach: Letter or phone.

Professional Nurse Traineeships $8,800–$609,500

Department of Health and Human Services, Room 5C–13
5600 Fishers Lane
Rockville, MD 20857
(301) 443-5763

Field of Interest: Scholarships – Health Professions
Average Amount Given: $6,500 per year plus tuition and expenses
Purpose: To prepare registered nurses as administrators, research-ers, teachers, and other roles requiring advanced training.
Who May Apply: Schools of nursing and public health, public or non-profit hospitals and other public or nonprofit entities, and qualified individuals associated with these entities.
Requirements: None.
Contact: Anastasia Buchanan.
Application Information: Application required.
Initial Approach: Letter or phone.

Public Health Traineeships $31,000–$290,000

Health Resources and Services Administration, PHS
Department of Health and Human Services, Rm 8C–09
5600 Fishers Lane
Rockville, MD 20857
(301) 443-6896

Field of Interest: Scholarships – Health Professions
Average Amount Given: $116,300
Purpose: To promote graduate education in public health and re-lated fields.
Who May Apply: Accredited schools of public health and qualified individuals attending these schools.
Requirements: None.
Contact: E. Coleman Santucci.
Application Information: Application required.
Initial Approach: Letter or phone.

Scholarships for the Undergraduate Education of Professional Nurses $100–$10,000

Department of Health and Human Services, Room 8A-55
5600 Fishers Lane
Rockville, MD 20857
(301) 443-1530

Field of Interest: Scholarships – Health Professions
Average Amount Given: N/A
Purpose: To provide financial assistance to undergraduate nursing students who are in need and who agree to work for the DHHS after graduation.
Who May Apply: Undergraduate nursing students at accredited schools.
Requirements: None.
Contact: Office of Program Development, Bureau of Health Profes-sions
Application Information: Application required.
Initial Approach: Letter or phone.

Bicentennial Educational Grant Program $1,000–$164,000

Commission on the Bicentennial of the U.S. Constitution
808 17th Street, NW
Washington, DC 20006
(202) 653-5110

Field of Interest: Scholarships – Humanities
Average Amount Given: $47,000
Purpose: To help elementary and secondary school teachers develop a better understanding of the history and development of the U.S. Constitution and the Bill of Rights so they can better teach these con-cepts to young learners.
Who May Apply: Individuals and private organizations and schools.
Requirements: None.
Contact: Education Grant Programs Office.
Application Information: Application required.
Initial Approach: Letter or phone.

Bilingual Education Training Fellowships $70,000–$210,000

Office of Bilingual and Minority Languages Affairs
330 C Street, SW
Washington, DC 20202
(202) 732-5722

Field of Interest: Scholarships – Humanities
Average Amount Given: $125,000
Purpose: To support training for personnel involved in bilingual education.
Who May Apply: Undergraduates at accredited institutions.
Requirements: None.
Contact: Dr. John S. Ovard.
Application Information: Application required.
Initial Approach: Letter or phone.

Fellowships for College Teachers and Independent Scholars $3,200,000

National Endowment for the Humanities
Room 316
Washington, DC 20506
(202) 786-0466

Field of Interest: Scholarships – Humanities
Average Amount Given: $30,000
Purpose: To enable college teachers and independent scholars to pursue research that will enhance their capabilities as teachers.
Who May Apply: Faculty of qualified colleges and independent scholars and writers, including retired faculty.
Requirements: None.
Contact: Division of Research Programs.
Application Information: Application required.
Initial Approach: Letter or phone.

Jacob K. Javits Fellowships $5,400,000

Department of Education
400 Maryland Ave., SW
Washington, DC 20202
(202) 732-4412

Field of Interest: Scholarships – Humanities
Average Amount Given: $9,000 plus tuition
Purpose: To provide fellowships to individuals of superior ability in the arts and humanities.
Who May Apply: Qualified individuals.
Requirements: U.S. citizenship required.
Contact: Alan P. Cissell.
Application Information: Application required.
Initial Approach: Letter or phone.

Library Career Fellowships

Office of Educational Research and Improvement
Department of Education
555 New Jersey Ave., NW
Washington, DC 20208
(202) 357-6319

Field of Interest: Scholarships – Humanities
Average Amount Given: $12,500
Purpose: To assist universities and libraries in training personnel for library careers.
Who May Apply: Educational institutions and library organizations and agencies and qualified individuals associated with them.
Requirements: None.
Contact: Ray Fry.
Application Information: Application required.
Initial Approach: Letter or phone.

Library Career Training   **$10,800–$33,400**

Office of Educational Research and Improvement
Department of Education
555 New Jersey Ave., NW
Washington, DC 20208
(202) 357-6319

Field of Interest: Scholarships – Humanities
Average Amount Given: N/A
Purpose: To assist universities and libraries train personnel for library careers.
Who May Apply: Educational institutions and library organizations and agencies and qualified individuals associated with them.
Requirements: None.
Contact: Ray Fry.
Application Information: Application required.
Initial Approach: Letter or phone.

**Summer Seminars for
College Teachers**   **$65,000–$90,000**

National Endowment for the Humanities
Room 316
Washington, DC 20506
(202) 786-0463

Field of Interest: Scholarships – Humanities
Average Amount Given: $81,750
Purpose: To provide opportunities for college teachers and independent scholars to work in the humanities during summers, under the tutelage of a humanities scholar.
Who May Apply: Distinguished scholars and teachers at institutions with libraries suitable for specialized research in the humanities.
Requirements: None.
Contact: Division of Fellowships and Seminars.
Application Information: Application required.
Initial Approach: Letter or phone.

**Summer Seminars for
School Teachers**   **$40,000–$87,000**

National Endowment for the Humanities
Room 316
Washington, DC 20506
(202) 786-0463

Field of Interest: Scholarships – Humanities
Average Amount Given: $62,000
Purpose: To provide teachers with the opportunity to work during the summer under the tutelage of distinguished scholars in the humanities.
Who May Apply: Distinguished teachers and active scholars in the humanities.
Requirements: None.
Contact: Summer Seminars Division.
Application Information: Application required.
Initial Approach: Letter or phone.

Summer Stipend Project Grants   **$800,000**

National Endowment for the Humanities
Room 316
Washington, DC 20506
(202) 786-0466

Field of Interest: Scholarships – Humanities
Average Amount Given: $3,750
Purpose: For two months of consecutive study for college teachers in the humanities.
Who May Apply: Qualified individuals, including college teachers and individual scholars.
Requirements: None.
Contact: Division of Fellowships and Seminars.
Application Information: Application required.
Initial Approach: Letter or phone.

Undergraduate Foreign Language Programs $22,000–$80,000

Department of Education
ROB-3, 7th and D Streets, SW
Washington, DC 20202
(202) 732-3293

Field of Interest: Scholarships – Humanities
Average Amount Given: $50,000
Purpose: To help educational institutions strengthen their foreign language programs.
Who May Apply: Accredited colleges and universities, public and private nonprofit entities and individuals.
Requirements: None.
Contact: Ralph Hines.
Application Information: Application required.
Initial Approach: Letter or phone.

Younger Scholars Project Grants $1,800–$2,200

National Endowment for the Humanities
Room 316
Washington, DC 20506
(202) 786-0463

Field of Interest: Scholarships – Humanities
Average Amount Given: $2,000
Purpose: To support noncredit humanities projects during the summer by advanced high school and college students, closely supervised by a humanities scholar.
Who may apply: U.S. citizens who have not received a bachelor's degree; if over 22 years old, individuals must be enrolled in college full time.
Requirements: None.
Contact: Division of Fellowships and seminars.
Application Information: Application required.
Initial Approach: Letter or phone.

Fulbright–Hays Doctoral Dissertation Research Abroad $3,400–$58,500

Center for International Education
Department of Education
ROB-3, 7th and D Streets, SW
Washington, DC 20202
(202) 732-3291

Field of Interest: Scholarships – International Understanding
Average Amount Given: $20,000
Purpose: To allow graduate students to engage in full-time research abroad in modern foreign languages and area studies.
Who May Apply: Institutions of higher education and qualified graduate students associated with them.
Requirements: None.
Contact: Vida Moattar.
Application Information: Application required.
Initial Approach: Letter or phone.

Fulbright–Hays Faculty Research Abroad Training Grants $5,000–$57,000

Center for International Education
Department of Education
ROB-3, 7th and D Streets, SW
Washington, DC 20202
(202) 732-3301

Field of Interest: Scholarships – International Understanding
Average Amount Given: $31,500
Purpose: To enable college faculty members to conduct research abroad in order to strengthen their foreign language skills.
Who May Apply: Educational institutions and the individuals associated with them.
Requirements: None.
Contact: Merion Kane.
Application Information: Application required.
Initial Approach: Letter or phone.

Fulbright–Hays Group Projects Abroad $28,000–$202,000

Department of Education
ROB-3, 7th and D Streets, SW
Washington, DC 20202
(202) 732-3283

Field of Interest: Scholarships – International Understanding
Average Amount Given: $68,000
Purpose: To help educational institutions improve their modern foreign language and area studies.
Who May Apply: Colleges and universities and qualified individuals associated with them.
Requirements: None.
Contact: Gwendolyn N. Weaver.
Application Information: Application required.
Initial Approach: Letter or phone.

Graduate Student Educational Exchange $1,000–$15,000

United States Information Agency
Institute of International Education
809 United Nations Plaza
New York, NY 10017

Field of Interest: Scholarships – International Understanding
Average Amount Given: $10,525
Purpose: To strengthen international relations by giving U.S. students the opportunity to live and study in another country.
Who May Apply: U.S. citizens who are graduate students at the time of application with foreign language proficiency and good health.
Requirements: None.
Contact: Director.
Application Information: Application required.
Initial Approach: Letter.

National Resource Fellowships for Language and International Studies

Department of Education
ROB-3, 7th and D Streets, SW
Washington, DC 20202
(202) 732-3298

Field of Interest: Scholarships – International Understanding
Average Amount Given: $12,500 per year
Purpose: To train experts in modern foreign languages and world affairs.
Who May Apply: Qualified individuals at accredited educational institutions.
Requirements: None.
Contact: Advanced Training and Research Branch.
Application Information: Application required.
Initial Approach: Letter or phone.

Undergraduate International Studies Programs $22,000–$80,000

Department of Education
ROB-3, 7th and D Streets, SW
Washington, DC 20202
(202) 732-3293

Field of Interest: Scholarships – International Understanding
Average Amount Given: $51,000
Purpose: To help educational institutions strengthen their undergraduate international studies programs.
Who May Apply: Accredited colleges and universities, public and private nonprofit entities and individuals.
Requirements: None.
Contact: Ralph Hines.
Application Information: Application required.
Initial Approach: Letter or phone.

**University Professors and Research
Scholars Educational Exchange**   **$2,000–$50,000**
United States Information Agency
Council for International Exchange of Scholars
3400 International Drive, NW
Washington, DC 20008-3097

Field of Interest: Scholarships – International Understanding
Average Amount Given: $20,000
Purpose: To support postdoctoral research for one year at overseas
colleges and universities.
Who May Apply: U.S. citizens with foreign language proficiency and
recognized professional standing.
Requirements: None.
Contact: Director.
Application Information: Application required.
Initial Approach: Letter.

**Aging Research Career
Development Awards**   **$20,000–$250,000**
National Institutes of Health, PHS
Bethesda, MD 20892
(301) 496-1472

Field of Interest: Scholarships – Medical Research
Average Amount Given: $120,000
Purpose: For research training in biomedical shortage areas.
Who May Apply: Qualified individuals at accredited institutions.
Requirements: None.
Contact: Carol Tippery.
Application Information: Application required.
Initial Approach: Letter or phone.

**Aging Research Clinical
Investigator Development Award**   **$54,000–$80,000**
National Institutes of Health, PHS
Bethesda, MD 20892
(301) 496-1472

Field of Interest: Scholarships – Medical Research
Average Amount Given: $70,000
Purpose: For research training in biomedical shortage areas.
Who May Apply: Qualified individuals at accredited institutions.
Requirements: None.
Contact: Carol Tippery.
Application Information: Application required.
Initial Approach: Letter or phone.

**Aging Research National
Service Awards**   **$20,000–$250,000**
National Institutes of Health, PHS
Bethesda, MD 20892
(301) 496-1472

Field of Interest: Scholarships – Medical Research
Average Amount Given: $120,000
Purpose: For research training in biomedical shortage areas.
Who May Apply: Qualified individuals at accredited institutions.
Requirements: None.
Contact: Carol Tippery.
Application Information: Application required.
Initial Approach: Letter or phone.

**Alcohol National Research Service
Awards for Research Training $11,500–$286,000**
Department of Health and Human Services, Room 16–86
5600 Fishers Lane
Rockville, MD 20857
(301) 443-4703

Field of Interest: Scholarships – Medical Research
Average Amount Given: $103,555
Purpose: To maintain well-trained alcohol researchers at the pre- and postdoctoral levels.
Who May Apply: Qualified individuals and public and private non-profit entities.
Requirements: None.
Contact: Dr. Helen Chao.
Application Information: Application required.
Initial Approach: Letter or phone.

**Alcohol Scientist Development
Award for Clinicians $54,800–$72,000**
Department of Health and Human Services, Room 16–86
5600 Fishers Lane
Rockville, MD 20857
(301) 443-4703

Field of Interest: Scholarships – Medical Research
Average Amount Given: $61,160
Purpose: To increase research relating to the problems of alcohol abuse, prevention, and rehabilitation.
Who May Apply: Qualified medical educational institutions or hospitals on behalf of individuals.
Requirements: None.
Contact: Dr. Helen Chao.
Application Information: Application required.
Initial Approach: Letter or phone.

**Allergy, Immunology, and Transplantation
Research Career Development
Awards $20,000–$250,000**
National Institutes of Health, PHS
Bethesda, MD 20892
(301) 496-7075

Field of Interest: Scholarships – Medical Research
Average Amount Given: $120,000
Purpose: For research training in biomedical shortage areas.
Who May Apply: Qualified individuals at accredited institutions.
Requirements: None.
Contact: Gary Thompson.
Application Information: Application required.
Initial Approach: Letter or phone.

**Allergy, Immunology, and Transplantation
Clinical Investigator Development
Award $54,000–$80,000**
National Institutes of Health, PHS
Bethesda, MD 20892
(301) 496-7075

Field of Interest: Scholarships – Medical Research
Average Amount Given: $70,000
Purpose: For research training in biomedical shortage areas.
Who May Apply: Qualified individuals at accredited institutions.
Requirements: None.
Contact: Gary Thompson.
Application Information: Application required.
Initial Approach: Letter or phone.

Allergy, Immunology, and Transplantation
National Research Service Awards $20,000–$250,000
National Institutes of Health, PHS
Bethesda, MD 20892
(301) 496-7075

Field of Interest: Scholarships – Medical Research
Average Amount Given: $120,000
Purpose: For research training in biomedical shortage areas.
Who May Apply: Qualified individuals at accredited institutions.
Requirements: None.
Contact: Gary Thompson.
Application Information: Application required.
Initial Approach: Letter or phone.

Anterior Segment Diseases Research
Career Development Awards $20,000–$250,000
National Institutes of Health, PHS
Bethesda, MD 20892
(301) 496-5884

Field of Interest: Scholarships – Medical Research
Average Amount Given: $120,000
Purpose: For research training in biomedical shortage areas.
Who May Apply: Qualified individuals at accredited institutions.
Requirements: None.
Contact: Carolyn Grimes.
Application Information: Application required.
Initial Approach: Letter or phone.

Anterior Segment Diseases Clinical
Investigator Development Award $54,000–$80,000
National Institutes of Health, PHS
Bethesda, MD 20892
(301) 496-5884

Field of Interest: Scholarships – Medical Research
Average Amount Given: $70,000
Purpose: For research training in biomedical shortage areas.
Who May Apply: Qualified individuals at accredited institutions.
Requirements: None.
Contact: Carolyn Grimes.
Application Information: Application required.

Anterior Segment Diseases National
Research Service Awards $20,000–$250,000
National Institutes of Health, PHS
Bethesda, MD 20892
(301) 496-5884

Field of Interest: Scholarships – Medical Research
Average Amount Given: $120,000
Purpose: For research training in biomedical shortage areas.
Who May Apply: Qualified individuals at accredited institutions.
Requirements: None.
Contact: Carolyn Grimes.
Application Information: Application required.
Initial Approach: Letter or phone.

Arthritis, Musculoskeletal, and Skin Diseases Research Career Development Awards $20,000–$250,000

National Institutes of Health, PHS
Bethesda, MD 20892
(301) 496-7495

Field of Interest: Scholarships – Medical Research
Average Amount Given: $120,000
Purpose: For research training in biomedical shortage areas.
Who May Apply: Qualified individuals at accredited institutions.
Requirements: None.
Contact: Diane Watson.
Application Information: Application required.
Initial Approach: Letter or phone.

Arthritis, Musculoskeletal, and Skin Diseases Clinical Investigator Development Award $54,000–$80,000

National Institutes of Health, PHS
Bethesda, MD 20892
(301) 496-7495

Field of Interest: Scholarships – Medical Research
Average Amount Given: $70,000
Purpose: For research training in biomedical shortage areas.
Who May Apply: Qualified individuals at accredited institutions.
Requirements: None.
Contact: Diane Watson.
Application Information: Application required.
Initial Approach: Letter or phone.

Arthritis, Musculoskeletal, and Skin Diseases National Research Service Awards $6,700,000

National Institutes of Health, PHS
Bethesda, MD 20892
(301) 496-7495

Field of Interest: Scholarships – Medical Research
Average Amount Given: N/A
Purpose: For research training in biomedical shortage areas.
Who May Apply: Qualified individuals at accredited institutions.
Requirements: None.
Contact: Diane Watson.
Application Information: Application required.
Initial Approach: Letter or phone.

Biological Neurological Disorders Career Development Awards $40,000–$70,000

National Institutes of Health, PHS
Bethesda, MD 20892
(301) 496-9231

Field of Interest: Scholarships – Medical Research
Average Amount Given: $60,000
Purpose: For research training in biomedical shortage areas.
Who May Apply: Qualified individuals at accredited institutions.
Requirements: None.
Contact: Mary Whitehead.
Application Information: Application required.
Initial Approach: Letter or phone.

**Biological Neurological Disorders
Clinical Investigator Development
Awards**   **$54,000–$80,000**

National Institutes of Health, PHS
Bethesda, MD 20892
(301) 496-9231

Field of Interest: Scholarships – Medical Research
Average Amount Given: $70,000
Purpose: For research training in biomedical shortage areas.
Who May Apply: Qualified individuals at accredited institutions.
Requirements: None.
Contact: Mary Whitehead.
Application Information: Application required.
Initial Approach: Letter or phone.

**Biological Neurological Disorders
National Research Service Awards** **$20,000–$235,000**

National Institutes of Health, PHS
Bethesda, MD 20892
(301) 496-9231

Field of Interest: Scholarships – Medical Research
Average Amount Given: $120,000
Purpose: For research training in biomedical shortage areas.
Who May Apply: Qualified individuals at accredited institutions.
Requirements: None.
Contact: Mary Whitehead.
Application Information: Application required.
Initial Approach: Letter or phone.

**Biomedical Research – NIH Research
Awards**   **$3,000–$10,500**

National Center for Research Resources
National Institutes of Health, PHS
Department of Health and Human Services
Bethesda, MD 20892
(301) 496-6743

Field of Interest: Scholarships – Medical Research
Average Amount Given: $5,000
Purpose: To strengthen U.S. health-related research.
Who May Apply: Accredited academic institutions and individuals
associated with them.
Requirements: None.
Contact: Dr. Marjorie Tingle.
Application Information: Application required.
Initial Approach: Letter or phone.

**Biophysics National Research
Service Award**   **$7,000,000**

National Institutes of Health, PHS
Bethesda, MD 20892
(301) 496-7463

Field of Interest: Scholarships – Medical Research
Average Amount Given: N/A
Purpose: To physics and engineering research support in the study of
biomedical problems.
Who May Apply: Individuals associated with research or educational
institutions.
Requirements: None.
Contact: Dr. Marvin Cassman, Director.
Application Information: Application required.
Initial Approach: Letter or phone.

Blood Diseases Career Development Awards $20,000–$250,000

National Institutes of Health, PHS
Bethesda, MD 20892
(301) 496-7255

Field of Interest: Scholarships – Medical Research
Average Amount Given: $200,000
Purpose: For research training in biomedical shortage areas.
Who May Apply: Qualified individuals at accredited institutions.
Requirements: None.
Contact: Lois Hinde.
Application Information: Application required.
Initial Approach: Letter or phone.

Blood Diseases Clinical Investigator Development Award $54,000–$80,000

National Institutes of Health, PHS
Bethesda, MD 20892
(301) 496-7255

Field of Interest: Scholarships – Medical Research
Average Amount Given: $70,000
Purpose: For research training in biomedical shortage areas.
Who May Apply: Qualified individuals at accredited institutions.
Requirements: None.
Contact: Lois Hinde.
Application Information: Application required.
Initial Approach: Letter or phone.

Blood Diseases National Research Service Awards $1,000–$2,000,000

National Institutes of Health, PHS
Bethesda, MD 20892
(301) 496-7255

Field of Interest: Scholarships – Medical Research
Average Amount Given: $224,000
Purpose: For research training in biomedical shortage areas.
Who May Apply: Qualified individuals at accredited institutions.
Requirements: None.
Contact: Lois Hinde.
Application Information: Application required.
Initial Approach: Letter or phone.

Cancer Research Manpower – Cancer Education Grants $2,800–$388,800

National Institutes of Health, PHS
Department of Health and Human Services
Bethesda, MD 20892
(301) 496-7753

Field of Interest: Scholarships – Medical Research
Average Amount Given: $88,000
Purpose: To support biomedical training opportunities.
Who May Apply: Academic institutions, nonprofit entities, and the individuals associated with them.
Requirements: None.
Contact: Leo Buscher.
Application Information: Application required.
Initial Approach: Letter or phone.

**Cancer Research Manpower –
NRSA Individual Fellowship Awards $2,800–$388,800**

National Institutes of Health, PHS
Department of Health and Human Services
Bethesda, MD 20892
(301) 496-7753

Field of Interest: Scholarships – Medical Research
Average Amount Given: $88,000
Purpose: To support biomedical training opportunities.
Who May Apply: Academic institutions, nonprofit entities, and the
individuals associated with them.
Requirements: None.
Contact: Leo Buscher.
Application Information: Application required.
Initial Approach: Letter or phone.

**Cancer Research Manpower –
Cancer Education Program for
Short-Term Support $2,800–$388,800**

National Institutes of Health, PHS
Department of Health and Human Services
Bethesda, MD 20892
(301) 496-7753

Field of Interest: Scholarships – Medical Research
Average Amount Given: $88,000
Purpose: To support biomedical training opportunities.
Who May Apply: Academic institutions, nonprofit entities and the
individuals associated with them.
Requirements: None.
Contact: Leo Buscher.
Application Information: Application required.
Initial Approach: Letter or phone.

**Cellular and Molecular Basis for Disease
Research Career Development
Awards $20,000–$250,000**

National Institutes of Health, PHS
Bethesda, MD 20892
(301) 496-7746

Field of Interest: Scholarships – Medical Research
Average Amount Given: $120,000
Purpose: For research training in biomedical shortage areas.
Who May Apply: Qualified individuals at accredited institutions.
Requirements: None.
Contact: Evelin Carlin.
Application Information: Application required.
Initial Approach: Letter or phone.

**Cellular and Molecular Basis for Disease
Clinical Investigator Development
Award $54,000–$80,000**

National Institutes of Health, PHS
Bethesda, MD 20892
(301) 496-7746

Field of Interest: Scholarships – Medical Research
Average Amount Given: $70,000
Purpose: For research training in biomedical shortage areas.
Who May Apply: Qualified individuals at accredited institutions.
Requirements: None.
Contact: Evelin Carlin.
Application Information: Application required.
Initial Approach: Letter or phone.

Cellular and Molecular Basis for Disease
National Research Service Awards $20,000–$250,000

National Institutes of Health, PHS
Bethesda, MD 20892
(301) 496-7746

Field of Interest: Scholarships – Medical Research
Average Amount Given: $120,000
Purpose: For research training in biomedical shortage areas.
Who May Apply: Qualified individuals at accredited institutions.
Requirements: None.
Contact: Evelin Carlin.
Application Information: Application required.
Initial Approach: Letter or phone.

Clinical Neurological Disorders Research
Career Development Awards $40,000–$70,000

National Institutes of Health, PHS
Bethesda, MD 20892
(301) 496-9231

Field of Interest: Scholarships – Medical Research
Average Amount Given: $60,000
Purpose: For research training in biomedical shortage areas.
Who May Apply: Qualified individuals at accredited institutions.
Requirements: None.
Contact: Mary Whitehead.
Application Information: Application required.
Initial Approach: Letter or phone.

Clinical Neurological Disorders
National Service Award $40,000–$70,000

National Institutes of Health, PHS
Bethesda, MD 20892
(301) 496-9231

Field of Interest: Scholarships – Medical Research
Average Amount Given: $60,000
Purpose: For research training in biomedical shortage areas.
Who May Apply: Qualified individuals at accredited institutions.
Requirements: None.
Contact: Mary Whitehead.
Application Information: Application required.
Initial Approach: Letter or phone.

Diabetes, Endocrinology, and Metabolism
Research Career Development
Awards $20,000–$250,000

National Institutes of Health, PHS
Bethesda, MD 20892
(301) 496-7793

Field of Interest: Scholarships – Medical Research
Average Amount Given: $120,000
Purpose: For research training in biomedical shortage areas.
Who May Apply: Qualified individuals at accredited institutions.
Requirements: None.
Contact: John Garthune.
Application Information: Application required.
Initial Approach: Letter or phone.

Diabetes, Endocrinology, and Metabolism Clinical Investigator Development Award $54,000–$80,000

National Institutes of Health, PHS
Bethesda, MD 20892
(301) 496-7793

Field of Interest: Scholarships – Medical Research
Average Amount Given: $70,000
Purpose: For research training in biomedical shortage areas.
Who May Apply: Qualified individuals at accredited institutions.
Requirements: None.
Contact: John Garthune.
Application Information: Application required.
Initial Approach: Letter or phone.

Diabetes, Endocrinology, and Metabolism National Research Service Awards $11,000,000

National Institutes of Health, PHS
Bethesda, MD 20892
(301) 496-7793

Field of Interest: Scholarships – Medical Research
Average Amount Given: N/A
Purpose: For research training in biomedical shortage areas.
Who May Apply: Qualified individuals at accredited institutions.
Requirements: None.
Contact: John Garthune.
Application Information: Application required.
Initial Approach: Letter or phone.

Digestive Diseases and Nutrition Career Development Awards $20,000–$250,000

National Institutes of Health, PHS
Bethesda, MD 20892
(301) 496-7793

Field of Interest: Scholarships – Medical Research
Average Amount Given: $120,000
Purpose: For research training in biomedical shortage areas.
Who May Apply: Qualified individuals at accredited institutions.
Requirements: None.
Contact: John Garthune.
Application Information: Application required.
Initial Approach: Letter or phone.

Digestive Diseases and Nutrition Clinical Investigator Development Award $54,000–$80,000

National Institutes of Health, PHS
Bethesda, MD 20892
(301) 496-7793

Field of Interest: Scholarships – Medical Research
Average Amount Given: $70,000
Purpose: For research training in biomedical shortage areas.
Who May Apply: Qualified individuals at accredited institutions.
Requirements: None.
Contact: John Garthune.
Application Information: Application required.
Initial Approach: Letter or phone.

Digestive Diseases and Nutrition
National Research Service Awards   **$5,800,000**

National Institutes of Health, PHS
Bethesda, MD 20892
(301) 496-7793

Field of Interest: Scholarships – Medical Research
Average Amount Given: N/A
Purpose: For research training in biomedical shortage areas.
Who May Apply: Qualified individuals at accredited institutions.
Requirements: None.
Contact: John Garthune.
Application Information: Application required.
Initial Approach: Letter or phone.

Drug Abuse Clinician
Development Award   **$45,000–$100,000**

Department of Health and Human Services, PHS
5600 Fishers Lane
Rockville, MD 20857
(301) 443-6021

Field of Interest: Scholarships – Medical Research
Average Amount Given: $63,000
Purpose: To support research relating to narcotic addictions.
Who May Apply: Individuals associated with accredited academic or medical institutions.
Requirements: None.
Contact: Dr. Jack Manischewitz.
Application Information: Application required.
Initial Approach: Letter or phone.

Drug Abuse National Research
Service Awards   **$8,500–$31,500**

Department of Health and Human Services, Room 8A–54
5600 Fishers Lane
Rockville, MD 20857
(301) 443-6021

Field of Interest: Scholarships – Medical Research
Average Amount Given: $20,000
Purpose: To provide high-quality training in the drug abuse field by supporting young scientists just beginning their research careers.
Who May Apply: Qualified individuals with at least two years graduate work in a doctoral program completed in the field.
Requirements: Individuals must be U.S. citizens or nationals.
Contact: Dr. Jack Manischewitz.
Application Information: Application required.
Initial Approach: Letter or phone.

Drug Abuse National Research Service
Awards – Institutional Grants   **$35,000–$424,000**

Department of Health and Human Services, PHS
5600 Fishers Lane
Rockville, MD 20857
(301) 443-6021

Field of Interest: Scholarships – Medical Research
Average Amount Given: $216,000
Purpose: To support research relating to narcotic addictions.
Who May Apply: Individuals associated with accredited academic or medical institutions.
Requirements: None.
Contact: Dr. Jack Manischewitz.
Application Information: Application required.
Initial Approach: Letter or phone.

Drug Abuse National Research Service Awards – Predoctoral Stipends

Department of Health and Human Services, PHS
5600 Fishers Lane
Rockville, MD 20857
(301) 443-6021

Field of Interest: Scholarships – Medical Research
Average Amount Given: $8,500
Purpose: To support research relating to narcotic addictions.
Who May Apply: Individuals associated with accredited academic or medical institutions.
Requirements: None.
Contact: Dr. Jack Manischewitz.
Application Information: Application required.
Initial Approach: Letter or phone.

Drug Abuse National Research Service Awards – Postdoctoral Stipends $17,000–$31,000

Department of Health and Human Services, PHS
5600 Fishers Lane
Rockville, MD 20857
(301) 443-6021

Field of Interest: Scholarships – Medical Research
Average Amount Given: $22,000
Purpose: To support research relating to narcotic addictions.
Who May Apply: Individuals associated with accredited academic or medical institutions.
Requirements: None.
Contact: Dr. Jack Manischewitz.
Application Information: Application required.
Initial Approach: Letter or phone.

Drug Abuse Research Scientist Award $45,000–$100,000

Department of Health and Human Services, PHS
5600 Fishers Lane
Rockville, MD 20857
(301) 443-6021

Field of Interest: Scholarships – Medical Research
Average Amount Given: $63,000
Purpose: To support research relating to narcotic addictions.
Who May Apply: Individuals associated with accredited academic or medical institutions.
Requirements: None.
Contact: Dr. Jack Manischewitz.
Application Information: Application required.
Initial Approach: Letter or phone.

Drug Abuse Scientist Development Award $45,000–$100,000

Department of Health and Human Services, PHS
5600 Fishers Lane
Rockville, MD 20857
(301) 443-6021

Field of Interest: Scholarships – Medical Research
Average Amount Given: $63,000
Purpose: To support research relating to narcotic addictions.
Who May Apply: Individuals associated with accredited academic or medical institutions.
Requirements: None.
Contact: Dr. Jack Manischewitz.
Application Information: Application required.
Initial Approach: Letter or phone.

Genetics Research Career Development Awards $20,000–$250,000

National Institutes of Health, PHS
Bethesda, MD 20892
(301) 496-7746

Field of Interest: Scholarships – Medical Research
Average Amount Given: $120,000
Purpose: For research training in biomedical shortage areas.
Who May Apply: Qualified individuals at accredited institutions.
Requirements: None.
Contact: Evelin Carlin.
Application Information: Application required.
Initial Approach: Letter or phone.

Genetics Research Clinical Investigator Development Award $54,000–$80,000

National Institutes of Health, PHS
Bethesda, MD 20892
(301) 496-7746

Field of Interest: Scholarships – Medical Research
Average Amount Given: $70,000
Purpose: For research training in biomedical shortage areas.
Who May Apply: Qualified individuals at accredited institutions.
Requirements: None.
Contact: Evelin Carlin.
Application Information: Application required.
Initial Approach: Letter or phone.

Genetics Research National Research Service Awards $20,000–$250,000

National Institutes of Health, PHS
Bethesda, MD 20892
(301) 496-7746

Field of Interest: Scholarships – Medical Research
Average Amount Given: $120,000
Purpose: For research training in biomedical shortage areas.
Who May Apply: Qualified individuals at accredited institutions.
Requirements: None.
Contact: Evelin Carlin.
Application Information: Application required.
Initial Approach: Letter or phone.

Grants for Faculty Development in Family Medicine $864–$289,000

Health Resources and Services Administration, PHS
Department of Health and Human Services, 4C–25
5600 Fishers Lane
Rockville, MD 20857
(301) 443-6190

Field of Interest: Scholarships – Medical Research
Average Amount Given: $152,000
Purpose: To increase the number of physicians available to teach family medicine.
Who May Apply: Public or private nonprofit hospitals or schools of medicine or osteopathy and individuals at these institutions.
Requirements: None.
Contact: Dr. Marilyn Gaston.
Application Information: Application required.
Initial Approach: Letter or phone.

Grants for Faculty Development in General Internal Medicine and/or Pediatrics   **$73,500–$334,000**

Health Resources and Services Administration, PHS
Department of Health and Human Services, 4C-25
5600 Fishers Lane
Rockville, MD 20857
(301) 443-6190

Field of Interest: Scholarships – Medical Research
Average Amount Given: $148,000
Purpose: To improve the development of faculty skills in physicians who teach or plan teaching careers in these fields.
Who May Apply: Accredited public or private nonprofit medical entities and qualified individuals at these institutions.
Requirements: None.
Contact: Dr. Marilyn Gaston.
Application Information: Application required.
Initial Approach: Letter or phone.

Grants for Faculty Training Projects in Geriatric Medicine and Dentistry   **$90,000–$198,000**

Department of Health and Human Services, Room 4C-25
5600 Fishers Lane
Rockville, MD 20857
(301) 443-6190

Field of Interest: Scholarships – Medical Research
Average Amount Given: $142,600
Purpose: To develop physicians and instructors for leadership roles in geriatric medicine and dentistry.
Who May Apply: Qualified individuals at schools of medicine, osteopathy, and teaching hospitals.
Requirements: None.
Contact: Dr. Marilyn Gaston.
Application Information: Application required.
Initial Approach: Letter or phone.

Heart and Vascular Diseases Career Development Awards   **$20,000–$250,000**

National Institutes of Health, PHS
Bethesda, MD 20892
(301) 496-7255

Field of Interest: Scholarships – Medical Research
Average Amount Given: $120,000
Purpose: For research training in biomedical shortage areas.
Who May Apply: Qualified individuals at accredited institutions.
Requirements: None.
Contact: Lois Hinde.
Application Information: Application required.
Initial Approach: Letter or phone.

Heart and Vascular Diseases Clinical Investigator Development Award   **$54,000–$80,000**

National Institutes of Health, PHS
Bethesda, MD 20892
(301) 496-7255

Field of Interest: Scholarships – Medical Research
Average Amount Given: $70,000
Purpose: For research training in biomedical shortage areas.
Who May Apply: Qualified individuals at accredited institutions.
Requirements: None.
Contact: Lois Hinde.
Application Information: Application required.
Initial Approach: Letter or phone.

**Heart and Vascular Diseases National
Research Service Awards**   **$8,000–$3,000,000**

National Institutes of Health, PHS
Bethesda, MD 20892
(301) 496-7255

Field of Interest: Scholarships – Medical Research
Average Amount Given: $230,000
Purpose: For research training in biomedical shortage areas.
Who May Apply: Qualified individuals at accredited institutions.
Requirements: None.
Contact: Lois Hinde.
Application Information: Application required.
Initial Approach: Letter or phone.

Intramural Research Training Award $24,000–$27,000

Department of Health and Human Services
Shannon Bldg., Room 140
Bethesda, MD 20892
(301) 496-4920

Field of Interest: Scholarships – Medical Research
Average Amount Given: $25,500
Purpose: To provide advanced training to physicians and doctoral-level investigators who are at the beginning of their careers.
Who May Apply: Individuals only.
Requirements: None.
Contact: Director for Intramural Affairs.
Application Information: Application required.
Initial Approach: Letter or phone.

**Kidney Diseases, Urology, and Hematology
Research Career Development
Awards**   **$20,000–$250,000**

National Institutes of Health, PHS
Bethesda, MD 20892
(301) 496-7793

Field of Interest: Scholarships – Medical Research
Average Amount Given: $120,000
Purpose: For research training in biomedical shortage areas.
Who May Apply: Qualified individuals at accredited institutions.
Requirements: None.
Contact: John Garthune.
Application Information: Application required.

**Kidney Diseases, Urology, and Hematology
Clinical Investigator
Development Award**   **$54,000–$80,000**

National Institutes of Health, PHS
Bethesda, MD 20892
(301) 496-7793

Field of Interest: Scholarships – Medical Research
Average Amount Given: $70,000
Purpose: For research training in biomedical shortage areas.
Who May Apply: Qualified individuals at accredited institutions.
Requirements: None.
Contact: John Garthune.
Application Information: Application required.
Initial Approach: Letter or phone.

Kidney Diseases, Urology, and Hematology National Research Service Awards $6,600,000

National Institutes of Health, PHS
Bethesda, MD 20892
(301) 496-7793

Field of Interest: Scholarships – Medical Research
Average Amount Given: N/A
Purpose: For research training in biomedical shortage areas.
Who May Apply: Qualified individuals at accredited institutions.
Requirements: None.
Contact: John Garthune.
Application Information: Application required.
Initial Approach: Letter or phone.

Laboratory Animal and Primate Research Fellowships

National Center for Research Resources
National Institutes of Health, PHS
Department of Health and Human Services
Bethesda, MD 20892
(301) 496-9840

Field of Interest: Scholarships – Medical Research
Average Amount Given: $17,000 per year
Purpose: To develop scientists skilled in this area.
Who May Apply: Individual postdoctoral scholars at accredited institutions.
Requirements: None.
Contact: Lacey Durham.
Application Information: Application required.
Initial Approach: Letter or phone.

Lung Diseases Research Career Development Awards $20,000–$250,000

National Institutes of Health, PHS
Bethesda, MD 20892
(301) 496-7255

Field of Interest: Scholarships – Medical Research
Average Amount Given: $120,000
Purpose: For research training in biomedical shortage areas.
Who May Apply: Qualified individuals at accredited institutions.
Requirements: None.
Contact: Lois Hinde.
Application Information: Application required.
Initial Approach: Letter or phone.

Lung Diseases Clinical Investigator Development Award $54,000–$80,000

National Institutes of Health, PHS
Bethesda, MD 20892
(301) 496-7255

Field of Interest: Scholarships – Medical Research
Average Amount Given: $70,000
Purpose: For research training in biomedical shortage areas.
Who May Apply: Qualified individuals at accredited institutions.
Requirements: None.
Contact: Lois Hinde.
Application Information: Application required.
Initial Approach: Letter or phone.

Lung Diseases National Research
Service Awards   **$2,000–$2,000,000**

National Institutes of Health, PHS
Bethesda, MD 20892
(301) 496-7255

Field of Interest: Scholarships – Medical Research
Average Amount Given: $196,000
Purpose: For research training in biomedical shortage areas.
Who May Apply: Qualified individuals at accredited institutions.
Requirements: None.
Contact: Lois Hinde.
Application Information: Application required.
Initial Approach: Letter or phone

Mental Health National Research
Service Awards   **$14,000–$100,000**

Department of Health and Human Services, PHS
5600 Fishers Lane
Rockville, MD 20857
(301) 443-3065

Field of Interest: Scholarships – Medical Research
Average Amount Given: $60,000
Purpose: To support research relating to mental health and illness issues.
Who May Apply: Individuals associated with accredited academic or medical institutions.
Requirements: None.
Contact: Bruce Ringler.
Application Information: Application required.
Initial Approach: Letter or phone.

Mental Health National Research
Service Awards for Research Training **$8,500–$31,000**

Department of Health and Human Services, Room 7C-15
5600 Fishers Lane
Rockville, MD 20857
(301) 443-3065

Field of Interest: Scholarships – Medical Research
Average Amount Given: N/A
Purpose: To ensure a supply of well-trained mental health professionals.
Who May Apply: Qualified individuals and appropriate medical training entities.
Requirements: None.
Contact: Bruce Ringler.
Application Information: Application required.
Initial Approach: Letter or phone.

Mental Health National Research
Service Predoctoral Stipends   **$17,000–$31,000**

Department of Health and Human Services, PHS
5600 Fishers Lane
Rockville, MD 20857
(301) 443-3065

Field of Interest: Scholarships – Medical Research
Average Amount Given: N/A
Purpose: To support research relating to mental health and illness issues.
Who May Apply: Individuals associated with accredited academic or medical institutions.
Requirements: None.
Contact: Bruce Ringler.
Application Information: Application required.
Initial Approach: Letter or phone.

**Mental Health National Research
Service Postdoctoral Stipends**   **$17,000–$31,000**

Department of Health and Human Services, PHS
5600 Fishers Lane
Rockville, MD 20857
(301) 443-3065

Field of Interest: Scholarships – Medical Research
Average Amount Given: $20,000
Purpose: To support research relating to mental health and illness issues.
Who May Apply: Individuals associated with accredited academic or medical institutions.
Requirements: None.
Contact: Bruce Ringler.
Application Information: Application required.
Initial Approach: Letter or phone.

**Mental Health Research Clinician
Development Award**   **$14,000–$100,000**

Department of Health and Human Services, PHS
5600 Fishers Lane
Rockville, MD 20857
(301) 443-3065

Field of Interest: Scholarships – Medical Research
Average Amount Given: $60,000
Purpose: To support research relating to mental health and illness issues.
Who May Apply: Individuals associated with accredited academic or medical institutions.
Requirements: None.
Contact: Bruce Ringler.
Application Information: Application required.
Initial Approach: Letter or phone.

**Mental Health Research Faculty
Fellowships**   **$17,000–$31,000**

Department of Health and Human Services, PHS
5600 Fishers Lane
Rockville, MD 20857
(301) 443-3065

Field of Interest: Scholarships – Medical Research
Average Amount Given: $20,000
Purpose: To support research relating to mental health and illness issues.
Who May Apply: Individuals associated with accredited academic or medical institutions.
Requirements: None.
Contact: Bruce Ringler.
Application Information: Application required.
Initial Approach: Letter or phone.

**Mental Health Research Scientist
Development Award**   **$14,000–$100,000**

Department of Health and Human Services, Room 7C-15
5600 Fishers Lane
Rockville, MD 20857
(301) 443-3065

Field of Interest: Scholarships – Medical Research
Average Amount Given: $60,000
Purpose: For research relating to mental illness and mental health.
Who May Apply: Qualified individuals at appropriate medical entities.
Requirements: None.
Contact: Bruce Ringler.
Application Information: Application required.
Initial Approach: Letter or phone.

Microbiology and Infectious Diseases Research Career Development Awards $20,000–$250,000

National Institutes of Health, PHS
Bethesda, MD 20892
(301) 496-7075

Field of Interest: Scholarships – Medical Research
Average Amount Given: $120,000
Purpose: For research training in biomedical shortage areas.
Who May Apply: Qualified individuals at accredited institutions.
Requirements: None.
Contact: Gary Thompson.
Application Information: Application required.
Initial Approach: Letter or phone.

Microbiology and Infectious Diseases Clinical Investigator Development Award $54,000–$80,000

National Institutes of Health, PHS
Bethesda, MD 20892
(301) 496-7075

Field of Interest: Scholarships – Medical Research
Average Amount Given: $70,000
Purpose: For research training in biomedical shortage areas.
Who May Apply: Qualified individuals at accredited institutions.
Requirements: None.
Contact: Gary Thompson.
Application Information: Application required.
Initial Approach: Letter or phone.

Microbiology and Infectious Diseases National Research Service Awards $20,000–$250,000

National Institutes of Health, PHS
Bethesda, MD 20892
(301) 496-7075

Field of Interest: Scholarships – Medical Research
Average Amount Given: $120,000
Purpose: For research training in biomedical shortage areas.
Who May Apply: Qualified individuals at accredited institutions.
Requirements: None.
Contact: Gary Thompson.
Application Information: Application required.
Initial Approach: Letter or phone.

National Research Services Awards $88,600–$184,500

Department of Health and Human Services, Room 4C-25
5600 Fishers Lane
Rockville, MD 20857
(301) 443-6190

Field of Interest: Scholarships – Medical Research
Average Amount Given: $132,300
Purpose: To promote postdoctoral research training programs in primary medical care.
Who May Apply: Qualified individuals with Ph.D.'s associated with public or private nonprofit entities.
Requirements: Individuals must be U.S. citizens or nationals.
Contact: Dr. Marilyn Gaston.
Application Information: Application required.
Initial Approach: Letter or phone.

Neurological Disorders Clinical Investigator Development Awards $54,000–$80,000

National Institutes of Health, PHS
Bethesda, MD 20892
(301) 496-9231

Field of Interest: Scholarships – Medical Research
Average Amount Given: $70,000
Purpose: For research training in biomedical shortage areas.
Who May Apply: Qualified individuals at accredited institutions.
Requirements: None.
Contact: Mary Whitehead.
Application Information: Application required.
Initial Approach: Letter or phone.

Post–Baccalaureate Faculty Fellowships $91,800–$200,000

Department of Health and Human Services, Room 5C-13
5600 Fishers Lane
Rockville, MD 20857
(301) 443-5763

Field of Interest: Scholarships – Medical Research
Average Amount Given: $146,000
Purpose: To schools of nursing to develop cost-effective alternatives to traditional health care, especially for at-risk populations.
Who May Apply: Public or private nonprofit schools of nursing with eligible faculty members.
Requirements: None.
Contact: Anastasia Buchanan.
Application Information: Application required.
Initial Approach: Letter or phone.

Pharmacological Sciences Research Career Development Awards $20,000–$250,000

National Institutes of Health, PHS
Bethesda, MD 20892
(301) 496-7746

Field of Interest: Scholarships – Medical Research
Average Amount Given: $120,000
Purpose: For research training in biomedical shortage areas.
Who May Apply: Qualified individuals at accredited institutions.
Requirements: None.
Contact: Evelin Carlin.
Application Information: Application required.
Initial Approach: Letter or phone.

Pharmacological Sciences Clinical Investigator Development Award $54,000–$80,000

National Institutes of Health, PHS
Bethesda, MD 20892
(301) 496-7746

Field of Interest: Scholarships – Medical Research
Average Amount Given: $70,000
Purpose: For research training in biomedical shortage areas.
Who May Apply: Qualified individuals at accredited institutions.
Requirements: None.
Contact: Evelin Carlin.
Application Information: Application required.
Initial Approach: Letter or phone.

Pharmacological Sciences National Research Service Awards $20,000–$250,000

National Institutes of Health, PHS
Bethesda, MD 20892
(301) 496-7746

Field of Interest: Scholarships – Medical Research
Average Amount Given: $120,000
Purpose: For research training in biomedical shortage areas.
Who May Apply: Qualified individuals at accredited institutions.
Requirements: None.
Contact: Evelin Carlin.
Application Information: Application required.
Initial Approach: Letter or phone.

Physiological Sciences National Research Service Award $7,000,000

National Institutes of Health, PHS
Bethesda, MD 20892
(301) 496-7463

Field of Interest: Scholarships – Medical Research
Average Amount Given: N/A
Purpose: To award physics and engineering research for the study of biomedical problems.
Who May Apply: Individuals associated with research or educational institutions.
Requirements: None.
Contact: Dr. Marvin Cassman, Director.
Application Information: Application required.
Initial Approach: Letter or phone.

Population Research Career Development Awards $20,000–$250,000

National Institutes of Health, PHS
Bethesda, MD 20892
(301) 496-5001

Field of Interest: Scholarships – Medical Research
Average Amount Given: $120,000
Purpose: For research training in biomedical shortage areas.
Who May Apply: Qualified individuals at accredited institutions.
Requirements: None.
Contact: Donald Clark.
Application Information: Application required.
Initial Approach: Letter or phone.

Population Research Clinical Investigator Development Award $54,000–$80,000

National Institutes of Health, PHS
Bethesda, MD 20892
(301) 496-5001

Field of Interest: Scholarships – Medical Research
Average Amount Given: $70,000
Purpose: For research training in biomedical shortage areas.
Who May Apply: Qualified individuals at accredited institutions.
Requirements: None.
Contact: Donald Clark.
Application Information: Application required.
Initial Approach: Letter or phone.

**Population Research National
Research Service Awards** $20,000–$250,000

National Institutes of Health, PHS
Bethesda, MD 20892
(301) 496-5001

Field of Interest: Scholarships – Medical Research
Average Amount Given: $120,000
Purpose: For research training in biomedical shortage areas.
Who May Apply: Qualified individuals at accredited institutions.
Requirements: None.
Contact: Donald Clark.
Application Information: Application required.
Initial Approach: Letter or phone.

**Research for Mothers and Children Research
Career Development Awards** $20,000–$250,000

National Institutes of Health, PHS
Bethesda, MD 20892
(301) 496-5001

Field of Interest: Scholarships – Medical Research
Average Amount Given: $120,000
Purpose: For research training in biomedical shortage areas.
Who May Apply: Qualified individuals at accredited institutions.
Requirements: None.
Contact: Donald Clark.
Application Information: Application required.
Initial Approach: Letter or phone.

**Research for Mothers and Children Clinical
Investigator Development Award** $54,000–$80,000

National Institutes of Health, PHS
Bethesda, MD 20892
(301) 496-5001

Field of Interest: Scholarships – Medical Research
Average Amount Given: $70,000
Purpose: For research training in biomedical shortage areas.
Who May Apply: Qualified individuals at accredited institutions.
Requirements: None.
Contact: Donald Clark.
Application Information: Application required.
Initial Approach: Letter or phone.

**Research for Mothers and Children National
Research Service Awards** $20,000–$250,000

National Institutes of Health, PHS
Bethesda, MD 20892
(301) 496-5001

Field of Interest: Scholarships – Medical Research
Average Amount Given: $120,000
Purpose: For research training in biomedical shortage areas.
Who May Apply: Qualified individuals at accredited institutions.
Requirements: None.
Contact: Donald Clark.
Application Information: Application required.
Initial Approach: Letter or phone.

**Retinal and Choroidal Diseases National
Research Service Awards $20,000–$250,000**

National Institutes of Health, PHS
Bethesda, MD 20892
(301) 496-5884

Field of Interest: Scholarships – Medical Research
Average Amount Given: $120,000
Purpose: For research training in biomedical shortage areas.
Who May Apply: Qualified individuals at accredited institutions.
Requirements: None.
Contact: Carolyn Grimes.
Application Information: Application required.
Initial Approach: Letter or phone.

**Retinal and Choroidal Diseases Research
Career Development Awards $20,000–$250,000**

National Institutes of Health, PHS
Bethesda, MD 20892
(301) 496-5884

Field of Interest: Scholarships – Medical Research
Average Amount Given: $120,000
Purpose: For research training in biomedical shortage areas.
Who May Apply: Qualified individuals at accredited institutions.
Requirements: None.
Contact: Carolyn Grimes.
Application Information: Application required.
Initial Approach: Letter or phone.

**Retinal and Choroidal Diseases Clinical
Investigator Development Award $54,000–$80,000**

National Institutes of Health, PHS
Bethesda, MD 20892
(301) 496-5884

Field of Interest: Scholarships – Medical Research
Average Amount Given: $70,000
Purpose: For research training in biomedical shortage areas.
Who May Apply: Qualified individuals at accredited institutions.
Requirements: None.
Contact: Carolyn Grimes.
Application Information: Application required.
Initial Approach: Letter or phone.

**Research Scientist Development Award
for Clinicians $54,800–$72,000**

Department of Health and Human Services, Room 16–86
5600 Fishers Lane
Rockville, MD 20857
(301) 443-4703

Field of Interest: Scholarships – Medical Research
Average Amount Given: $61,160
Purpose: To increase research relating to the problems of alcohol abuse, prevention, and rehabilitation.
Who May Apply: Qualified medical educational institutions or hospitals on behalf of individuals.
Requirements: None.
Contact: Dr. Helen Chao.
Application Information: Application required.
Initial Approach: Letter or phone.

Senior International Fellowships $9,500–$37,000

Fogarty International Center
National Institutes of Health, PHS
Department of Health and Human Services
Bethesda, MD 20892
(301) 496-4161

Field of Interest: Scholarships – Medical Research
Average Amount Given: $25,000
Purpose: To promote the international exchange of information about biomedical and behavioral sciences.
Who May Apply: Qualified individuals.
Requirements: None.
Contact: Dr. Jack Schmidt.
Application Information: Application required.
Initial Approach: Letter or phone.

Special International Postdoctoral Research Program in AIDS

Fogarty International Center
National Institutes of Health, PHS
Bethesda, MD 20892
(301) 496-4146

Field of Interest: Scholarships – Medical Research
Money Given: $200,000 each
Purpose: To support collaborative international AIDS research.
Who May Apply: U.S. nonprofits with qualified individual scientists.
Requirements: None.
Contact: Dr. Jack Schmidt.
Application Information: Application required.
Initial Approach: Letter or phone.

Fellowships for Native Americans $765–$33,000

Department of Education
400 Maryland Ave., SW
Washington, DC 20202
(202) 732-1887

Field of Interest: Scholarships – Minority and Disadvantaged
Average Amount Given: $12,900
Purpose: To enable Native Americans to pursue graduate education in medicine, psychology, law, education, or related fields.
Who May Apply: Full-time Native American graduate students at accredited institutions.
Requirements: None.
Contact: Aaron Shedd.
Application Information: Application required.
Initial Approach: Letter or phone.

Nursing Education Opportunities for Individuals from Disadvantaged Backgrounds $7,142–$233,000

Department of Health and Human Services, Room 5C13
5600 Fishers Lane
Rockville, MD 20857
(301) 443-6193

Field of Interest: Scholarships – Health Care
Average Amount Given: $150,000
Purpose: To provide opportunities for nursing education for individuals from disadvantaged backgrounds and to help nursing schools create appropriate programs.
Who May Apply: Public and private, profit and nonprofit entities, including nursing schools.
Requirements: None.
Contact: Dr. Mary Hill.
Application Information: Application required.
Initial Approach: Letter or phone.

Financial Assistance for Disadvantaged Health Professions Students $6,300,000

Department of Health and Human Services, Room 8-48
Parklawn Bldg.
5600 Fishers Lane
Rockville, MD 20857
(301) 443-4776

Field of Interest: Scholarships
Average Amount Given: $10,000 per student
Purpose: To assist health professions students with exceptional financial need by supporting their costs for education.
Who May Apply: Accredited schools of medicine, dentistry, and osteopathy; students at these schools.
Requirements: None.
Contact: Bruce Bagget.
Application Information: Application required.
Initial Approach: Letter or phone.

Health Careers Opportunity Program $33,800–$565,837

Health Resources and Services Administration
Department of Health and Human Services
5600 Fishers Lane
Rockville, MD 20857
(301) 443-4493

Field of Interest: Scholarships – Health Care
Average Amount Given: $140,000
Purpose: To identify and recruit students from disadvantaged backgrounds for education in health care.
Who May Apply: Health professions schools and public or nonprofit private health and education entities and qualified individuals who plan to attend these schools.
Requirements: None.
Contact: Chief, Program Coordination Branch.
Application Information: Application required.
Initial Approach: Letter or phone.

Legal Training for the Disadvantaged

Department of Education
400 Maryland Ave., SW
Washington, DC 20202
(202) 732-4393

Field of Interest: Scholarships – Minority and Disadvantaged
Average Amount Given: $2,100
Purpose: To provide disadvantaged students with an opportunity to attend an ABA accredited law school.
Who May Apply: Qualified individuals of low income.
Requirements: U.S. citizenship required.
Contact: Walter Lewis.
Application Information: Application required.
Initial Approach: Letter or phone.

*Migrant Education College Assistance Program $1,700,000

Department of Education
400 Maryland Ave., SW
Washington, DC 20202
(202) 732-4742

Field of Interest: Scholarships – Minority and Disadvantaged
Average Amount Given: N/A
Purpose: To assist students who are migrant workers or who belong to migrant worker families in receiving a college education.
Who May Apply: Private nonprofit entities.
Requirements: None.
Contact: William L. Stormer.
Application Information: Application required.
Initial Approach: Letter or phone.

Minority Access to Research
Careers $10,000–$406,000
National Institutes of Health, PHS
Department of Health and Human Services
Bethesda, MD 20892
(301) 496-7941

Field of Interest: Scholarships – Minority Development
Average Amount Given: $67,500
Purpose: To assist minority institutions in training greater numbers of biomedical scientists and health professionals.
Who May Apply: Any nonfederal, public or private nonprofit with majority minority enrollment and individuals at these institutions.
Requirements: None.
Contact: Edward Bynum, Director of the MARC Program.
Application Information: Application required.
Initial Approach: Letter or phone.

Minority Honors Training and Industrial
Assistance Program $33,000–$80,000
Department of Energy
1000 Independence Ave., SW
Washington, DC 20585
(202) 586-1953

Field of Interest: Scholarships – Minority and Disadvantaged
Average Amount Given: $60,000
Purpose: To fund needy minority honor students pursuing training in energy-related technologies.
Who May Apply: Minority honor students attending qualified universities.
Requirements: None.
Contact: Isiah O. Sewell, Office of Minority Economic Impact.
Application Information: Application required.
Initial Approach: Letter or phone.

Minority Participation in Graduate
Education $13,000–$120,000
Department of Education
400 Maryland Ave., SW
Washington, DC 20202
(202) 732-4393

Field of Interest: Scholarships – Minority and Disadvantaged
Average Amount Given: $77,200
Purpose: To identify and fund talented undergraduate minority students for graduate education.
Who May Apply: Accredited educational institutions and individuals associated with them.
Requirements: None.
Contact: Walter T. Lewis.
Application Information: Application required.
Initial Approach: Letter or phone.

Minority Research and Teaching
Program Grants $3,000–$15,000
Office of Advocacy and Enterprise
Department of Agriculture
14th and Independence Ave., SW
Washington, DC 20250
(202) 447-4423

Field of Interest: Scholarships – Minority Development
Average Amount Given: N/A
Purpose: To increase minority participation in agriculture and related fields and to improve the educational resources which prepare students for these fields.
Who May Apply: Public, private, and other colleges and universities.
Requirements: Second Morrill Act compliance necessary.
Contact: Dr. Ezra Naughton.
Application Information: Application required.
Initial Approach: Letter or phone.

Minority Science Improvement $18,600–$472,000

Department of Education
400 Maryland Ave., SW
Washington, DC 20202
(202) 732-4396

Field of Interest: Scholarships – Minority and Disadvantaged
Average Amount Given: $250,000
Purpose: To improve the access of minority students to careers in science and mathematics and to assist institutions in this goal.
Who May Apply: Educational institutions which have a majority population of minority students and the individual students attending these institutions.
Requirements: None.
Contact: Argelia Velez-Rodriguez.
Application Information: Application required.
Initial Approach: Letter or phone.

Nursing Education Opportunities for Individuals from Disadvantaged Backgrounds $7,142–$233,000

Department of Health and Human Services, Room 5C13
5600 Fishers Lane
Rockville, MD 20857
(301) 443-6193

Field of Interest: Health Care
Average Amount Given: $150,000
Purpose: To provide opportunities for nursing education for individuals from disadvantaged backgrounds and to help nursing schools create appropriate programs.
Who May Apply: Public and private, profit and nonprofit entities, including nursing schools.
Requirements: None.
Contact: Dr. Mary Hill.
Application Information: Application required.
Initial Approach: Letter or phone.

Patricia Roberts Harris Fellowships $1,100,000

Department of Education
400 Maryland Ave., SW
Washington, DC 20202
(202) 732-4395

Field of Interest: Scholarships – Minority and Disadvantaged
Average Amount Given: $16,000
Purpose: To fund graduate and professional education for students in finacial need.
Who May Apply: Qualified graduate students at accredited institutions.
Requirements: None.
Contact: Charles H. Miller.
Application Information: Application required.
Initial Approach: Letter or phone.

Pre-Freshman Enrichment Project Grants $350,000

Division of University and Industry Programs
Department of Energy
Forrestal Bldg.
1000 Independence Ave., SW
Washington, DC 20585
(202) 586-1634

Field of Interest: Scholarships – Minority and Disadvantaged
Average Amount Given: $14,000
Purpose: To prepare minority and women high school students for careers in mathematics, science, and engineering.
Who May Apply: Qualified educational institutions and individuals planning to attend these colleges and universitites.
Requirements: Matching funding required.
Contact: John Ortman.
Application Information: Application required.
Initial Approach: Letter or phone.

**Ronald E. McNair Post Baccalaureate
Achievement Awards**   **$80,000–$120,000**

Department of Education
400 Maryland Ave., SW
Washington, DC 20202
(202) 732-4804

Field of Interest: Scholarships – Minority and Disadvantaged
Average Amount Given: $100,000
Purpose: To prepare low-income and first generation college students for doctoral study.
Who May Apply: Accredited educational institutions and qualified students enrolled at these institutions.
Requirements: None.
Contact: May J. Weaver.
Application Information: Application required.
Initial Approach: Letter or phone.

**Scholarships for Students of Exceptional
Financial Need**

Health Resources and Services Administration
Department of Health and Human Services
5600 Fishers Lane
Rockville, MD 20857
(301) 443-4776

Field of Interest: Scholarships – Health Care
Average Amount Given: $18,448 per year
Purpose: To award scholarships to students in exceptional financial need.
Who May Apply: Qualified students at accredited schools in the health professions, including veterinary medicine.
Requirements: None.
Contact: Bruce Bagget, Division of Student Assistance.
Application Information: Application required.
Initial Approach: Letter or phone.

**Supplemental Educational Opportunity
Grants**   **$418,000,000**

Department of Education
400 Maryland Ave., SW
Washington, DC 20202-5446
(202) 732-4490

Field of Interest: Scholarships – Minority and Disadvantaged
Average Amount Given: $700
Purpose: To provide educational assistance to undergraduate post secondary students with demonstrated financial need.
Who May Apply: Higher educational institutions and qualified students attending them.
Requirements: None.
Contact: Chief, Student Financial Assistance Programs.
Application Information: Application required.
Initial Approach: Letter or phone.

**Applied Toxicological Research and Testing –
Academic Awards**   **$63,100–$700,000**

Department of Health and Human Services
PO Box 12233
Research Triangle Park, NC 27709
(919) 541-7634

Field of Interest: Scholarships – Science Research
Average Amount Given: $60,000
Purpose: To develop scientific information about potentially toxic or hazardous chemicals through research.
Who May Apply: Profit or nonprofit medical, educational, or research institutions and the individuals associated with them.
Requirements: None.
Contact: David Mineo, Grants Management Officer.
Application Information: Application required.
Initial Approach: Letter or phone.

Applied Toxicological Research and Testing Career Development Awards $63,100–$700,000

Department of Health and Human Services
PO Box 12233
Research Triangle Park, NC 27709
(919) 541-7634

Field of Interest: Scholarships – Science Research
Average Amount Given: $50,000
Purpose: To develop scientific information about potentially toxic or hazardous chemicals through research.
Who May Apply: Profit or nonprofit medical, educational, or research institutions and the individuals associated with them.
Requirements: None.
Contact: David Mineo, Grants Management Officer.
Application Information: Application required.
Initial Approach: Letter or phone.

Applied Toxicological Research and Testing Mid-Career Development Awards $63,100–$700,000

Department of Health and Human Services
PO Box 12233
Research Triangle Park, NC 27709
(919) 541-7634

Field of Interest: Scholarships – Science Research
Average Amount Given: $60,000
Purpose: To develop scientific information about potentially toxic or hazardous chemicals through research.
Who May Apply: Profit or nonprofit medical, educational, or research institutions and the individuals associated with them.
Requirements: None.
Contact: David Mineo, Grants Management Officer.
Application Information: Application required.
Initial Approach: Letter or phone.

Applied Toxicological Research and Testing Physician–Scientist Awards $63,100–$700,000

Department of Health and Human Services
PO Box 12233
Research Triangle Park, NC 27709
(919) 541-7634

Field of Interest: Scholarships – Science Research
Average Amount Given: $60,000
Purpose: To develop scientific information about potentially toxic or hazardous chemicals through research.
Who May Apply: Profit or nonprofit medical, educational, or research institutions and the individuals associated with them.
Requirements: None.
Contact: David Mineo, Grants Management Officer.
Application Information: Application required.
Initial Approach: Letter or phone.

Biological Response to Environmental Health Hazards Academic Awards $53,800–$1,600,000

Department of Health and Human Services
PO Box 12233
Research Triangle Park, NC 27709
(919) 541-7634

Field of Interest: Scholarships – Science Research
Average Amount Given: $60,000 and expenses
Purpose: To understand how chemical agents cause pathological changes in cells.
Who May Apply: Profit or nonprofit medical, educational, or research institutions and the individuals associated with them.
Requirements: None.
Contact: David Mineo, Grants Management Officer.
Application Information: Application required.
Initial Approach: Letter or phone.

Biological Response to Environmental Health Hazards Research
Career Development Awards $53,800–$1,600,000
Department of Health and Human Services
PO Box 12233
Research Triangle Park, NC 27709
(919) 541-7634

Field of Interest: Scholarships – Science Research
Average Amount Given: $50,000
Purpose: To understand how chemical agents cause pathological changes in cells.
Who May Apply: Profit or nonprofit medical, educational, or research institutions and the individuals associated with them.
Requirements: None.
Contact: David Mineo, Grants Management Officer.
Application Information: Application required.
Initial Approach: Letter or phone.

Biological Response to Environmental Health Hazards
Mid–Career Development Awards $53,800–$1,600,000
Department of Health and Human Services
PO Box 12233
Research Triangle Park, NC 27709
(919) 541-7634

Field of Interest: Scholarships – Science Research
Average Amount Given: $50,000 and expenses
Purpose: To understand how chemical agents cause pathological changes in cells.
Who May Apply: Profit or nonprofit medical, educational, or research institutions and the individuals associated with them.
Requirements: None.
Contact: David Mineo, Grants Management Officer.
Application Information: Application required.
Initial Approach: Letter or phone.

Biological Response to Environmental Health Hazards Physician–Scientist
Awards $53,800–$1,600,000
Department of Health and Human Services
PO Box 12233
Research Triangle Park, NC 27709
(919) 541-7634

Field of Interest: Scholarships – Science Research
Average Amount Given: $60,000 and expenses
Purpose: To understand how chemical agents cause pathological changes in cells.
Who May Apply: Profit or nonprofit medical, educational, or research institutions and the individuals associated with them.
Requirements: None.
Contact: David Mineo, Grants Management Officer.
Application Information: Application required.
Initial Approach: Letter or phone.

Environmental Health Hazards Research
Career Development Award $46,700–$1,100,000
Department of Health and Human Services
PO Box 12233
Research Triangle Park, NC 27709
(919) 541-7634

Field of Interest: Scholarships – Science Research
Average Amount Given: N/A
Purpose: To identify and measure the biological, chemical, and physical factors in the human environment, with an emphasis on possible human injury.
Who May Apply: Qualified individuals with at least three years professional experience.
Requirements: None.
Contact: David Mineo, Grants Management Officer.
Application Information: Application required.
Initial Approach: Letter or phone.

Environmental Health Hazards Mid–Career Development Award   **$46,700–$1,100,000**

Department of Health and Human Services
PO Box 12233
Research Triangle Park, NC 27709
(919) 541-7634

Field of Interest: Scholarships – Science Research
Average Amount Given: $147,000
Purpose: To identify and measure the biological, chemical, and physical factors in the human environment, with an emphasis on possible human injury.
Who May Apply: Qualified individuals with at least three years professional experience.
Requirements: None.
Contact: David Mineo, Grants Management Officer.
Application Information: Application required.
Initial Approach: Letter or phone.

Environmental Health Hazards Physician–Scientist Award   **$46,700–$1,100,000**

Department of Health and Human Services
PO Box 12233
Research Triangle Park, NC 27709
(919) 541-7634

Field of Interest: Scholarships – Science Research
Average Amount Given: $100,000
Purpose: To identify and measure the biological, chemical, and physical factors in the human environment, with an emphasis on possible human injury.
Who May Apply: Qualified individuals with at least three years professional experience.
Requirements: None.
Contact: David Mineo, Grants Management Officer.
Application Information: Application required.
Initial Approach: Letter or phone.

Graduate Research Fellowships   **$29,900,000**

Division of Research Career Development
National Science Foundation
1800 G Street, NW
Washington, DC 20550
(202) 357-7856

Field of Interest: Scholarships – Science Research
Average Amount Given: $18,300
Purpose: To support talented graduate students for advanced study in the sciences, mathematics, and engineering.
Who May Apply: Beginning graduate students.
Requirements: Individuals must be U.S. citizens.
Contact: Dr. Douglas S. Chapin.
Application Information: Application required.
Initial Approach: Letter or phone.

Science and Engineering Research Semester   **$2,600,000**

Department of Energy
1000 Independence Ave., SW
Washington, DC 20585
(202) 586-8949

Field of Interest: Scholarships – Science Research
Average Amount Given: $200 per week plus housing and transportation
Purpose: To give college juniors and seniors the opportunity to participate in hands-on research at DOE national laboratories.
Who May Apply: Qualified individuals at accredited U.S. colleges and universities.
Requirements: Candidates must be U.S. citizens with 3.0 GPAs.
Contact: Donna J. Prokop, Division of University and Industry Programs.
Application Information: Application required.
Initial Approach: Letter or phone.

Community Development Work–Study
Program Project Grants $33,000–$150,000
Office of Program Policy Development
Department of Housing and Urban Development
451 W. 7th St., SW
Washington, DC 20410
(202) 755-6092

Field of Interest: Scholarships – Social Services
Average Amount Given: $11,000 per year for undergraduates;
$15,000 per year for graduate students
Purpose: To assist economically disadvantaged and minority students prepare for careers in community affairs.
Who May Apply: Urban, educational institutions offering the appropriate degrees and qualified individuals at these schools.
Requirements: None.
Contact: Community Planning and Development Office.
Application Information: Application required.
Initial Approach: Letter or phone.

Emergency Management Institute $1,000,000
National Emergency Training Center
Support Services Branch
16825 S. Seton Avenue
Emmitsburg, MD 21727
(301) 447-1000

Field of Interest: Scholarships – Social Services
Average Amount Given: $500
Purpose: For travel and per diem expenses while attending the Emergency Management Institute.
Who May Apply: Individuals who need emergency management training or who are assigned to emergency or civil defense positions.
Requirements: None.
Contact: Director.
Application Information: Application required.
Initial Approach: Letter or phone.

National Fire Academy Training Assistance $1,200,000
National Emergency Training Center
Support Services Branch
16825 S. Seton Avenue
Emmitsburg, MD 21727
(301) 447-1000

Field of Interest: Scholarships – Social Services
Average Amount Given: $300
Purpose: To provide travel stipends to individuals attending Academy courses.
Who May Apply: Any student who has been accepted by the Academy.
Requirements: None.
Contact: Training Program Director.
Application Information: Application required.
Initial Approach: Letter or phone.

National Fire Academy Educational
Program $3,100,000
National Emergency Training Center
Support Services Branch
16825 S. Seton Avenue
Emmitsburg, MD 21727
(301) 447-1000

Field of Interest: Scholarships – Social Services
Average Amount Given: N/A
Purpose: To increase the professional level of fire service, prevention, and control.
Who May Apply: Any individual who is a member of a fire department or who has significant responsibility for fire prevention and control.
Requirements: None.
Contact: Director.
Application Information: Application required.
Initial Approach: Letter or phone.

Christa McAuliffe Fellowships $15,600–$31,200

Department of Education
400 Maryland Ave., SW
Washington, DC 20202
(202) 732-4342

Field of Interest: Scholarships
Average Amount Given: $25,700
Purpose: To reward excellent teachers by funding innovative programs that will improve their knowledge and skills and the education of their students.
Who May Apply: Teachers who are U.S. citizens.
Requirements: None.
Contact: Director.
Application Information: Application required.
Initial Approach: Letter or phone.

*Criminal Justice Discretionary Grant Program $15,000–$1,700,000

Bureau of Justice Assistance
Department of Justice
Washington, DC 20531
(202) 514-5943

Field of Interest: Scholarships
Average Amount Given: N/A
Purpose: To enhance criminal justice education and training and to promote national demonstration programs in the field.
Who May Apply: Public and private nonprofit organizations.
Requirements: None.
Contact: Eugene Dzikiewicz.
Application Information: Application required.
Initial Approach: Letter or phone.

Criminal Justice Research and Development Fellowships $150,000

National Institute of Justice
Department of Justice
Washington, DC 20531
(202) 307-0645

Field of Interest: Scholarships
Average Amount Given: $11,000
Purpose: To improve the quality and quantity of knowledge about crime and the criminal justice system and to increase the number of people qualified to teach criminal justice at the college level.
Who May Apply: Accredited institutions offering a doctoral program and individuals at these institutions.
Requirements: None.
Contact: Director.
Application Information: Application required.
Initial Approach: Letter or phone.

Graduate Assistance in Areas of National Need $100,000–$500,000

Department of Education
400 Maryland Ave., SW
Washington, DC 20202
(202) 732-4412

Field of Interest: Scholarships
Average Amount Given: $173,000
Purpose: To support graduate education in areas of need by funding graduate students of superior ability.
Who May Apply: Accredited educational institutions and the students associated with them.
Requirements: None.
Contact: Allen P. Cissell.
Application Information: Application required.
Initial Approach: Letter or phone.

Grants for Mining and Mineral Resources $138,000–$1,000,000

Office of Mineral Institutes
Bureau of Mines
2401 E St., NW
Washington, DC 20241
(202) 634-1328

Field of Interest: Scholarships
Average Amount Given: N/A
Purpose: To support research and training in mining and mineral resources related to the need of the Department of the Interior.
Who May Apply: One designated college or university per state and qualified individuals at these institutions.
Requirements: None.
Contact: Dr. Ronald Munson.
Application Information: Application required.
Initial Approach: Letter or phone.

Harry S. Truman Scholarship Program $1,000–$7,000

712 Jackson Place, NW
Washington, DC 20006
(202) 395-4831

Field of Interest: Scholarships
Average Amount Given: $6,500
Purpose: To allow young Americans to prepare for careers in public service.
Who May Apply: Undergraduate sophomore college students at accredited U.S. institutions of higher education.
Requirements: None.
Contact: Louis Blair, Executive Secretary.
Application Information: Application required.
Initial Approach: Letter or phone.

National Institute on Disability and Rehabilitation Research Fellowships $10,000–$750,000

Department of Education
400 Maryland Ave., SW
Washington, DC 20202
(202) 732-1143

Field of Interest: Scholarships
Average Amount Given: $150,000
Purpose: To support research that will improve the lives of handicapped people.
Who May Apply: Individuals.
Requirements: None.
Contact: Joseph Fenton.
Application Information: Application required.
Initial Approach: Letter or phone.

National Institute of Justice Visiting Fellowships $300,000

National Institute of Justice
Department of Justice
Washington, DC 20531
(202) 307-0645

Field of Interest: Scholarships
Average Amount Given: N/A
Purpose: To provide experienced criminal justice practitioners and researchers to create projects of their own design aimed at improved understanding of crime, delinquency, and criminal justice administration.
Who May Apply: Individuals or their parent organizations or agencies.
Requirements: None.
Contact: Director.
Application Information: Application required.
Initial Approach: Letter or phone.

Pell Grant Program $100–$2,300

Department of Education
400 Maryland Ave., SW
Washington, DC 20202
(202) 732-4888

Field of Interest: Scholarships
Average Amount Given: $1,500
Purpose: To support undergraduate students at colleges and universities.
Who May Apply: Any undergraduate in good standing at an accredited university.
Requirements: None.
Contact: Chief, Pell Grant Program.
Application Information: Application required.
Initial Approach: Letter or phone.

State Marine Schools $100,000 to each school

Office of Maritime Labor and Training
Maritime Administration
Department of Transportation
400 Seventh Street, SW
Washington, DC 20590
(202) 366-5755

Field of Interest: Scholarships
Average Amount Given: $1,200 per academic year for four years
Purpose: To train Merchant Marine officers.
Who may apply: One university or college per state and qualified students at these institutions.
Requirements: None.
Contact: Bruce J. Carlton.
Application Information: Application required.
Initial Approach: Letter or phone.

U.S. Merchant Marine Academy $25,000,000

Maritime Administration
Department of Transportation
400 Seventh Street, SW
Washington, DC 20590
(202) 366-0364

Field of Interest: Scholarships
Average Amount Given: $525 per month during the sea year plus total support for tuition, room, board, medical care, program travel, books, and uniforms.
Purpose: To attract students to the maritime professions.
Who may apply: High school graduates as recommended by senators or congressmen.
Requirements: Individuals must be U.S. citizens.
Contact: Bruce J. Carlton.
Application Information: Application required.
Initial Approach: Letter or phone.

Urban Mass Transportation Training Grants $600,000

Urban Mass Transportation Administration
Department of Transportation
400 Seventh Street, SW
Washington, DC 20590
(202) 366-0080

Field of Interest: Scholarships
Average Amount Given: $85,000
Purpose: To develop and train professionals in the field of transportation.
Who May Apply: Individual students at qualified educational institutions.
Requirements: None.
Contact: Office of Technical Assistance and Safety.
Application Information: Application required.
Initial Approach: Letter or phone.

Veterans Education Outreach Program $1,000–$70,000

Department of Education
400 Maryland Ave., SW
Washington, DC 20202
(202) 732-4406

Field of Interest: Scholarships
Average Amount Given: $5,000
Purpose: To serve the needs of veterans, especially disabled veterans.
Who May Apply: Qualified individuals at accredited educational institutions.
Requirements: None.
Contact: L. Neil McArthur.
Application Information: Application required.
Initial Approach: Letter or phone.

SCIENCE RESEARCH

Scientific, Technological, and
International Affairs $1,000–$200,000

National Science Foundation
1800 G Street, NW
Washington, DC 20550
(202) 357-7631

Field of Interest: Science Research – Business Development
Average Amount Given: $41,000
Purpose: To allow small, high-technology firms to participate in NSF research and to promote international research cooperation.
Who May Apply: Small businesses, individuals associated with universities on international travel, and profit and nonprofit entities of all types.
Requirements: None.
Contact: Assistant Director.
Application Information: Application required.
Initial Approach: Letter or phone.

Conservation Research and
Development $50,000–$500,000

Department of Energy
1000 Independence Ave., SW
Washington, DC 20585
(202) 586-9232

Field of Interest: Science Research – Energy
Average Amount Given: $200,000
Purpose: To conduct long-term research in building, industry, transportation, and energy systems technology.
Who May Apply: Businesses and private profit or nonprofit entities.
Requirements: Cost-sharing is encouraged.
Contact: Noel K. Cole, Office of the Deputy Assistant Secretary.
Application Information: Application required.
Initial Approach: Letter or phone.

Energy and Field Operations Research
in Energy and Related Fields $10,000–$2,000,000

Division of Acquisition and Assistance Management
Office of Energy Research, Department of Energy
Mail Stop G-236
Washington, DC 20545
(301) 353-4946

Field of Interest: Science Research – Energy
Average Amount Given: $150,000
Purpose: To support fundamental research in the basic energy sciences and advanced energy technology.
Who May Apply: Educational institutions and nonprofit entities and industries, including small businesses of all sorts.
Requirements: None.
Contact: William Burrier.
Application Information: Application required.
Initial Approach: Letter or phone.

*Energy Policy, Planning, and Development
Project Grants $25,000–$125,000

Department of Energy
1000 Independence Ave., SW
Washington, DC 20585
(202) 586-5325

Field of Interest: Science Research – Energy
Average Amount Given: $75,000
Purpose: To fund conferences, seminars, and work groups centered upon energy policy issues.
Who May Apply: Educational and nonprofit institutions.
Requirements: None.
Contact: Stephen F. Durbin, Management Office.
Application Information: Application required.
Initial Approach: Letter or phone.

Energy-Related Inventions Project Grants $5,000,000

Office of Energy Related Inventions
National Institute of Standards and Technology
Gaithersburg, MD 20899
(202) 586-1479

Field of Interest: Science Research – Energy
Average Amount Given: $70,000
Purpose: To develop non-nuclear energy technology.
Who May Apply: No restrictions; individuals, small businesses, and entrepreneurs are especially encouraged to apply.
Requirements: None.
Contact: George Lewitt.
Application Information: Application required.
Initial Approach: Letter or phone.

**Fossil Energy Research and Development
Project Grants $20,000–$1,700,000**

Department of Energy
Fossil Energy Program, FE–122
Germantown, MD 20545
(202) 353-2621

Field of Interest: Science Research – Energy
Average Amount Given: $660,000
Purpose: To support long-term, high-risk research and development in oil, gas, and shale resources.
Who May Apply: Individuals, corporations, small businesses, non-profit entities of all types, and educational institutions.
Requirements: Variable.
Contact: Dwight Mottet.
Application Information: Application required.
Initial Approach: Letter or phone.

**Industrial Energy Conservation
Project Grants $10,000–$5,000,000**

Office of Industrial Programs CE–14
Department of Energy
Washington, DC 20585
(202) 586-2097

Field of Interest: Science Research – Energy
Average Amount Given: $1,400,000
Purpose: To research and develop high-risk technologies to assist in the transfer of energy-efficient technologies.
Who May Apply: Businesses and private profit or nonprofit organizations.
Requirements: Cost-sharing is encouraged.
Contact: Marsha Quinn.
Application Information: Application required.
Initial Approach: Letter or phone.

**International Affairs and Energy
Emergencies $10,000–$200,000**

Management Services Staff, 4G–039
Department of Energy
1000 Independence Ave., SW
Washington, DC 20585
(202) 586-2995

Field of Interest: Science Research – Energy
Average Amount Given: N/A
Purpose: To develop emergency contingency plans and to promote international energy research and development agreements.
Who May Apply: No restrictions; all public, private, profit, and non-profit concerns may apply.
Requirements: Cost-sharing is desirable.
Contact: Fredrick Faine.
Application Information: Application required.
Initial Approach: Letter or phone.

**Minority Educational Institution Research
Travel Fund** $200–$800

Department of Energy
1000 Independence Ave., SW
Washington, DC 20585
(202) 586-1953

Field of Interest: Science Research – Energy
Average Amount Given: $500
Purpose: To provide travel funds to faculty and graduate students doing energy-related research.
Who May Apply: Qualified individuals at minority educational institutions.
Requirements: None.
Contact: Isiah O. Sewell, Office of Minority Economic Impact.
Application Information: Application required.
Initial Approach: Letter or phone.

***Nuclear Energy Policy, Planning, and
Development** $500–$1,000

Office of Nuclear Energy, D–407
Germantown Bldg.
Washington, DC 20545
(202) 353-5153

Field of Interest: Science Research – Energy
Average Amount Given: N/A
Purpose: To support the gathering of outside experts at seminars and conferences to discuss nuclear policy issues.
Who May Apply: Educational and nonprofit institutions.
Requirements: None.
Contact: Chief.
Application Information: Application required.
Initial Approach: Letter or phone.

***Nuclear Energy Process and Safety Information
Project Grants** $5,000–$50,000

Division of Contracts and Property Management
Nuclear Regulatory Commission
Washington, DC 20555
(301) 492-4297

Field of Interest: Science Research – Energy
Average Amount Given: N/A
Purpose: To stimulate technological research applicable to nuclear safety issues.
Who May Apply: Public and private nonprofit entities as well as educational institutions.
Requirements: None.
Contact: Mary H. Mace, Chief of Contract Negotiations.
Application Information: Application required.
Initial Approach: Letter or phone.

**Renewable Energy Research and
Development** $50,000–$90,000

Research and Technology Integration
Department of Energy
1000 Independence Ave., SW
Washington, DC 20585
(202) 586-9282

Field of Interest: Science Research – Energy
Average Amount Given: N/A
Purpose: To develop energy technologies for solar buildings, alcohol fuels, and urban waste, among related projects.
Who May Apply: Profit organizations, private nonprofit organizations, and educational institutions.
Requirements: None.
Contact: Judy Florance.
Application Information: Application required.
Initial Approach: Letter or phone.

University Coal Research $84,000–$200,000

Office of Technical Coordination
Assistant Secretary of Fossil Energy
Washington, DC 20545
(301) 353-4251

Field of Interest: Science Research – Energy
Average Amount Given: $175,000
Purpose: To improve scientific understanding of the chemistry and physics involved in the conversion and utilization of coal.
Who May Apply: Qualified educational institutions and faculty and students associated with them.
Requirements: None.
Contact: Jack Jennings.
Application Information: Application required.
Initial Approach: Letter or phone.

University–Laboratory Cooperative Program $7,000,000

Office of Energy Research
Department of Energy
Washington, DC 20585
(202) 586-8947

Field of Interest: Science Research – Energy
Average Amount Given: Variable.
Purpose: To provide research opportunities at Department of Energy facilities for college engineering and science faculty with specific projects.
Who May Apply: Qualified individuals, including faculty as well as graduate students in appropriate fields.
Requirements: None.
Contact: Larry L. Barker.
Application Information: Application required.
Initial Approach: Letter or phone.

Applied Toxicological Research and Testing Research Grants $63,100–$700,000

Department of Health and Human Services
PO Box 12233
Research Triangle Park, NC 27709
(919) 541-7634

Field of Interest: Science Research – Environment
Average Amount Given: N/A
Purpose: To develop scientific information about potentially toxic or hazardous chemicals through research.
Who May Apply: Profit or nonprofit medical, educational, or research institutions and the individuals associated with them.
Requirements: None.
Contact: David Mineo, Grants Management Officer.
Application Information: Application required.
Initial Approach: Letter or phone.

Applied Toxicological Research and Testing Small Business Project Grants $50,000–$500,000

Department of Health and Human Services
PO Box 12233
Research Triangle Park, NC 27709
(919) 541-7634

Field of Interest: Science Research – Environment
Average Amount Given: N/A
Purpose: To develop scientific information about potentially toxic or hazardous chemicals through research.
Who May Apply: Small businesses.
Requirements: None.
Contact: David Mineo, Grants Management Officer.
Application Information: Application required.
Initial Approach: Letter or phone.

**Applied Toxicological Research and Testing
Small Instrumentation Grants $5,000–$60,000**

Department of Health and Human Services
PO Box 12233
Research Triangle Park, NC 27709
(919) 541-7634

Field of Interest: Science Research – Environment
Average Amount Given: N/A
Purpose: To develop scientific information about potentially toxic or hazardous chemicals through research and to develop technology for this research.
Who May Apply: Profit or nonprofit medical, educational, or research institutions and the individuals associated with them.
Requirements: None.
Contact: David Mineo, Grants Management Officer.
Application Information: Application required.
Initial Approach: Letter or phone.

**Biometry and Risk Estimation
Academic Awards $41,000–$1,600,000**

Department of Health and Human Services
PO Box 12233
Research Triangle Park, NC 27709
(919) 541-7634

Field of Interest: Science Research – Environment
Average Amount Given: $60,000
Purpose: To conduct research in statistics, biomathematics, and epidemiology towards estimating probable health risks from human exposure to various environmental hazards.
Who May Apply: Profit or nonprofit medical, educational, or research institutions and the individuals associated with them.
Requirements: None.
Contact: David Mineo, Grants Management Officer.
Application Information: Application required.
Initial Approach: Letter or phone.

**Biometry and Risk Estimation Career
Development Awards $41,000–$1,600,000**

Department of Health and Human Services
PO Box 12233
Research Triangle Park, NC 27709
(919) 541-7634

Field of Interest: Science Research – Environment
Average Amount Given: $50,000
Purpose: To conduct research in statistics, biomathematics, and epidemiology towards estimating probable health risks from human exposure to various environmental hazards.
Who May Apply: Profit or nonprofit medical, educational, or research institutions and the individuals associated with them.
Requirements: None.
Contact: David Mineo, Grants Management Officer.
Application Information: Application required.
Initial Approach: Letter or phone.

**Biometry and Risk Estimation Mid–Career
Development Awards $41,000–$1,600,000**

Department of Health and Human Services
PO Box 12233
Research Triangle Park, NC 27709
(919) 541-7634

Field of Interest: Science Research – Environment
Average Amount Given: $60,000
Purpose: To conduct research in statistics, biomathematics, and epidemiology towards estimating probable health risks from human exposure to various environmental hazards.
Who May Apply: Profit or nonprofit medical, educational, or research institutions and the individuals associated with them.
Requirements: None.
Contact: David Mineo, Grants Management Officer.
Application Information: Application required.
Initial Approach: Letter or phone.

Biometry and Risk Estimation Physician–Scientist Awards $41,000–$1,600,000

Department of Health and Human Services
PO Box 12233
Research Triangle Park, NC 27709
(919) 541-7634

Field of Interest: Science Research – Environment
Average Amount Given: $60,000
Purpose: To conduct research in statistics, biomathematics, and epidemiology towards estimating probable health risks from human exposure to various environmental hazards.
Who May Apply: Profit or nonprofit medical, educational, or research institutions and the individuals associated with them.
Requirements: None.
Contact: David Mineo, Grants Management Officer.
Application Information: Application required.
Initial Approach: Letter or phone.

Biometry and Risk Estimation Research Grants $41,000–$1,600,000

Department of Health and Human Services
PO Box 12233
Research Triangle Park, NC 27709
(919) 541-7634

Field of Interest: Science Research – Environment
Average Amount Given: $646,000
Purpose: To conduct research in statistics, biomathematics, and epidemiology towards estimating probable health risks from human exposure to various environmental hazards.
Who May Apply: Profit or nonprofit medical, educational, or research institutions and the individuals associated with them.
Requirements: None.
Contact: David Mineo, Grants Management Officer.
Application Information: Application required.
Initial Approach: Letter or phone.

Biometry and Risk Estimation Small Instrumentation Grants $5,000–$50,000

Department of Health and Human Services
PO Box 12233
Research Triangle Park, NC 27709
(919) 541-7634

Field of Interest: Science Research – Environment
Average Amount Given: N/A
Purpose: To conduct research in statistics, biomathematics, and epidemiology towards estimating probable health risks from human exposure to various environmental hazards and to develop technical means to conduct this research.
Who May Apply: Profit or nonprofit medical, educational, or research institutions and the individuals associated with them.
Requirements: None.
Contact: David Mineo, Grants Management Officer.
Application Information: Application required.
Initial Approach: Letter or phone.

Minority Educational Institution Assistance $95,000–$180,000

Department of Energy
1000 Independence Ave., SW
Washington, DC 20585
(202) 586-1593

Field of Interest: Science Research – Minority Development
Average Amount Given: $140,000
Purpose: To encourage minorities to participate in Department of Energy Programs and to improve facilities and curriculum at minority institutions.
Who May Apply: Minority educational institutions and qualified individual faculty and students associated with them.
Requirements: Cost-sharing encouraged.
Contact: Isiah O. Sewell, Office of Minority Impact.
Application Information: Application required.
Initial Approach: Letter or phone.

Research Initiation and Improvement $10,000–$285,000

National Science Foundation
1800 G Street, NW
Washington, DC 20550
(202) 357-7552

Field of Interest: Science Research – Minority Development
Average Amount Given: $170,000
Purpose: To increase professional science and engineering opportunities for women and minorities.
Who May Apply: Individuals, especially women, minorities, and the disabled and all U.S. colleges and universities.
Requirements: None.
Contact: Program Director.
Application Information: Application required.
Initial Approach: Letter or phone.

Undergraduate Science, Mathematics, and Engineering Career Access Opportunities $1,000,000 for each of five years

National Science Foundation
1800 G Street, NW
Washington, DC 20550
(202) 357-7051

Field of Interest: Science Research – Minority Development
Average Amount Given: N/A
Purpose: To help colleges and universities maintain strong, high quality science instructional programs for all their students, especially for women and minorities.
Who May Apply: All U.S. colleges and universities, especially those with significant minority populations, and individuals at these institutions.
Requirements: None.
Contact: Program Director.
Application Information: Application required.
Initial Approach: Letter or phone.

Undergraduate Science, Mathematics, and Engineering Model Projects $200,000

National Science Foundation
1800 G Street, NW
Washington, DC 20550
(202) 357-7051

Field of Interest: Science Research – Minority Development
Average Amount Given: N/A
Purpose: To help colleges and universities maintain strong, high quality science instructional programs for all their students.
Who May Apply: All U.S. colleges and universities, especially those with significant minority populations, and individuals associated with these institutions.
Requirements: None.
Contact: Program Director.
Application Information: Application required.
Initial Approach: Letter or phone.

Young Scholars Project Grants $21,000–$232,368

National Science Foundation
1800 G Street, NW
Washington, DC 20550
(202) 357-7538

Field of Interest: Science Research – Minority Development
Average Amount Given: $46,000
Purpose: To identify secondary students with high potential for careers in science, mathematics, and engineering and to facilitate their career path, with special emphasis on women, minorities, the disabled, and students from rural areas.
Who May Apply: Colleges and universities, related educational entities, and individuals associated with them, and for-profit organizations.
Requirements: None.
Contact: Dr. Elmina C. Johnson.
Application Information: Application required.
Initial Approach: Letter or phone.

Behavioral Science Project Grants $5,000–$1,000,000

National Science Foundation
1800 G Street, NW
Washington, DC 20550
(202) 357-9854

Field of Interest: Science Research – Social Sciences
Average Amount Given: $77,000
Purpose: To support basic research in behavioral and neural sciences.
Who May Apply: Unaffiliated scientists, all profit or nonprofit entities, and colleges and universities and individuals associated with them.
Requirements: None.
Contact: Director.
Application Information: Application required.
Initial Approach: Letter or phone.

Biometry and Risk Estimation Small Business Project Grants $50,000–$500,000

Department of Health and Human Services
PO Box 12233
Research Triangle Park, NC 27709
(919) 541-7634

Field of Interest: Science Research – Social Sciences
Average Amount Given: N/A
Purpose: To conduct research in statistics, biomathematics, and epidemiology towards estimating probable health risks from human exposure to various environmental hazards.
Who May Apply: Small businesses.
Requirements: None.
Contact: David Mineo, Grants Management Officer.
Application Information: Application required.
Initial Approach: Letter or phone.

Population Research $7,000–$1,400,000

National Institutes of Health, PHS
Department of Health and Human Services
Bethesda, MD 20892
(301) 496-1848

Field of Interest: Science Research – Social Sciences
Average Amount Given: $151,000
Purpose: To research reproductive processes, to develop safer and more effective contraceptives, and to understand how population structure and change affect the health of society.
Who May Apply: Individuals, small businesses, and public and private, profit and nonprofit entities.
Requirements: None.
Contact: Hildegard P. Topper
Application Information: Application required.
Initial Approach: Letter or phone.

Social Sciences Project Grants $5,000–$1,000,000

National Science Foundation
1800 G Street, NW
Washington, DC 20550
(202) 357-9854

Field of Interest: Science Research – Social Sciences
Average Amount Given: $77,000
Purpose: To support basic research in social and economic science.
Who May Apply: Unaffiliated scientists, all profit or nonprofit entities and colleges, universities, and individuals associated with them.
Requirements: None.
Contact: Director.
Application Information: Application required.
Initial Approach: Letter or phone.

Socioeconomic and Demographic Research Project Grants $819,000

Department of Energy
1000 Independence Ave., SW
Washington, DC 20585
(202) 586-1593

Field of Interest: Science Research – Social Sciences
Average Amount Given: N/A
Purpose: To support socioeconomic data and research, especially data on minority spending on energy-related issues, and thereby develop Department of Energy policy and strategies.
Who May Apply: Energy-related small businesses, educational institutions, and nonprofit institutions.
Requirements: None.
Contact: Georgia R. Johnson.
Application Information: Application required.
Initial Approach: Letter or phone.

Atmospheric Sciences Project Grants $1,000–$300,000,000

National Science Foundation
1800 G Street, NW
Washington, DC 20550
(202) 357-9874

Field of Interest: Science Research – General
Average Amount Given: $100,000
Purpose: To expand fundamental knowledge of the earth's natural environment through basic research, science and technology centers, and instrumentation and lab equipment.
Who May Apply: All individuals, private profit organizations, and colleges and universities.
Requirements: None.
Contact: Dr. Eugene W. Bierly.
Application Information: Application required.
Initial Approach: Letter or phone.

Biological Science Project Grants $5,000–$1,000,000

National Science Foundation
1800 G Street, NW
Washington, DC 20550
(202) 357-9854

Field of Interest: Science Research – General
Average Amount Given: $77,000
Purpose: To support basic research in cellular and molecular biosciences.
Who May Apply: Unaffiliated scientists, all profit or nonprofit entities, and colleges and universities and individuals associated with them.
Requirements: None.
Contact: Director.
Application Information: Application required.
Initial Approach: Letter or phone.

Computer and Information Science and Engineering $15,000–$5,000,000

National Science Foundation
1800 G Street, NW
Washington, DC 20550
(202) 357-7936

Field of Interest: Science Research – General
Average Amount Given: $145,000
Purpose: To support basic research in computer science, information processing, and engineering and to provide access to very advanced computer networking capabilities.
Who May Apply: Small businesses and public or private, profit or nonprofit entities, especially educational institutions.
Requirements: None.
Contact: Assistant Director.
Application Information: Application required.
Initial Approach: Letter or phone.

Earth Sciences Project Grants $1,000–$300,000,000

National Science Foundation
1800 G Street, NW
Washington, DC 20550
(202) 357-7958

Field of Interest: Science Research – General
Average Amount Given: $100,000
Purpose: To expand fundamental knowledge of the earth's natural environment through basic research, science and technology centers, and instrumentation and lab equipment.
Who May Apply: All individuals, private profit organizations, and colleges and universities.
Requirements: None.
Contact: Dr. James F. Hayes.
Application Information: Application required.
Initial Approach: Letter or phone.

Engineering Grants $ 1,000–$5,000,000

Division of Research Career Development
National Science Foundation
1800 G Street, NW
Room 1126C
Washington, DC 20550(202) 357-9774

Field of Interest: Science Research – General
Average Amount Given: $78,000
Purpose: To promote the progress of engineering and technology.
Who May Apply: Public and private universities and colleges and qualified individuals at these institutions.
Requirements: None.
Contact: Paul Herer.
Application Information: Application required.
Initial Approach: Letter or phone.

Mathematical and Physical Sciences Research Grants $10,000–$4,200,000

National Science Foundation
1800 G Street, NW
Washington, DC 20550
(202) 357-9742

Field of Interest: Science Research – General
Average Amount Given: $70,000
Purpose: To support basic scientific research, especially that which aims toward solving America's problems.
Who May Apply: Unaffiliated scientists, public and private educational institutions and individual scientists associated with them and private profit and nonprofit agencies.
Requirements: None.
Contact: Assistant Director.
Application Information: Application required.
Initial Approach: Letter or phone.

Ocean Sciences Project Grants $1,000–$300,000,000

National Science Foundation
1800 G Street, NW
Washington, DC 20550
(202) 357-9639

Field of Interest: Science Research – General
Average Amount Given: $100,000
Purpose: To expand fundamental knowledge of the earth's natural environment through basic research, science and technology centers, and instrumentation and lab equipment.
Who May Apply: All individuals, private profit organizations, and colleges and universities.
Requirements: None.
Contact: Dr. M. Grant Gross.
Application Information: Application required.
Initial Approach: Letter or phone.

Polar Programs Project Grants $1,000–$300,000,000

National Science Foundation
1800 G Street, NW
Washington, DC 20550
(202) 357-7766

Field of Interest: Science Research – General
Average Amount Given: $100,000
Purpose: To expand fundamental knowledge of the earth's natural environment through basic research, science and technology centers, and instrumentation and lab equipment.
Who May Apply: All individuals, private profit organizations, and colleges and universities.
Requirements: None.
Contact: Dr. Peter Wilkniss.
Application Information: Application required.
Initial Approach: Letter or phone.

Undergraduate Science, Mathematics, and Engineering Undergraduate Faculty Enhancement

National Science Foundation
1800 G Street, NW
Washington, DC 20550
(202) 357-7051

Field of Interest: Science Research – General
Average Amount Given: $65,000
Purpose: To help colleges and universities maintain strong, high quality science instructional programs for all their students.
Who May Apply: All U.S. colleges and universities and qualified individuals associated with them.
Requirements: None.
Contact: Program Director.
Application Information: Application required.
Initial Approach: Letter or phone.

Undergraduate Science, Mathematics, and Engineering Instrumentation and Laboratory Improvement $5,000–$100,000

National Science Foundation
1800 G Street, NW
Washington, DC 20550
(202) 357-7051

Field of Interest: Science Research – General
Average Amount Given: N/A
Purpose: To help colleges and universities maintain strong, high quality science instructional programs for all their students.
Who May Apply: All U.S. colleges and universities and educational consortia, and qualified individuals associated with them.
Requirements: None.
Contact: Program Director.
Application Information: Application required.
Initial Approach: Letter or phone.

SOCIAL SERVICES

Capital Assistance for Elderly and Handicapped Persons $35,000,000

Urban Mass Transportation Administration
Department of Transportation
400 Seventh Street, SW
Washington, DC 20590
(202) 366-2053

Field of Interest: Social Services – Aged
Average Amount Given: N/A
Purpose: To assist the elderly and handicapped when transportation services are not sufficient.
Who May Apply: Private nonprofit entities.
Requirements: 20% matching funding required.
Contact: Office of Grants Management.
Application Information: Application required.
Initial Approach: Letter or phone.

---

*Foster Grandparent Program
Project Grants $2,000–$1,300,000

ACTION
1100 Vermont Avenue, NW
Washington, DC 20525
(202) 634-9349

Field of Interest: Social Services – Aged
Average Amount Given: $225,000
Purpose: To provide part-time volunteer service opportunities for low-income people over 60 and to give person-to-person service in health, education, and welfare to help alleviate social problems.
Who May Apply: Private nonprofit agencies.
Requirements: 10% matching funding required.
Contact: Program Officer.
Application Information: Application required.
Initial Approach: Letter or phone.

---

*Retired Senior Volunteer Program $10,000–$600,000

ACTION
1100 Vermont Avenue, NW
Washington, DC 20525
(202) 634-9353

Field of Interest: Social Services – Aged
Average Amount Given: $40,700
Purpose: To provide retired individuals over 60 to help their communities through volunteer service.
Who May Apply: Private nonprofit agencies.
Requirements: Variable.
Contact: Program Officer.
Application Information: Application required.
Initial Approach: Letter or phone.

---

*Senior Community Service Employment
Program $342,800,000

Office of Special Targeted Programs
Employment and Training Administration
Department of Labor
200 Constitution Ave., NW
Washington, DC 20210
(202) 535-0500

Field of Interest: Social Services – Aged
Average Amount Given: N/A
Purpose: To provide and promote part-time work opportunities in community service activities for low-income persons 55 or older.
Who May Apply: National public and private nonprofit entities.
Requirements: Details given at time of application.
Contact: Paul Mayrand.
Application Information: Application required.
Initial Approach: Letter or phone.

*Senior Companion Program $7,500–$365,000

ACTION
1100 Vermont Avenue, NW
Washington, DC 20525
(202) 634-9351

Field of Interest: Social Services – Aged
Average Amount Given: $195,000
Purpose: To provide volunteer opportunities for low-income individuals over 60 by assisting other older people who are physically or mentally impaired.
Who May Apply: Private nonprofit agencies.
Requirements: 10% matching funding required.
Contact: Program Officer.
Application Information: Application required.
Initial Approach: Letter or phone.

*Special Programs for the Aging $9,000–$400,000

Office of Program Development
Administration on Aging
Department of Health and Human Services
Washington, DC 20201
(202) 245-0442

Field of Interest: Social Services – Aged
Average Amount Given: $125,000
Purpose: To train personnel to work with the aging.
Who May Apply: Any public or private nonprofit entity.
Requirements: None.
Contact: Mike Suzuki.
Application Information: Application required.
Initial Approach: Letter or phone.

Assistance Payments Research Project Grants $55,000–$350,000

Office of Family Assistance
Family Support Administration
370 L'Enfant Promenade, SW
Washington DC 20447
(202) 252-4681

Field of Interest: Social Services – Business Development
Average Amount Given: $144,000
Purpose: To discover and demonstrate new concepts and methods which will increase cost-effectiveness and reduce welfare dependency and generally improve the Aid to Families with Dependent Children program.
Who May Apply: Profit and nonprofit organizations.
Requirements: At least 5% matching funds required.
Contact: Gary Ashcraft.
Application Information: Application required.
Initial Approach: Letter or phone.

Health Care Financing Research Project Grants $25,000–$1,000,000

Health Care Financing Administration
Department of Health and Human Services
6325 Security Blvd.
Baltimore, MD 21207

Field of Interest: Social Services – Business Development
Average Amount Given: $235,000
Purpose: For pilot projects to resolve major health care financing issues or to develop innovative methods for the administration of Medicare and Medicaid.
Who May Apply: Any private or public, profit or nonprofit entites.
Requirements: 5% matching funding required.
Contact: John R. Antos, Director.
Application Information: Application required.
Initial Approach: Letter.

Social Security Research and Demonstration
Project Grants $26,250–$450,000

Social Security Administration 1-E-4
Gwynn Oak Building
Gwynn Oak Ave.
Baltimore, MD 21207
(301) 965-9502

Field of Interest: Social Services – Business Development
Average Amount Given: $160,000
Purpose: To conduct research on all aspects of aging and the aged; and to research the rates of return on various investments and related issues.
Who May Apply: Profit and nonprofit entities and educational institutions.
Requirements: 5% to 25% of cost is shared.
Contact: Lawrence H. Pullen.
Application Information: Application required.
Initial Approach: Letter or phone.

Abandoned Infants Project Grants $50,000–$200,000

Children's Bureau, Program Support Division
Office of Human Development Services
330 C Street, SW
Washington, DC 20201
(202) 245-0709

Field of Interest: Social Services – Children
Average Amount Given: N/A
Purpose: To prevent the abandonment of infants and young children; to meet the needs of those who are abandoned, especially those infants with AIDS, in their natural families or foster care; and to train caregivers.
Who May Apply: Nonprofit organizations.
Requirements: 25% matching funding required.
Contact: Joan Gaffney.
Application Information: Application required.
Initial Approach: Letter or phone.

*Adolescent Family Life Demonstration
Project Grants $25,000–$400,000

Department of Health and Human Services, PHS
Hubert H. Humphrey Bldg., Rm 736E
200 Independence Ave., SW
Washington, DC 20201
(202) 245-7476

Field of Interest: Social Services – Children
Average Amount Given: $160,000
Purpose: To promote adoption as an alternative for adolescent parents and to promote community-based solutions to the issues of adolescent out-of-wedlock pregnancy.
Who May Apply: Public and private nonprofit entities.
Requirements: 30% in matching funds required.
Contact: Patricia Funderbunk, Director.
Application Information: Application required.
Initial Approach: Letter or phone.

Adoption Opportunities
Project Grants $50,000–$250,000

Children's Bureau
Administration for Children, Youth and Families
PO Box 1182
Washington, DC 20013
(202) 426-2822

Field of Interest: Social Services – Children
Average Amount Given: N/A
Purpose: To improve adoption practices and services.
Who May Apply: Educational or nonprofit entities.
Requirements: None.
Contact: Delmar Weathers.
Application Information: Application required.
Initial Approach: Letter or phone.

*Appalachian Child Development   **$10,000–$60,000**

Appalachian Regional Commission
1666 Connecticut Ave., NW
Washington, DC 20235
(202) 673-7874

Field of Interest: Social Services – Children
Average Amount Given: $35,000
Purpose: To provide child development services in the region.
Who may apply: Public and private nonprofit entities.
Requirements: None.
Contact: Executive Director.
Application Information: Application required.
Initial Approach: Letter or phone.

***Child Abuse and Neglect
Discretionary Activities**   **$20,000–$300,000**

Administration for Children, Youth and Families
NCCAN
PO Box 1182
Washington, DC 20013
(202) 245-2056

Field of Interest: Social Services – Children
Average Amount Given: $100,000
Purpose: To prevent, identify, and treat child abuse and neglect through research, services improvement, and technical assistance.
Who May Apply: Qualified nonprofit agencies.
Requirements: 5% matching funds required.
Contact: Director, National Center on Child Abuse and Neglect.
Application Information: Application required.
Initial Approach: Letter or phone.

**Child Support Enforcement Research
Project Grants**   **$440,000–$119,000,000**

Policy and Planning Division, Office of Child Support Enforcement
Department of Health and Human Services, 4th Floor
370 L'Enfant Promenade, SW
Washington DC 20447
(202) 252-4620

Field of Interest: Social Services – Children
Average Amount Given: $17,000,000
Purpose: To discover and demonstrate new concepts which will increase child support collections from absent parents.
Who May Apply: Profit and nonprofit organizations.
Requirements: At least 5% matching funding required.
Contact: Gaile Maller, Chief.
Application Information: Application required.
Initial Approach: Letter or phone.

**Child Welfare Research and Demonstration
Project Grants**   **$10,000–$250,000**

Administration for Children, Youth and Families
Office of Human Development Services
PO Box 1182
Washington, DC 20013
(202) 755-7420

Field of Interest: Social Services – Children
Average Amount Given: $100,000
Purpose: To finance demonstration projects in the area of child and family development and welfare.
Who May Apply: Nonprofit organizations, institutions of higher learning, and any entity engaged in research or child welfare activities.
Requirements: 5% matching funding required.
Contact: Chief, Discretionary Branch Program.
Application Information: Application required.
Initial Approach: Letter or phone.

Child Welfare Services Training Grants $3,600,000

Children's Bureau
Administration for Children, Youth and Families
PO Box 1182
Washington, DC 20013
(202) 755-7820

Field of Interest: Social Services – Children
Average Amount Given: $50,000
Purpose: To develop and maintain qualified and trained professionals in social services to children and their families.
Who May Apply: Qualified individuals at accredited institutions of higher learning.
Requirements: None.
Contact: Director, Program Support Division.
Application Information: Application required.
Initial Approach: Letter or phone.

*Comprehensive Child Development Centers $35,000 for planning; $300,000 –$1,800,000 for operating

Administration for Children, Youth and Families
PO Box 1182
Washington, DC 20013
(202) 755-7782

Field of Interest: Social Services – Children
Average Amount Given: N/A
Purpose: To create centers where low-income infants, toddlers, and pre-schoolers can enhance their social, intellectual, emotional, and physical development.
Who May Apply: Qualified public or private nonprofit entities.
Requirements: 20% in matching funds required.
Contact: Allen Smith.
Application Information: Application required.
Initial Approach: Letter or phone.

Drug Abuse Prevention and Education for Runaway and Homeless Youth $50,000–$150,000

Children's Bureau
Administration for Children, Youth and Families
PO Box 1182
Washington, DC 20013
(202) 426-2822

Field of Interest: Social Services – Children
Average Amount Given: N/A
Purpose: To expand and improve existing drug abuse and prevention services to runaway and homeless youth and their families.
Who May Apply: Individuals, public and private nonprofit entities.
Requirements: 25% in matching funds or in kind services required.
Contact: Frank Fuentes.
Application Information: Application required.
Initial Approach: Letter or phone.

Missing Children's Assistance $7,900,000

Office of Juvenile Justice and Delinquency Prevention
Office of Justice Programs
Department of Justice
Washington, DC 20531
(202) 307-0751

Field of Interest: Social Services – Children
Average Amount Given: N/A
Purpose: To ensure coordination among all federally funded programs related to missing children.
Who May Apply: Individuals and public or private nonprofit organizations.
Requirements: None.
Contact: Director.
Application Information: Application required.
Initial Approach: Letter or phone.

Runaway and Homeless Youth
Project Grants $12,000–$150,000
Administration for Children, Youth and Families
Office of Human Development Services
PO Box 1182
Washington, DC 20013
(202) 245-0049

Field of Interest: Social Services – Children
Average Amount Given: $78,000
Purpose: To develop local facilities to address the immediate needs of runaway and homeless youth and their families.
Who May Apply: Profit and nonprofit private agencies.
Requirements: 10% matching funds in cash or kind.
Contact: Associate Commissioner, Family and Youth Services Bureau.
Application Information: Application required.
Initial Approach: Letter or phone.

Transitional Living for Runaway and Homeless Youth
Project Grants $50,000–$150,000
Family and Youth Services Bureau
Program Operations Division
Office of Human Development Services
330 C Street, SW
Washington, DC 20201(202) 245-0043

Field of Interest: Social Services – Children
Average Amount Given: N/A
Purpose: To assist homeless youth in making a smooth transition toward a productive adulthood and self-sufficiency.
Who May Apply: Nonprofit organizations.
Requirements: 10% matching funding required.
Contact: Preston Bruce.
Application Information: Application required.
Initial Approach: Letter or phone.

*Crime Victim Assistance
Discretionary Grants $5,000–$350,000
Office for Victims of Crime
Office of Justice Programs
Department of Justice
633 Indiana Avenue, NW, Room 1352
Washington, DC 20531
(202) 514-6444

Field of Interest: Social Services – Crime
Average Amount Given: N/A
Purpose: For training and technical assistance and for direct services to crime victims.
Who May Apply: Private nonprofit agencies.
Requirements: None.
Contact: Marti Speights, Director.
Application Information: Application required.
Initial Approach: Letter or phone.

Justice Research and Development
Project Grants $24,000,000
National Institute of Justice
Department of Justice
Washington, DC 20531
(202) 307-2942

Field of Interest: Social Services – Crime
Average Amount Given: N/A
Purpose: To research the causes and control of crime and to improve the criminal justice system.
Who May Apply: Public or private, profit or nonprofit entities and qualified individuals.
Requirements: None.
Contact: Director.
Application Information: Application required.
Initial Approach: Letter or phone.

Juvenile Gangs and Drug Abuse and Drug Trafficking $2,000,000

Office of Juvenile Justice and Delinquency Prevention
Office of Justice Programs, Department of Justice
Washington, DC 20531
(202) 724-7751

Field of Interest: Social Services – Crime
Average Amount Given: N/A
Purpose: To establish programs which reduce juvenile participation in drug-related crimes; create innovative solutions for convicted juveniles; facilitate identification of those juveniles at risk; and to educate juveniles away from gangs.
Who May Apply: Individuals and public or private nonprofit agencies.
Requirements: None.
Contact: Director.
Application Information: Application required.
Initial Approach: Letter or phone.

Juvenile Justice and Delinquency Prevention Project Grants $4,810,000

Office of Justice Programs, Department of Justice
Washington, DC 20531
(202) 307-5914

Field of Interest: Social Services – Crime
Average Amount Given: N/A
Purpose: To develop programs which prevent and control juvenile delinquency through community-based alternatives, diverting them from the traditional juvenile justice system and developing advocacy activities of every type.
Who May Apply: Individuals and public or private nonprofit entities.
Requirements: 50% in matching funds required.
Contact: Office of Juvenile Justice and Delinquency Prevention.
Application Information: Application required.
Initial Approach: Letter or phone.

National Institute for Juvenile Justice and Delinquency Prevention $2,467,000

Office of Juvenile Justice and Delinquency Prevention
Office of Justice Programs, Department of Justice
Washington, DC 20531
(202) 307-5929

Field of Interest: Social Services – Crime
Average Amount Given: N/A
Purpose: To conduct and coordinate research of juvenile justice and delinquency prevention activities including publishing information and conducting national training programs on juvenile justice issues.
Who May Apply: Individuals and public or private agencies and organizations.
Requirements: None.
Contact: Irving Slott.
Application Information: Application required.
Initial Approach: Letter or phone.

*Fair Housing Education Initiatives Program $2,000,000

Department of Housing and Urban Development
451 W. 7th St., SW
Washington, DC 20410
(202) 755-0455

Field of Interest: Social Services – Housing
Average Amount Given: N/A
Purpose: To coordinate and implement outreach and educational programs designed to inform the public of the fair housing laws of the U.S.
Who May Apply: Private nonprofits.
Requirements: None.
Contact: Assistant Secretary for Fair Housing and Equal Opportunity.
Application Information: Application required.
Initial Approach: Letter or phone.

***Fair Housing Private Enforcement Initiative
Program**   **$3,500,000**

Department of Housing and Urban Development
451 W. 7th St., SW
Washington, DC 20410
(202) 755-0455

Field of Interest: Social Services – Housing
Average Amount Given: N/A
Purpose: To carry out activities designed to enforce the fair housing laws of the U.S.
Who May Apply: Private nonprofit organizations.
Requirements: None.
Contact: Assistant Secretary for Fair Housing and Equal Opportunity.
Application Information: Application required.
Initial Approach: Letter or phone.

**Housing Counseling Assistance
Program Project Grants**   **$3,500,000**

Secretary–Help and Counseling Services Branch
Department of Housing and Urban Development
451 W. 7th St., SW
Washington, DC 20410
(202) 755-6664

Field of Interest: Social Services – Housing
Average Amount Given: $40,000 maximum
Purpose: To counsel UHD homeowners and tenants and thereby prevent delinquencies, defaults, and foreclosures.
Who May Apply: Community-based public or private nonprofit entities.
Requirements: None.
Contact: Office of Insured Single-Family Housing.
Application Information: Application required.
Initial Approach: Letter or phone.

**Lower Income Housing Assistance
Program**   **$11,500,000**

Department of Housing and Urban Development
451 W. 7th St., SW
Washington, DC 20410
(202) 755-6887

Field of Interest: Social Services – Housing
Average Amount Given: N/A
Purpose: To aid very low income families in obtaining decent, safe, and sanitary housing.
Who May Apply: Property owners authorized to develop low-income housing.
Requirements: None.
Contact: Office of Elderly and Assisted Housing.
Application Information: Application required.
Initial Approach: Letter or phone.

***Nehemiah Housing Opportunity Grant
Program**   **$44,200,000**

Department of Housing and Urban Development
451 W. 7th St., SW
Washington, DC 20410
(202) 755-6700

Field of Interest: Social Services – Housing
Average Amount Given: $15,000 per family
Purpose: To aid low income families in buying homes and to create employment in low-income areas.
Who May Apply: Nonprofit organizations.
Requirements: None.
Contact: Morris E. Carter.
Application Information: Application required.
Initial Approach: Letter or phone.

Rehabilitation Mortgage Insurance $26,750,000

Office of Insured Single-Family Housing
Department of Housing and Urban Development
451 W. 7th St., SW
Washington, DC 20410
(202) 755-6720

Field of Interest: Social Services – Housing
Average Amount Given: 6,468 homes insured in 1989
Purpose: To help families repair, purchase, or refinance existing residential structures more than a year old.
Who May Apply: Individual purchasers or investors.
Requirements: Determined on case basis.
Contact: Director, Single Family Development Division.
Application Information: Application required.
Initial Approach: Letter or phone.

*Supplemental Assistance for Facilities to Assist the Homeless $15,000–$1,000,000

Department of Housing and Urban Development
451 W. 7th St., SW
Washington, DC 20410
(202) 755-6300

Field of Interest: Social Services – Housing
Average Amount Given: $330,000
Purpose: To create innovative programs for, or alternative methods of, meeting the housing needs of the homeless.
Who May Apply: Private nonprofit organizations.
Requirements: None.
Contact: James. M. Forsberg.
Application Information: Application required.
Initial Approach: Letter or phone.

*Supportive Housing Demonstration Program Project Grants $135,000,000

Department of Housing and Urban Development
451 W. 7th St., SW
Washington, DC 20410
(202) 755-6300

Field of Interest: Social Services – Housing
Average Amount Given: N/A
Purpose: To develop innovative approaches to supportive housing for disadvantaged or at-risk populations.
Who May Apply: Private nonprofit organizations.
Requirements: None.
Contact: James M. Forsberg.
Application Information: Application required.
Initial Approach: Letter or phone.

Employment Services and Job Training Pilot and Demonstration Programs $100,000–$1,800,000

Employment and Training Administration
Department of Labor
200 Constitution Ave., NW
Washington, DC 20210
(202) 535-0677

Field of Interest: Social Services – Job Retraining and Development
Average Amount Given: $350,000
Purpose: To provide and promote job training and other services at the national level and to coordinate linkages between federal, state, and local employment and human resource agencies.
Who May Apply: Private profit and nonprofit agencies.
Requirements: None.
Contact: Lafayette Grisby.
Application Information: Application required.
Initial Approach: Letter or phone.

Employment and Training Research and Development Projects $1,000–$1,000,000

Employment and Training Administration
Department of Labor
200 Constitution Ave., NW
Washington, DC 20210
(202) 535-0677

Field of Interest: Social Services – Job Retraining and Development
Average Amount Given: $175,000
Purpose: To develop policy and programs to fully utilize U.S. human resources.
Who May Apply: Qualified individuals and any qualified entity.
Requirements: Discretionary matching funding required.
Contact: Lafayette Grisby.
Application Information: Application required.
Initial Approach: Letter or phone.

*Migrant and Seasonal Farmworkers Project Grant $120,000–$5,600,000

Office of Special Targeted Programs
Employment and Training Administration
Department of Labor
200 Constitution Ave., NW
Washington, DC 20210
(202) 535-0500

Field of Interest: Social Services – Job Retraining and Development
Average Amount Given: $1,250,000
Purpose: To provide job training and assistance and other support services to those suffering chronic seasonal unemployment in agriculture.
Who May Apply: Private nonprofit agencies.
Requirements: None.
Contact: Paul Mayrand.
Application Information: Application required.
Initial Approach: Letter or phone.

*Veterans Employment Program $55,000–$767,000

Office of the Assistant Secretary for
Veterans' Employment
Room S1316
200 Constitution Ave. NW
Washington, DC 20210
(202) 523-9110

Field of Interest: Social Services – Job Retraining and Development
Average Amount Given: $147,000
Purpose: To develop programs employing and training U.S. veterans.
Who May Apply: Private nonprofit organizations.
Requirements: None.
Contact: Headquarters, Veterans' Employment and Training Service.
Application Information: Application required.
Initial Approach: Letter or phone.

Corrections Research, Evaluation, and Policy Formation $15,000–$200,000

National Institute of Corrections
320 First Street, NW, Room 200
Washington, DC 20534
(202) 724-3106

Field of Interest: Social Services – Prisons
Average Amount Given: $75,000
Purpose: To conduct and coordinate research relating to corrections, including causes, prevention, diagnosis, and treatment of criminal offenders.
Who May Apply: Qualified individuals, public and private agencies and educational institutions.
Requirements: None.
Contact: Chief, Community Services Division.
Application Information: Application required.
Initial Approach: Letter or phone.

Corrections – Technical Assistance Clearinghouse $1,500–$50,000

National Institute of Corrections
320 First Street, NW, Room 200
Washington, DC 20534
(202) 724-3106

Field of Interest: Social Services – Prisons
Average Amount Given: $7,500
Purpose: To develop and implement improved corrections programs and to consult to Federal, state, local, public, and private agencies in this field.
Who May Apply: Qualified individuals, public and private agencies, and educational institutions.
Requirements: None.
Contact: Technical Assistance Coordinator.
Application Information: Application required.
Initial Approach: Letter or phone.

Corrections Training and Staff Development $1,500–$300,000

National Institute of Corrections
320 First Street, NW, Room 200
Washington, DC 20534
(202) 724-3106

Field of Interest: Social Services – Prisons
Average Amount Given: $100,000
Purpose: To devise and conduct workshops and training programs for law enforcement and judicial personnel.
Who May Apply: Individuals, public and private agencies, and educational institutions.
Requirements: None.
Contact: Director.
Application Information: Application required.
Initial Approach: Letter or phone.

*Prison Capacity Discretionary Project Grants $55,000–$325,000

Bureau of Justice Assistance
Department of Justice
Washington, DC 20531
(202) 514-5943

Field of Interest: Social Services – Prisons
Average Amount Given: N/A
Purpose: To provide technical assistance and training to entities dealing with state prison capacities and their alternatives.
Who May Apply: Private nonprofit organizations.
Requirements: None.
Contact: John Gregrich.
Application Information: Application required.
Initial Approach: Letter or phone.

Drug Abuse Prevention and Education Relating to Youth Gangs $50,000–$1,000,000

Administration for Children, Youth and Families
330 C Street, SW
Washington, DC 20201
(202) 245-0078

Field of Interest: Social Services – Substance Abuse
Average Amount Given: N/A
Purpose: To prevent and reduce the participation of youth in gangs that engage in illicit drug-related activities.
Who May Apply: Individuals and public and nonprofit private agencies.
Requirements: 25% in matching funds required.
Contact: Frank Fuentes.
Application Information: Application required.
Initial Approach: Letter or phone.

*Drug Alliance Project Grants   **$9,000–$50,000**
ACTION
1100 Vermont Avenue, NW
Washington, DC 20525
(202) 634-9757

Field of Interest: Social Services – Substance Abuse
Average Amount Given: $35,000
Purpose: To strengthen and expand the efforts of community-based volunteer groups working to prevent illicit drug use.
Who May Apply: Private nonprofit organizations.
Requirements: None.
Contact: Director.
Application Information: Application required.
Initial Approach: Letter or phone.

Communications Program Aimed Toward the Prevention of Alcohol and Other Drug Problems   **$100,000–$300,000**

Health Resources and Services Administration, PHS
Department of Health and Human Services
5600 Fishers Lane
Rockville, MD 20857
(301) 443-0373

Field of Interest: Social Services – Substance Abuse
Average Amount Given: $200,000
Purpose: To develop communications based approaches to the prevention of alcohol and other drug problems.
Who May Apply: Any public or private, profit or nonprofit entities.
Requirements: None.
Contact: Robert W. Denniston.
Application Information: Application required.
Initial Approach: Letter or phone.

*Drug Control and System Improvement   **$50,000–$2,500,000**
Bureau of Justice Assistance
Department of Justice
Washington, DC 20531
(202) 514-5943

Field of Interest: Social Services – Substance Abuse
Average Amount Given: N/A
Purpose: For criminal justice education and training and projects in the field which are national in scope.
Who May Apply: Public and private nonprofit agencies.
Requirements: None.
Contact: Eugene Dzikiewicz.
Application Information: Application required.
Initial Approach: Letter or phone.

*Employee Assistance Program for Drug and Alcohol Abuse   **$11,000–$189,000**
Occupational Health and Safety Administration
Department of Labor
200 Constitution Ave., NW
Washington, DC 20210
(202) 523-9361

Field of Interest: Social Services – Substance Abuse
Average Amount Given: $65,200
Purpose: To help employers establish employee assistance programs for drug and alcohol abuse.
Who May Apply: Any nonprofit that is an employer or employer representative.
Requirements: 25% matching funds in year one of the grant; 50% in year two; and 75% in year three.
Contact: Assistant Secretary.
Application Information: Application required.
Initial Approach: Letter or phone.

Airport Improvement Program $17,500–$60,000,000

Office of Airport Planning and Programming
Grants-in-Aid Division, APP-500
800 Independence Ave., SW
Washington, DC 20591
(202) 267-3831

Field of Interest: Social Services – General
Average Amount Given: $1,000,000
Purpose: To assist airport owners in developing a nationwide system to meet the needs of civil aeronautics.
Who May Apply: Individual owners of public-use reliever airports or airports enplaning over 2,500 passengers annually.
Requirements: Detailed in application process.
Contact: Federal Aviation Administration.
Application Information: Application required.
Initial Approach: Letter or phone.

*Boating Safety Financial Assistance $10,000–$167,000

Commandant, U.S. Coast Guard
Washington, DC 20593-0001
(202) 267-0954

Field of Interest: Social Services – General
Average Amount Given: $79,000
Purpose: To promote boating safety through education, assistance, and enforcement.
Who May Apply: National nonprofit organizations.
Requirements: None.
Contact: Robert Dewees.
Application Information: Application required.
Initial Approach: Letter or phone.

*Centers for Independent Living $24,000–$622,000

Department of Education
400 Maryland Ave., SW
Washington, DC 20202
(202) 732-1326

Field of Interest: Social Services – General
Average Amount Given: $175,000
Purpose: To provide independent living services to severely handicapped individuals.
Who May Apply: Public or private nonprofit entities.
Requirements: None.
Contact: Dierdra Davis.
Application Information: Application required.
Initial Approach: Letter or phone.

*Community-Based Anti-Arson Program $10,000–$15,000

U.S. Fire Administration
500 C Street, SW
Federal Center Plaza
Washington, DC 20472
(301) 447-1080

Field of Interest: Social Services – General
Average Amount Given: N/A
Purpose: To assist local community-based anti-arson organizations.
Who May Apply: Local nonprofit organizations.
Requirements: None.
Contact: Administrator.
Application Information: Application required.
Initial Approach: Letter or phone.

Cuban and Haitian Resettlement
Program $150,000–$3,000,000
Community Relations Service
5550 Friendship Blvd.
Chevy Chase, MD 20815
(301) 492-5929

Field of Interest: Social Services – General
Average Amount Given: $560,000
Purpose: To provide outplacement for Mariel Cubans, Haitian and Cuban detainees, and unaccompanied minors to make them productive members of society and to provide follow-up care for the mentally ill.
Who May Apply: Public or private, profit or nonprofit entities.
Requirements: None.
Contact: Grace Flores Hughes.
Application Information: Application required.
Initial Approach: Letter or phone.

Disaster Assistance Project
Grants and Payments $60,000–$190,000,000
Federal Emergency Management Agency
Office of Disaster Assistance Programs
Washington, DC 20472
(202) 646-4174

Field of Interest: Social Services – General
Average Amount Given: $13,000,000
Purpose: To alleviate suffering and hardship resulting from major emergencies and disasters.
Who May Apply: Private nonprofit organizations and qualifying individuals.
Requirements: Some cost-sharing required on a case-by-case basis.
Contact: Deborah Hart.
Application Information: Application required.
Initial Approach: Letter or phone.

*Family Violence Prevention and Services
Discretionary Grants $8,273,000
Office of Human Development Services
200 Independence Avenue, SW
Washington, DC 20201
(202) 245-2892

Field of Interest: Social Services – General
Average Amount Given: N/A
Purpose: To assist states and Native Americans prevent family violence and to provide immediate shelter and related assistance for victims of family violence and their dependents.
Who May Apply: Qualified nonprofit entities.
Requirements: None.
Contact: Office of Policy, Planning and Legislation.
Application Information: Application required.
Initial Approach: Letter or phone.

General Research and Technology
Activity $10,000–$300,000
Budget, Contracts and Program Control Division
Department of Housing and Urban Development
451 W. 7th St., SW
Washington, DC 20410
(202) 755-6996

Field of Interest: Social Services – General
Average Amount Given: $60,000
Purpose: To carry out research and demonstration projects pre-selected by the Department of Housing and Urban Development.
Who May Apply: Public and private, profit and nonprofit agencies.
Requirements: None.
Contact: Assistant Secretary, Policy Development and Research.
Application Information: Application required.
Initial Approach: Letter or phone.

Minigrant Program $500–$9,000

ACTION
1100 Vermont Avenue, NW
Washington, DC 20525
(202) 634-9757

Field of Interest: Social Services – General
Average Amount Given: N/A
Purpose: To initiate and strengthen broad-based volunteer efforts in the U.S. and its communities.
Who May Apply: Private nonprofit organizations.
Requirements: 10% matching funding required for grants over $3,500.
Contact: Technical Assistance Officer.
Application Information: Application required.
Initial Approach: Letter or phone.

Occupational Health and Safety Project Grants $219,000,000

Occupational Safety and Health Administration
Department of Labor
200 Constitution Ave., NW
Washington, DC 20210
(202) 523-8677

Field of Interest: Social Services – General
Average Amount Given: $135,000
Purpose: Advisory services and counseling for employees and employers and project grants to administer and enforce state OHSA programs.
Who May Apply: Individuals, nonprofit organizations.
Requirements: 10% to 50% matching funds required.
Contact: E. Tyna Coles.
Application Information: Application required.
Initial Approach: Letter or phone.

Services Delivery Improvement Research Grants for Family Planning $58,000–$136,000

Department of Health and Human Services, PHS
Hubert H. Humphrey Bldg., Rm 736E
200 Independence Ave., SW
Washington, DC 20201
(202) 245-1811

Field of Interest: Social Services – General
Average Amount Given: $100,000
Purpose: Promote service delivery improvement through research studies and application of knowledge.
Who May Apply: Any public or private nonprofit entity.
Requirements: None.
Contact: Patricia Thompson, Office of Population Affairs.
Application Information: Application required.
Initial Approach: Letter or phone.

Social Services Research and Demonstration Project Grants $30,000–$200,000

Department of Health and Human Services
Hubert H. Humphrey Bldg., Room 322-B
200 Independence Ave., SW
Washington, DC 20201
(202) 472-3026

Field of Interest: Social Services – General
Average Amount Given: $100,000
Purpose: To promote effective social services for vulnerable populations, such as the poor, the aged, children, and the disabled.
Who May Apply: Educational institutions and profit and nonprofit entities.
Requirements: 25% in matching funds required.
Contact: Ann Queen.
Application Information: Application required.
Initial Approach: Letter or phone.

*Student Community Service Program $5,000–$15,000

ACTION
1100 Vermont Avenue, NW
Washington, DC 20525
(202) 634-9424

Field of Interest: Social Services – General
Average Amount Given: N/A
Purpose: To encourage secondary students to participate in community service projects addressing poverty-related problems.
Who May Apply: Private nonprofit agencies.
Requirements: $3,000 a year required in matching funding.
Contact: Program Director.
Application Information: Application required.
Initial Approach: Letter or phone.

*Technical Assistance Program

ACTION
1100 Vermont Avenue, NW
Washington, DC 20525
(202) 634-9757

Field of Interest: Social Services – General
Average Amount Given: $28,000
Purpose: To help volunteer and nonprofit organizations with technical equipment and assistance.
Who May Apply: Private nonprofit organizations.
Requirements: None.
Contact: Technical Assistance Officer.
Application Information: Application required.
Initial Approach: Letter or phone.

*Volunteer Demonstration Program Project Grants $5,500–$150,000

ACTION
1100 Vermont Avenue, NW
Washington, DC 20525
(202) 634-9757

Field of Interest: Social Services – General
Average Amount Given: N/A
Purpose: To determine innovative areas for volunteerism and demonstrate the effectiveness of these new programs.
Who May Apply: Private nonprofit organizations.
Requirements: None.
Contact: Assistant Director.
Application Information: Application required.
Initial Approach: Letter or phone.

REGIONAL – ARTS AND LITERATURE

Promotion of the Arts in Alabama $200–$65,400
Alabama State Council on the Arts
1 Dexter Ave.
Montgomery, AL 36130
(205) 242-4076

Field of Interest: Arts and Literature – General
Average Amount Given: $2,578
Purpose: To develop programs for the encouragement of arts and artists in each state.
Who May Apply: Individuals and arts organizations, by state.
Requirements: Variable by state.
Contact: Albert B. Head.
Application Information: Application required.
Initial Approach: Letter or phone.

Promotion of the Arts in Arizona $200–$65,400
Arizona Commission on the Arts
417 W. Roosevelt St.
Phoenix, AZ 85003
(802) 255-5882

Field of Interest: Arts and Literature – General
Average Amount Given: $3,250
Purpose: To develop programs for the encouragement of arts and artists in each state.
Who May Apply: Individuals and arts organizations, by state.
Requirements: Variable by state.
Contact: Shelley Cohn.
Application Information: Application required.
Initial Approach: Letter or phone.

Promotion of the Arts in Alaska $200–$65,400
Alaska State Council on the Arts
679 Warehouse Ave., Suite 220
Anchorage, AK 99501
(907) 279-1559

Field of Interest: Arts and Literature – General
Average Amount Given: $2,620
Purpose: To develop programs for the encouragement of arts and artists in each state.
Who May Apply: Individuals and arts organizations, by state.
Requirements: Variable by state.
Contact: Christine D'Arcy.
Application Information: Application required.
Initial Approach: Letter or phone.

Promotion of the Arts in Arkansas $200–$65,400
Arkansas Arts Council
225 E. Markham, Suite 200
Little Rock, AR 72201
(501) 371-2539

Field of Interest: Arts and Literature – General
Average Amount Given: $2,884
Purpose: To develop programs for the encouragement of arts and artists in each state.
Who May Apply: Individuals and arts organizations, by state.
Requirements: Variable by state.
Contact: Bev Lindsay.
Application Information: Application required.
Initial Approach: Letter or phone.

*Indicates grants for which fiscal sponsorship is required.

Promotion of the Arts in California $200–$65,400

California Arts Council
1901 Broadway, Suite A
Sacramento, CA 95818
(916) 445-1530

Field of Interest: Arts and Literature – General
Average Amount Given: $5,330
Purpose: To develop programs for the encouragement of arts and artists in each state.
Who May Apply: Individuals and arts organizations, by state.
Requirements: Variable by state.
Contact: Robert H. Reid.
Application Information: Application required.
Initial Approach: Letter or phone.

Promotion of the Arts in Connecticut $200–$65,400

Connecticut Commission on the Arts
227 Lawrence Street
Hartford, CT 06106
(203) 566-4770

Field of Interest: Arts and Literature – General
Average Amount Given: $2,000
Purpose: To develop programs for the encouragement of arts and artists in each state.
Who May Apply: Individuals and arts organizations, by state.
Requirements: Variable by state.
Contact: Gary Young.
Application Information: Application required.
Initial Approach: Letter or phone.

Promotion of the Arts in Colorado $200–$65,400

Colorado Council on the Arts and Humanities
750 Pennsylvania Street
Denver, CO 80203
(303) 894-2617

Field of Interest: Arts and Literature – General
Average Amount Given: $2,440
Purpose: To develop programs for the encouragement of arts and artists in each state.
Who May Apply: Individuals and arts organizations, by state.
Requirements: Variable by state.
Contact: Barbara Neal.
Application Information: Application required.
Initial Approach: Letter or phone.

Promotion of the Arts in Delaware $200–$65,400

Delaware State Arts Council
820 N. French Street
Wilmington, DE 19801
(302) 571-3540

Field of Interest: Arts and Literature – General
Average Amount Given: $1,618
Purpose: To develop programs for the encouragement of arts and artists in each state.
Who May Apply: Individuals and arts organizations, by state.
Requirements: Variable by state.
Contact: Cecelia Fitzgibbon.
Application Information: Application required.
Initial Approach: Letter or phone.

Promotion of the Arts in Florida $200–$65,400

Florida Arts Council
Department of State, The Capitol
Tallahassee, FL 32399
(904) 487-2980

Field of Interest: Arts and Literature – General
Average Amount Given: $1,159
Purpose: To develop programs for the encouragement of arts and artists in each state.
Who May Apply: Individuals and arts organizations, by state.
Requirements: Variable by state.
Contact: Peyton Fearrington.
Application Information: Application required.
Initial Approach: Letter or phone.

Promotion of the Arts in Georgia $200–$65,400

Georgia Council for the Arts
2082 East Exchange Place, Suite 100
Tucker, GA 30084
(404) 493-5780

Field of Interest: Arts and Literature – General
Average Amount Given: $690
Purpose: To develop programs for the encouragement of arts and artists in each state.
Who May Apply: Individuals and arts organizations, by state.
Requirements: Variable by state.
Contact: Frank Ratka.
Application Information: Application required.
Initial Approach: Letter or phone.

Promotion of the Arts in Hawaii $200–$65,400

Hawaii State Foundation on Culture and the Arts
335 Merchant St., Suite 202
Honolulu, HI 96013
(808) 548-4145

Field of Interest: Arts and Literature – General
Average Amount Given: $1,540
Purpose: To develop programs for the encouragement of arts and artists in each state.
Who May Apply: Individuals and arts organizations, by state.
Requirements: Variable by state.
Contact: Wendell Silva.
Application Information: Application required.
Initial Approach: Letter or phone.

Promotion of the Arts in Idaho $200–$65,400

Idaho Commission on the Arts
304 W. State Street
Boise, ID 83720
(208) 334-2119

Field of Interest: Arts and Literature – General
Average Amount Given: $750
Purpose: To develop programs for the encouragement of arts and artists in each state.
Who May Apply: Individuals and arts organizations, by state.
Requirements: Variable by state.
Contact: Margot Knight.
Application Information: Application required.
Initial Approach: Letter or phone.

Promotion of the Arts in Illinois   **$200–$65,400**

Illinois Arts Council
100 W. Randolph St.
Chicago, IL 60601
(312) 917-6750

Field of Interest: Arts and Literature – General
Average Amount Given: $2,650
Purpose: To develop programs for the encouragement of arts and artists in each state.
Who May Apply: Individuals and arts organizations, by state.
Requirements: Variable by state.
Contact: Lori Spaar Montana.
Application Information: Application required.
Initial Approach: Letter or phone.

Promotion of the Arts in Indiana   **$200–$65,400**

Indiana Arts Commission
47 S. Pennsylvania Ave., 6th Floor
Indianapolis, IN 46204
(317) 232-1266

Field of Interest: Arts and Literature – General
Average Amount Given: $1,860
Purpose: To develop programs for the encouragement of arts and artists in each state.
Who May Apply: Individuals and arts organizations, by state.
Requirements: Variable by state.
Contact: Thomas Schorgl.
Application Information: Application required.
Initial Approach: Letter or phone.

Promotion of the Arts in Iowa   **$200–$65,400**

Iowa Arts Council
Capitol Complex
Des Moines, IA 50319
(515) 281-4451

Field of Interest: Arts and Literature – General
Average Amount Given: $1,060
Purpose: To develop programs for the encouragement of arts and artists in each state.
Who May Apply: Individuals and arts organizations, by state.
Requirements: Variable by state.
Contact: Natalie A. Hala.
Application Information: Application required.
Initial Approach: Letter or phone.

Promotion of the Arts in Kansas   **$200–$65,400**

Kansas Arts Commission
700 Jackson, Suite 1004
Topeka, KS 66603
(913) 296-3335

Field of Interest: Arts and Literature – General
Average Amount Given: $1,035
Purpose: To develop programs for the encouragement of arts and artists in each state.
Who May Apply: Individuals and arts organizations, by state.
Requirements: Variable by state.
Contact: Dorothy L. Ilgen.
Application Information: Application required.
Initial Approach: Letter or phone.

Promotion of the Arts in Kentucky $200–$65,000

Kentucky Arts Council
Berry Hill
Frankfort, KY 40601
(502) 564-3757

Field of Interest: Arts and Literature – General
Average Amount Given: $1,347
Purpose: To develop programs for the encouragement of arts and artists in each state.
Who May Apply: Individuals and arts organizations, by state.
Requirements: Variable by state.
Contact: Charles Newell.
Application Information: Application required.
Initial Approach: Letter or phone.

Promotion of the Arts in Louisiana $200–$65,000

Louisiana Division of the Arts
PO Box 44247
Baton Rouge, LA 70804
(504) 342-8180

Field of Interest: Arts and Literature – General
Average Amount Given: $950
Purpose: To develop programs for the encouragement of arts and artists in each state.
Who May Apply: Individuals and arts organizations, by state.
Requirements: Variable by state.
Contact: Emma Burnen.
Application Information: Application required.
Initial Approach: Letter or phone.

Promotion of the Arts in Maine $200–$65,000

Maine Arts Commission
55 Capitol Street, State House Station 25
Augusta, ME 04333
(207) 289-2724

Field of Interest: Arts and Literature – General
Average Amount Given: $793
Purpose: To develop programs for the encouragement of arts and artists in each state.
Who May Apply: Individuals and arts organizations, by state.
Requirements: Variable by state.
Contact: Alden C. Wilson.
Application Information: Application required.
Initial Approach: Letter or phone.

Promotion of the Arts in Maryland $200–$65,000

Maryland State Arts Council
15 West Mulberry St.
Baltimore, MD 21201
(301) 333-8232

Field of Interest: Arts and Literature – General
Average Amount Given: $1,249
Purpose: To develop programs for the encouragement of arts and artists in each state.
Who May Apply: Individuals and arts organizations, by state.
Requirements: Variable by state.
Contact: James Backas.
Application Information: Application required.
Initial Approach: Letter or phone.

Promotion of the Arts in Massachusetts $200–$65,000

Massachusetts Council on the Arts and Humanities
80 Boylston St., Room 1000
Boston, MA 02116
(617) 727-3668

Field of Interest: Arts and Literature – General
Average Amount Given: $1,322
Purpose: To develop programs for the encouragement of arts and artists in each state.
Who May Apply: Individuals and arts organizations, by state.
Requirements: Variable by state.
Contact: Mary Anne Piacenelli.
Application Information: Application required.
Initial Approach: Letter or phone.

Promotion of the Arts in Michigan $200–$65,000

Michigan Council for the Arts
1200 Sixth Street, 11th Floor
Detroit, MI 46226
(313) 256-3751

Field of Interest: Arts and Literature – General
Average Amount Given: $1,090
Purpose: To develop programs for the encouragement of arts and artists in each state.
Who May Apply: Individuals and arts organizations, by state.
Requirements: Variable by state.
Contact: Barbara K. Goldman, Director, States Programs.
Application Information: Application required.
Initial Approach: Letter or phone.

Promotion of the Arts in Minnesota $200–$65,000

Minnesota State Arts Board
432 Summit Ave.
St. Paul, MN 55102
(612) 297-2503

Field of Interest: Arts and Literature – General
Average Amount Given: $1,006
Purpose: To develop programs for the encouragement of arts and artists in each state.
Who May Apply: Individuals and arts organizations, by state.
Requirements: Variable by state.
Contact: Sam Grabarski.
Application Information: Application required.
Initial Approach: Letter or phone.

Promotion of the Arts in Mississippi $200–$65,000

Mississippi Arts Commission
239 N. Lamar St., Suite 207
Jackson, MS 39201
(601) 359-6030

Field of Interest: Arts and Literature – General
Average Amount Given: $647
Purpose: To develop programs for the encouragement of arts and artists in each state.
Who May Apply: Individuals and arts organizations, by state.
Requirements: Variable by state.
Contact: Jane Crater Hiatt.
Application Information: Application required.
Initial Approach: Letter or phone.

Promotion of the Arts in Missouri $200–$65,000

Missouri Arts Council
111 N. Seventh St., Suite 105
St. Louis, MO 63101
(314) 444-6945

Field of Interest: Arts and Literature – General
Average Amount Given: $1,449
Purpose: To develop programs for the encouragement of arts and artists in each state.
Who May Apply: Individuals and arts organizations, by state.
Requirements: Variable by state.
Contact: Anthony Radich.
Application Information: Application required.
Initial Approach: Letter or phone.

Promotion of the Arts in Montana $200–$65,000

Montana Arts Council
48 N. Last Chance Gulch
Helena, MT 59820
(405) 444-6430

Field of Interest: Arts and Literature – General
Average Amount Given: $734
Purpose: To develop programs for the encouragement of arts and artists in each state.
Who May Apply: Individuals and arts organizations, by state.
Requirements: Variable by state.
Contact: David Nelson.
Application Information: Application required.
Initial Approach: Letter or phone.

Promotion of the Arts in Nebraska $200–$65,000

Nebraska Arts Council
1313 Farnam on the Mall
Omaha, NE 68102
(402) 554-2122

Field of Interest: Arts and Literature – General
Average Amount Given: $1,243
Purpose: To develop programs for the encouragement of arts and artists in each state.
Who May Apply: Individuals and arts organizations, by state.
Requirements: Variable by state.
Contact: Jennifer S. Clark.
Application Information: Application required.
Initial Approach: Letter or phone.

Promotion of the Arts in Nevada $200–$65,000

Nevada State Council on the Arts
329 Flint Street
Reno, NV 89501
(702) 789-0225

Field of Interest: Arts and Literature – General
Average Amount Given: $1,333
Purpose: To develop programs for the encouragement of arts and artists in each state.
Who May Apply: Individuals and arts organizations, by state.
Requirements: Variable by state.
Contact: Bill Fox.
Application Information: Application required.
Initial Approach: Letter or phone.

Promotion of the Arts in New Hampshire $200–$65,000

New Hampshire State Council on the Arts
40 N. Main Street
Concord, NH 03301
(603) 271-2788

Field of Interest: Arts and Literature – General
Average Amount Given: $1,500
Purpose: To develop programs for the encouragement of arts and artists in each state.
Who May Apply: Individuals and arts organizations, by state.
Requirements: Variable by state.
Contact: Susan Bonaluto.
Application Information: Application required.
Initial Approach: Letter or phone.

Promotion of the Arts in New Jersey $200–$65,000

New Jersey State Council on the Arts
109 West State Street
Trenton, NJ 08808
(609) 292-8130

Field of Interest: Arts and Literature – General
Average Amount Given: $1,354
Purpose: To develop programs for the encouragement of arts and artists in each state.
Who May Apply: Individuals and arts organizations, by state.
Requirements: Variable by state.
Contact: Jeffrey Kasper.
Application Information: Application required.
Initial Approach: Letter or phone.

Promotion of the Arts in New Mexico $200–$65,000

New Mexico Arts Division
224 East Palace Ave.
Santa Fe, NM 87501
(505) 827-6490

Field of Interest: Arts and Literature – General
Average Amount Given: $975
Purpose: To develop programs for the encouragement of arts and artists in each state.
Who May Apply: Individuals and arts organizations, by state.
Requirements: Variable by state.
Contact: Lara C. Morrow.
Application Information: Application required.
Initial Approach: Letter or phone.

Promotion of the Arts in New York $200–$65,000

New York State Council on the Arts
915 Broadway
New York, NY 10010
(212) 614-2900

Field of Interest: Arts and Literature – General
Average Amount Given: $1,793
Purpose: To develop programs for the encouragement of arts and artists in each state.
Who May Apply: Individuals and arts organizations, by state.
Requirements: Variable by state.
Contact: Mary Hays.
Application Information: Application required.
Initial Approach: Letter or phone.

Promotion of the Arts in North Carolina $200–$65,000

North Carolina Arts Council
Department of Cultural Resources
Raleigh, NC 27601
(919) 733-2621

Field of Interest: Arts and Literature – General
Average Amount Given: $1,082
Purpose: To develop programs for the encouragement of arts and artists in each state.
Who May Apply: Individuals and arts organizations, by state.
Requirements: Variable by state.
Contact: Mary Reagan.
Application Information: Application required.
Initial Approach: Letter or phone.

Promotion of the Arts in North Dakota $200–$65,000

North Dakota Council on the Arts
114 Broadway, Suite 606
Fargo, ND 58102
(701) 237-8982

Field of Interest: Arts and Literature – General
Average Amount Given: $650
Purpose: To develop programs for the encouragement of arts and artists in each state.
Who May Apply: Individuals and arts organizations, by state.
Requirements: Variable by state.
Contact: Donna Evenson.
Application Information: Application required.
Initial Approach: Letter or phone.

Promotion of the Arts in Ohio $200–$65,400

Ohio Arts Council
727 East Main St.
Columbus, Ohio 43205
(614) 466-2613

Field of Interest: Arts and Literature – General
Average Amount Given: $1,830
Purpose: To develop programs for the encouragement of arts and artists in each state.
Who May Apply: Individuals and arts organizations, by state.
Requirements: Variable by state.
Contact: Wayne Lawson.
Application Information: Application required.
Initial Approach: Letter or phone.

Promotion of the Arts in Oklahoma $200–$65,400

State Arts Council of Oklahoma
2101 N. Lincoln Blvd., Room 640
Oklahoma City, OK 73105
(405) 521-2931

Field of Interest: Arts and Literature – General
Average Amount Given: $1,200
Purpose: To develop programs for the encouragement of arts and artists in each state.
Who May Apply: Individuals and arts organizations, by state.
Requirements: Variable by state.
Contact: Betty Price.
Application Information: Application required.
Initial Approach: Letter or phone.

Promotion of the Arts in Oregon $200–$65,400

Oregon Arts Commission
835 Summit St., NE
Salem, OR 97301

Field of Interest: Arts and Literature – General
Average Amount Given: $960
Purpose: To develop programs for the encouragement of arts and artists in each state.
Who May Apply: Individuals and arts organizations, by state.
Requirements: Variable by state.
Contact: Leslie Tuomi.
Application Information: Application required.
Initial Approach: Letter or phone.

Promotion of the Arts in Pennsylvania $200–$65,400

Pennsylvania Council on the Arts
216 Finance Building
Harrisburg, PA 17120
(717) 787-6883

Field of Interest: Arts and Literature – General
Average Amount Given: $1,554
Purpose: To develop programs for the encouragement of arts and artists in each state.
Who May Apply: Individuals and arts organizations, by state.
Requirements: Variable by state.
Contact: Derek E. Gordon.
Application Information: Application required.
Initial Approach: Letter or phone.

Promotion of the Arts in Rhode Island $200–$65,400

Rhode Island State Council on the Arts
95 Cedar St., Suite 103
Providence, RI 02903
(401) 277-3880

Field of Interest: Arts and Literature – General
Average Amount Given: $1,210
Purpose: To develop programs for the encouragement of arts and artists in each state.
Who May Apply: Individuals and arts organizations, by state.
Requirements: Variable by state.
Contact: Iona Dobbins.
Application Information: Application required.
Initial Approach: Letter or phone.

Promotion of the Arts in South Carolina $200–$65,400

South Carolina Arts Commission
1800 Gervais
Columbia, SC 29201
(803) 734-8698

Field of Interest: Arts and Literature – General
Average Amount Given: $1,240
Purpose: To develop programs for the encouragement of arts and artists in each state.
Who May Apply: Individuals and arts organizations, by state.
Requirements: Variable by state.
Contact: Scott Sanders.
Application Information: Application required.
Initial Approach: Letter or phone.

Promotion of the Arts in South Dakota $200–$65,400

South Dakota Arts Council
108 W. 11th Street
Sioux Falls, SD 57102
(605) 339-6646

Field of Interest: Arts and Literature – General
Average Amount Given: $950
Purpose: To develop programs for the encouragement of arts and artists in each state.
Who May Apply: Individuals and arts organizations, by state.
Requirements: Variable by state.
Contact: Dennis Holub.
Application Information: Application required.
Initial Approach: Letter or phone.

Promotion of the Arts in Tennessee $200–$65,400

Tennessee Arts Commission
320 Sixth Ave. North, Suite 100
Nashville, TN 37243
(615) 741-1701

Field of Interest: Arts and Literature – General
Average Amount Given: $1,401
Purpose: To develop programs for the encouragement of arts and artists in each state.
Who May Apply: Individuals and arts organizations, by state.
Requirements: Variable by state.
Contact: Bennett Tarleton.
Application Information: Application required.
Initial Approach: Letter or phone.

Promotion of the Arts in Texas $200–$65,400

Texas Commission on the Arts
PO Box 13106, Capitol Station
Austin, TX 78711
(512) 483-5535

Field of Interest: Arts and Literature – General
Average Amount Given: $1,520
Purpose: To develop programs for the encouragement of arts and artists in each state.
Who May Apply: Individuals and arts organizations, by state.
Requirements: Variable by state.
Contact: John Paul Batista.
Application Information: Application required.
Initial Approach: Letter or phone.

Promotion of the Arts in Utah $200–$65,400

Utah Arts Council
817 S. Temple
Salt Lake City, UT 94102
(801) 533-5898

Field of Interest: Arts and Literature – General
Average Amount Given: $1,243
Purpose: To develop programs for the encouragement of arts and artists in each state.
Who May Apply: Individuals and arts organizations, by state.
Requirements: Variable by state.
Contact: Carol Nixon.
Application Information: Application required.
Initial Approach: Letter or phone.

Promotion of the Arts in Vermont $200–$65,400

Vermont Council on the Arts
136 State Street
Montpelier, VT 05602
(802) 829-3291

Field of Interest: Arts and Literature – General
Average Amount Given: $1,333
Purpose: To develop programs for the encouragement of arts and artists in each state.
Who May Apply: Individuals and arts organizations, by state.
Requirements: Variable by state.
Contact: Joanne Chow Winship.
Application Information: Application required.
Initial Approach: Letter or phone.

Promotion of the Arts in Virginia $200–$65,400

Virginia Commission for the Arts
101 N. 14th Street, 17th Floor
Richmond, VA 23219
(804) 225-3132

Field of Interest: Arts and Literature – General
Average Amount Given: $1,606
Purpose: To develop programs for the encouragement of arts and artists in each state.
Who May Apply: Individuals and arts organizations, by state.
Requirements: Variable by state.
Contact: Peggy Baggett.
Application Information: Application required.
Initial Approach: Letter or phone.

Promotion of the Arts in Washington $200–$65,400

Washington State Arts Commission
Mail Stop GH–11
Olympia, WA 98504
(208) 750-0660

Field of Interest: Arts and Literature – General
Average Amount Given: $1,359
Purpose: To develop programs for the encouragement of arts and artists in each state.
Who May Apply: Individuals and arts organizations, by state.
Requirements: Variable by state.
Contact: John W. Firman.
Application Information: Application required.
Initial Approach: Letter or phone.

Promotion of the Arts in West Virginia $200–$65,400

West Virginia Division of Culture and History
Arts and Humanities Section
The Cultural Center, Capitol Complex
Charleston, WV 25305
(304) 348-0240

Field of Interest: Arts and Literature – General
Average Amount Given: $1,212
Purpose: To develop programs for the encouragement of arts and artists in each state.
Who May Apply: Individuals and arts organizations, by state.
Requirements: Variable by state.
Contact: Lakin Cook.
Application Information: Application required.
Initial Approach: Letter or phone.

Promotion of the Arts in Wisconsin $200–$65,400

Wisconsin Arts Board
131 W. Wilson St., Suite 301
Madison, WI 53703
(808) 266-0190

Field of Interest: Arts and Literature – General
Average Amount Given: $1,225
Purpose: To develop programs for the encouragement of arts and artists in each state.
Who May Apply: Individuals and arts organizations, by state.
Requirements: Variable by state.
Contact: Arley Curtz.
Application Information: Application required.
Initial Approach: Letter or phone.

Promotion of the Arts in Wyoming $200–$65,400

Wyoming Arts Council
2320 Capitol Ave.
Cheyenne, WY 82002
(307) 777-7742

Field of Interest: Arts and Literature – General
Average Amount Given: $793
Purpose: To develop programs for the encouragement of arts and artists in each state.
Who May Apply: Individuals and arts organizations, by state.
Requirements: Variable by state.
Contact: Joy Thompson.
Application Information: Application required.
Initial Approach: Letter or phone.

REGIONAL – BUSINESS DEVELOPMENT

Disabled Veterans Outreach Program
for Alabama $139,700–$9,500,000

Department of Labor – VETS
519 Industrial Relations Bldg.
Montgomery, AL 36130
(205) 261-5430

Field of Interest: Business Development – General
Average Amount Given: $567,000
Purpose: To provide jobs and job training opportunities for disabled and other veterans through employer contacts, on-the-job training, and apprenticeships.
Who May Apply: State Employment Security Agencies and small businesses and individuals associated with these agencies.
Requirements: Variable by state.
Contact: James C. Gates.
Application Information: Application required.
Initial Approach: Letter or phone.

Disabled Veterans Outreach Program
for Alaska $139,700–$9,500,000

Department of Labor – VETS
1111 W. 8th St.
Juneau, AK 99802
(907) 465-2723

Field of Interest: Business Development – General
Average Amount Given: $293,500
Purpose: To provide jobs and job training opportunities for disabled and other veterans through employer contacts, on-the-job training, and apprenticeships.
Who May Apply: State Employment Security Agencies and small businesses and individuals associated with these agencies.
Requirements: Variable by state.
Contact: Daniel Travis.
Application Information: Application required.
Initial Approach: Letter or phone.

Disabled Veterans Outreach Program
for Arizona $139,700–$9,500,000

Department of Labor – VETS
1300 West Washington
Phoenix, AZ 85005
(602) 261-4961

Field of Interest: Business Development – General
Average Amount Given: $1,905,000
Purpose: To provide jobs and job training opportunities for disabled and other veterans through employer contacts, on-the-job training, and apprenticeships.
Who May Apply: State Employment Security Agencies and small businesses and individuals associated with these agencies.
Requirements: Variable by state.
Contact: Marco A. Valenzuela.
Application Information: Application required.
Initial Approach: Letter or phone.

Disabled Veterans Outreach Program
for Arkansas $139,700–$9,500,000

Department of Labor – VETS
PO Box 128
Little Rock, AK 72203
(501) 682-3786

Field of Interest: Business Development – General
Average Amount Given: $1,320,000
Purpose: To provide jobs and job training opportunities for disabled and other veterans through employer contacts, on-the-job training, and apprenticeships.
Who May Apply: State Employment Security Agencies and small businesses and individuals associated with these agencies.
Requirements: Variable by state.
Contact: Billy Threlkeld.
Application Information: Application required.
Initial Approach: Letter or phone.

Disabled Veterans Outreach Program for California $139,700–$9,500,000

Department of Labor – VETS
800 Capitol Mall, Room W-2052
Sacramento, CA 94280
(916) 551-1422

Field of Interest: Business Development – General
Average Amount Given: $9,450,000
Purpose: To provide jobs and job training opportunities for disabled and other veterans through employer contacts, on-the-job training, and apprenticeships.
Who May Apply: State Employment Security Agencies and small businesses and individuals associated with these agencies.
Requirements: Variable by state.
Contact: Charles Martinez.
Application Information: Application required.
Initial Approach: Letter or phone.

Disabled Veterans Outreach Program for Colorado $139,700–$9,500,000

Department of Labor – VETS
600 Grant St., Suite 800
Denver, CO 80203
(303) 866-1114

Field of Interest: Business Development – General
Average Amount Given: $3,650,000
Purpose: To provide jobs and job training opportunities for disabled and other veterans through employer contacts, on-the-job training, and apprenticeships.
Who May Apply: State Employment Security Agencies and small businesses and individuals associated with these agencies.
Requirements: Variable by state.
Contact: Mark McGinty.
Application Information: Application required.
Initial Approach: Letter or phone.

Disabled Veterans Outreach Program for Connecticut $139,700–$9,500,000

Department of Labor – VETS
200 Folly Brook Blvd.
Wethersfield, CT 06109
(203) 566-3326

Field of Interest: Business Development – General
Average Amount Given: $2,540,000
Purpose: To provide jobs and job training opportunities for disabled and other veterans through employer contacts, on-the-job training, and apprenticeships.
Who May Apply: State Employment Security Agencies and small businesses and individuals associated with these agencies.
Requirements: Variable by state.
Contact: Robert B. Inman.
Application Information: Application required.
Initial Approach: Letter or phone.

Disabled Veterans Outreach Program for Delaware $139,700–$9,500,000

Department of Labor – VETS
Stockton Bldg., Room 104
Newark, DE 19702
(302) 368-6898

Field of Interest: Business Development – General
Average Amount Given: $875,000
Purpose: To provide jobs and job training opportunities for disabled and other veterans through employer contacts, on-the-job training, and apprenticeships.
Who May Apply: State Employment Security Agencies and small businesses and individuals associated with these agencies.
Requirements: Variable by state.
Contact: Joseph Hortiz.
Application Information: Application required.
Initial Approach: Letter or phone.

Disabled Veterans Outreach Program
for Florida $139,700–$9,500,000

Department of Labor – VETS
Suite 102, Atkins Bldg.
1320 Executive Center Dr.
Tallahassee, FL 32399
(904) 877-4164

Field of Interest: Business Development – General
Average Amount Given: $7,195,700
Purpose: To provide jobs and job training opportunities for disabled and other veterans through employer contacts, on-the-job training, and apprenticeships.
Who May Apply: State Employment Security Agencies and small businesses and individuals associated with these agencies.
Requirements: Variable by state.
Contact: Lewis E. Waggoner.
Application Information: Application required.
Initial Approach: Letter or phone.

Disabled Veterans Outreach Program
for Georgia $139,700–$9,500,000

Department of Labor – VETS
Sussex Place, Suite 438
148 International Blvd. NE
Atlanta, GA 30303
(404) 656-3138

Field of Interest: Business Development – General
Average Amount Given: $1,600,500
Purpose: To provide jobs and job training opportunities for disabled and other veterans through employer contacts, on-the-job training, and apprenticeships.
Who May Apply: State Employment Security Agencies and small businesses and individuals associated with these agencies.
Requirements: Variable by state.
Contact: Eugene R. Wagner.
Application Information: Application required.
Initial Approach: Letter or phone.

Disabled Veterans Outreach Program
for Hawaii $139,700–$9,500,000

Department of Labor – VETS
830 Punchbowl St., Room 232A
Honolulu, HI 96811
(808) 541-1780

Field of Interest: Business Development – General
Average Amount Given: $2,400,000
Purpose: To provide jobs and job training opportunities for disabled and other veterans through employer contacts, on-the-job training, and apprenticeships.
Who May Apply: State Employment Security Agencies and small businesses and individuals associated with these agencies.
Requirements: Variable by state.
Contact: Raymond Sumikawa.
Application Information: Application required.
Initial Approach: Letter or phone.

Disabled Veterans Outreach Program
for Idaho $139,700–$9,500,000

Department of Labor – VETS
317 Main Street, Room 303
Boise, ID 83735
(208) 334-6164

Field of Interest: Business Development – General
Average Amount Given: $942,000
Purpose: To provide jobs and job training opportunities for disabled and other veterans through employer contacts, on-the-job training, and apprenticeships.
Who May Apply: State Employment Security Agencies and small businesses and individuals associated with these agencies.
Requirements: Variable by state.
Contact: Robert M. Wilson.
Application Information: Application required.
Initial Approach: Letter or phone.

Disabled Veterans Outreach Program for Illinois $139,700–$9,500,000

Department of Labor – VETS
401 S. Park St., 2 North
Chicago, IL 60605
(312) 793-3433

Field of Interest: Business Development – General
Average Amount Given: $7,600,000
Purpose: To provide jobs and job training opportunities for disabled and other veterans through employer contacts, on-the-job training, and apprenticeships.
Who May Apply: State Employment Security Agencies and small businesses and individuals associated with these agencies.
Requirements: Variable by state.
Contact: Samuel L. Parks.
Application Information: Application required.
Initial Approach: Letter or phone.

Disabled Veterans Outreach Program for Indiana $139,700–$9,500,000

Department of Labor – VETS
10 North Senate Ave., Room 203
Indianapolis, IN 46204
(317) 232-6804

Field of Interest: Business Development – General
Average Amount Given: $5,333,000
Purpose: To provide jobs and job training opportunities for disabled and other veterans through employer contacts, on-the-job training, and apprenticeships.
Who May Apply: State Employment Security Agencies and small businesses and individuals associated with these agencies.
Requirements: Variable by state.
Contact: Bruce Redman.
Application Information: Application required.
Initial Approach: Letter or phone.

Disabled Veterans Outreach Program for Iowa $139,700–$9,500,000

Department of Labor – VETS
1000 East Grand Ave.
Des Moines, IA 50319
(515) 281-5106

Field of Interest: Business Development – General
Average Amount Given: $3,500,900
Purpose: To provide jobs and job training opportunities for disabled and other veterans through employer contacts, on-the-job training, and apprenticeships.
Who May Apply: State Employment Security Agencies and small businesses and individuals associated with these agencies.
Requirements: Variable by state.
Contact: Leonard E. Shaw.
Application Information: Application required.
Initial Approach: Letter or phone.

Disabled Veterans Outreach Program for Kansas $139,700–$9,500,000

Department of Labor – VETS
1309 Topeka Blvd.
Topeka, KS 66612
(913) 296-5032

Field of Interest: Business Development – General
Average Amount Given: $4,311,000
Purpose: To provide jobs and job training opportunities for disabled and other veterans through employer contacts, on-the-job training, and apprenticeships.
Who May Apply: State Employment Security Agencies and small businesses and individuals associated with these agencies.
Requirements: Variable by state.
Contact: John A. Hill.
Application Information: Application required.
Initial Approach: Letter or phone.

Disabled Veterans Outreach Program
for Kentucky   **$139,700–$9,500,000**
Department of Labor – VETS
275 E. Main St.
Frankfort, KY 40621
(502) 564-7062

Field of Interest: Business Development – General
Average Amount Given: $2,379,000
Purpose: To provide jobs and job training opportunities for disabled and other veterans through employer contacts, on-the-job training, and apprenticeships.
Who May Apply: State Employment Security Agencies and small businesses and individuals associated with these agencies.
Requirements: Variable by state.
Contact: Charles Netherton.
Application Information: Application required.
Initial Approach: Letter or phone.

Disabled Veterans Outreach Program
for Louisiana   **$139,700–$9,500,000**
Department of Labor – VETS
1001 N. 23rd St., Room 174
Baton Rouge, LA 70804
(504) 342-5691

Field of Interest: Business Development – General
Average Amount Given: $1,250,000
Purpose: To provide jobs and job training opportunities for disabled and other veterans through employer contacts, on-the-job training, and apprenticeships.
Who May Apply: State Employment Security Agencies and small businesses and individuals associated with these agencies.
Requirements: Variable by state.
Contact: Leonard Walters.
Application Information: Application required.
Initial Approach: Letter or phone.

Disabled Veterans Outreach Program
for Maine   **$139,700–$9,500,000**
Department of Labor – VETS
PO Box 3106
Lewiston, ME 04243
(207) 783-5352

Field of Interest: Business Development – General
Average Amount Given: $660,000
Purpose: To provide jobs and job training opportunities for disabled and other veterans through employer contacts, on-the-job training, and apprenticeships.
Who May Apply: State Employment Security Agencies and small businesses and individuals associated with these agencies.
Requirements: Variable by state.
Contact: William J. Rogers.
Application Information: Application required.
Initial Approach: Letter or phone.

Disabled Veterans Outreach Program
for Maryland   **$139,700–$9,500,000**
Department of Labor – VETS
1100 North Utah Street, Room 205
Baltimore, MD 21201
(301) 333-5194

Field of Interest: Business Development – General
Average Amount Given: $7,100,000
Purpose: To provide jobs and job training opportunities for disabled and other veterans through employer contacts, on-the-job training, and apprenticeships.
Who May Apply: State Employment Security Agencies and small businesses and individuals associated with these agencies.
Requirements: Variable by state.
Contact: Gary D. Lobdell.
Application Information: Application required.
Initial Approach: Letter or phone.

**Disabled Veterans Outreach Program
for Massachusetts**   **$139,700–$9,500,000**

Department of Labor – VETS
JFK Federal Bldg., Room 506
Boston, MA 02203
(617) 565-2080

Field of Interest: Business Development – General
Average Amount Given: $6,600,000
Purpose: To provide jobs and job training opportunities for disabled and other veterans through employer contacts, on-the-job training, and apprenticeships.
Who May Apply: State Employment Security Agencies and small businesses and individuals associated with these agencies.
Requirements: Variable by state.
Contact: Richard Brenan.
Application Information: Application required.
Initial Approach: Letter or phone.

**Disabled Veterans Outreach Program
for Michigan**   **$139,700–$9,500,000**

Department of Labor – VETS
7310 Woodward Ave.
Detroit, MI 48202
(313) 876-5613

Field of Interest: Business Development – General
Average Amount Given: $8,900,000
Purpose: To provide jobs and job training opportunities for disabled and other veterans through employer contacts, on-the-job training, and apprenticeships.
Who May Apply: State Employment Security Agencies and small businesses and individuals associated with these agencies.
Requirements: Variable by state.
Contact: John Kaarsberg.
Application Information: Application required.
Initial Approach: Letter or phone.

**Disabled Veterans Outreach Program
for Minnesota**   **$139,700–$9,500,000**

Department of Labor – VETS
390 N. Robert St., First Floor
St. Paul, MN 55101
(612) 296-3665

Field of Interest: Business Development – General
Average Amount Given: $3,800,000
Purpose: To provide jobs and job training opportunities for disabled and other veterans through employer contacts, on-the-job training, and apprenticeships.
Who May Apply: State Employment Security Agencies and small businesses and individuals associated with these agencies.
Requirements: Variable by state.
Contact: Michael D. Graham.
Application Information: Application required.
Initial Approach: Letter or phone.

**Disabled Veterans Outreach Program
for Mississippi**   **$139,700–$9,500,000**

Department of Labor – VETS
1520 West Capitol St.
Jackson, MS 39215
(601) 961-7588

Field of Interest: Business Development – General
Average Amount Given: $1,500,000
Purpose: To provide jobs and job training opportunities for disabled and other veterans through employer contacts, on-the-job training, and apprenticeships.
Who May Apply: State Employment Security Agencies and small businesses and individuals associated with these agencies.
Requirements: Variable by state.
Contact: Bill Cooper.
Application Information: Application required.
Initial Approach: Letter or phone.

**Disabled Veterans Outreach Program
for Missouri** $139,700–$9,500,000

Department of Labor – VETS
421 E. Dunklin St.
Jefferson City, MO 65104
(314) 751-3921

Field of Interest: Business Development – General
Average Amount Given: $5,900,000
Purpose: To provide jobs and job training opportunities for disabled and other veterans through employer contacts, on-the-job training, and apprenticeships.
Who May Apply: State Employment Security Agencies and small businesses and individuals associated with these agencies.
Requirements: Variable by state.
Contact: Jonas N. Matthews.
Application Information: Application required.
Initial Approach: Letter or phone.

**Disabled Veterans Outreach Program
for Montana** $139,700–$9,500,000

Department of Labor – VETS
515 North Sanders
Helena, MT 59624
(406) 449-5431

Field of Interest: Business Development – General
Average Amount Given: $761,000
Purpose: To provide jobs and job training opportunities for disabled and other veterans through employer contacts, on-the-job training, and apprenticeships.
Who May Apply: State Employment Security Agencies and small businesses and individuals associated with these agencies.
Requirements: Variable by state.
Contact: Daniel P. Antonietti.
Application Information: Application required.
Initial Approach: Letter or phone.

**Disabled Veterans Outreach Program
for Nebraska** $139,700–$9,500,000

Department of Labor – VETS
550 S. 16th St.
Lincoln, NE 68509
(401) 437-5289

Field of Interest: Business Development – General
Average Amount Given: $3,682,000
Purpose: To provide jobs and job training opportunities for disabled and other veterans through employer contacts, on-the-job training, and apprenticeships.
Who May Apply: State Employment Security Agencies and small businesses and individuals associated with these agencies.
Requirements: Variable by state.
Contact: Robert Manifold.
Application Information: Application required.
Initial Approach: Letter or phone.

**Disabled Veterans Outreach Program
for Nevada** $139,700–$9,500,000

Department of Labor – VETS
500 East 3rd St.
Carson City, NV 89710
(702) 885-4632

Field of Interest: Business Development – General
Average Amount Given: $1,987,000
Purpose: To provide jobs and job training opportunities for disabled and other veterans through employer contacts, on-the-job training, and apprenticeships.
Who May Apply: State Employment Security Agencies and small businesses and individuals associated with these agencies.
Requirements: Variable by state.
Contact: Claude Shipley.
Application Information: Application required.
Initial Approach: Letter or phone.

**Disabled Veterans Outreach Program
for New Hampshire**   **$139,700–$9,500,000**

Department of Labor – VETS
55 Pleasant St.
Concord, NH 03301
(603) 225-1425

Field of Interest: Business Development – General
Average Amount Given: $1,400,000
Purpose: To provide jobs and job training opportunities for disabled and other veterans through employer contacts, on-the-job training, and apprenticeships.
Who May Apply: State Employment Security Agencies and small businesses and individuals associated with these agencies.
Requirements: Variable by state.
Contact: David Houle.
Application Information: Application required.
Initial Approach: Letter or phone.

**Disabled Veterans Outreach Program
for New Jersey**   **$139,700–$9,500,000**

Department of Labor – VETS
28 Yard Ave., Room 200
Trenton, NJ 08609
(609) 292-2930

Field of Interest: Business Development – General
Average Amount Given: $7,445,200
Purpose: To provide jobs and job training opportunities for disabled and other veterans through employer contacts, on-the-job training, and apprenticeships.
Who May Apply: State Employment Security Agencies and small businesses and individuals associated with these agencies.
Requirements: Variable by state.
Contact: Alan Grohs.
Application Information: Application required.
Initial Approach: Letter or phone.

**Disabled Veterans Outreach Program
for New Mexico**   **$139,700–$9,500,000**

Department of Labor – VETS
5301 Central, NE, Suite 1214
Albuquerque, NM 87108
(505) 841-4592

Field of Interest: Business Development – General
Average Amount Given: $1,500,000
Purpose: To provide jobs and job training opportunities for disabled and other veterans through employer contacts, on-the-job training, and apprenticeships.
Who May Apply: State Employment Security Agencies and small businesses and individuals associated with these agencies.
Requirements: Variable by state.
Contact: Jacob Castillo.
Application Information: Application required.
Initial Approach: Letter or phone.

**Disabled Veterans Outreach Program
for New York**   **$139,700–$9,500,000**

Department of Labor – VETS
201 Varick St., Room 766
New York, NY 10014
(212) 337-2211

Field of Interest: Business Development – General
Average Amount Given: $9,230,000
Purpose: To provide jobs and job training opportunities for disabled and other veterans through employer contacts, on-the-job training, and apprenticeships.
Who May Apply: State Employment Security Agencies and small businesses and individuals associated with these agencies.
Requirements: Variable by state.
Contact: Miles Sisson.
Application Information: Application required.
Initial Approach: Letter or phone.

**Disabled Veterans Outreach Program
for North Carolina**   **$139,700–$9,500,000**

Department of Labor – VETS
700 Wade Ave.
Raleigh, NC 27611
(919) 733-7402

Field of Interest: Business Development – General
Average Amount Given: $2,250,000
Purpose: To provide jobs and job training opportunities for disabled
and other veterans through employer contacts, on-the-job training,
and apprenticeships.
Who May Apply: State Employment Security Agencies and small
businesses and individuals associated with these agencies.
Requirements: Variable by state.
Contact: S. Marvin Burton.
Application Information: Application required.
Initial Approach: Letter or phone.

**Disabled Veterans Outreach Program
for North Dakota**   **$139,700–$9,500,000**

Department of Labor – VETS
1000 Divide Ave.
Bismarck, ND 58501
(701) 224-2865

Field of Interest: Business Development – General
Average Amount Given: $320,000
Purpose: To provide jobs and job training opportunities for disabled
and other veterans through employer contacts, on-the-job training,
and apprenticeships.
Who May Apply: State Employment Security Agencies and small
businesses and individuals associated with these agencies.
Requirements: Variable by state.
Contact: Leo A. Swenson.
Application Information: Application required.
Initial Approach: Letter or phone.

**Disabled Veterans Outreach Program
for Ohio**   **$139,700–$9,500,000**

Department of Labor – VETS
145 Front Street
Columbus, OH 43216
(614) 466-2768

Field of Interest: Business Development – General
Average Amount Given: $7,600,000
Purpose: To provide jobs and job training opportunities for disabled
and other veterans through employer contacts, on-the-job training,
and apprenticeships.
Who May Apply: State Employment Security Agencies and small
businesses and individuals associated with these agencies.
Requirements: Variable by state.
Contact: William Bolls.
Application Information: Application required.
Initial Approach: Letter or phone.

**Disabled Veterans Outreach Program
for Oklahoma**   **$139,700–$9,500,000**

Department of Labor – VETS
Will Rogers Memorial Bldg.
Oklahoma City, OK 73105

Field of Interest: Business Development – General
Average Amount Given: $4,100,000
Purpose: To provide jobs and job training opportunities for disabled
and other veterans through employer contacts, on-the-job training,
and apprenticeships.
Who May Apply: State Employment Security Agencies and small
businesses and individuals associated with these agencies.
Requirements: Variable by state.
Contact: James D. Howard.
Application Information: Application required.
Initial Approach: Letter or phone.

**Disabled Veterans Outreach Program
for Oregon** $139,700–$9,500,000

Department of Labor – VETS
875 Union St., NE
Salem, OR 97311
(503) 378-3338

Field of Interest: Business Development – General
Average Amount Given: $5,500,000
Purpose: To provide jobs and job training opportunities for disabled
and other veterans through employer contacts, on-the-job training,
and apprenticeships.
Who May Apply: State Employment Security Agencies and small
businesses and individuals associated with these agencies.
Requirements: Variable by state.
Contact: Rex Newell.
Application Information: Application required.
Initial Approach: Letter or phone.

**Disabled Veterans Outreach Program
for Pennsylvania** $139,700–$9,500,000

Department of Labor – VETS
Seventh and Forster Streets, Room 625
Harrisburg, PA 17121
(717) 787-5834

Field of Interest: Business Development – General
Average Amount Given: $8,600,900
Purpose: To provide jobs and job training opportunities for disabled
and other veterans through employer contacts, on-the-job training,
and apprenticeships.
Who May Apply: State Employment Security Agencies and small
businesses and individuals associated with these agencies.
Requirements: Variable by state.
Contact: Carl G. Fisher.
Application Information: Application required.
Initial Approach: Letter or phone.

**Disabled Veterans Outreach Program
for Rhode Island** $139,700–$9,500,000

Department of Labor – VETS
507 Federal Bldg. and Courthouse
Providence, RI 02903
(401) 528-5134

Field of Interest: Business Development – General
Average Amount Given: $2,900,000
Purpose: To provide jobs and job training opportunities for disabled
and other veterans through employer contacts, on-the-job training,
and apprenticeships.
Who May Apply: State Employment Security Agencies and small
businesses and individuals associated with these agencies.
Requirements: Variable by state.
Contact: Arthur Dawson.
Application Information: Application required.
Initial Approach: Letter or phone.

**Disabled Veterans Outreach Program
for South Carolina** $139,700–$9,500,000

Department of Labor – VETS
914 Richland Street, Suite 101A
Columbia, SC 29201
(803) 737-1717

Field of Interest: Business Development – General
Average Amount Given: $2,330,300
Purpose: To provide jobs and job training opportunities for disabled
and other veterans through employer contacts, on-the-job training,
and apprenticeships.
Who May Apply: State Employment Security Agencies and small
businesses and individuals associated with these agencies.
Requirements: Variable by state.
Contact: William C. Plowden, Jr.
Application Information: Application required.
Initial Approach: Letter or phone.

**Disabled Veterans Outreach Program
for South Dakota**   **$139,700–$9,500,000**
Department of Labor – VETS
420 South Roosevelt St.
Aberdeen, SD 57402
(605) 226-7289

Field of Interest: Business Development – General
Average Amount Given: $476,000
Purpose: To provide jobs and job training opportunities for disabled
and other veterans through employer contacts, on-the-job training,
and apprenticeships.
Who May Apply: State Employment Security Agencies and small
businesses and individuals associated with these agencies.
Requirements: Variable by state.
Contact: Earl Schultz.
Application Information: Application required.
Initial Approach: Letter or phone.

**Disabled Veterans Outreach Program
for Tennessee**   **$139,700–$9,500,000**
Department of Labor – VETS
301 James Robertson Parkway, Room 317
Nashville, TN 37201
(615) 741-2135

Field of Interest: Business Development – General
Average Amount Given: $4,400,000
Purpose: To provide jobs and job training opportunities for disabled
and other veterans through employer contacts, on-the-job training,
and apprenticeships.
Who May Apply: State Employment Security Agencies and small
businesses and individuals associated with these agencies.
Requirements: Variable by state.
Contact: Clayton Lamberth.
Application Information: Application required.
Initial Approach: Letter or phone.

**Disabled Veterans Outreach Program
for Texas**   **$139,700–$9,500,000**
Department of Labor – VETS
525 Griffin St., Federal Bldg., Room 204
Dallas, TX 75202
(214) 767-4987

Field of Interest: Business Development – General
Average Amount Given: $7,430,700
Purpose: To provide jobs and job training opportunities for disabled
and other veterans through employer contacts, on-the-job training,
and apprenticeships.
Who May Apply: State Employment Security Agencies and small
businesses and individuals associated with these agencies.
Requirements: Variable by state.
Contact: Lester L. Williams.
Application Information: Application required.
Initial Approach: Letter or phone.

**Disabled Veterans Outreach Program
for Utah**   **$139,700–$9,500,000**
Department of Labor – VETS
178 Social Hall Ave.
Salt Lake City, UT 84111
(801) 524-5703

Field of Interest: Business Development – General
Average Amount Given: $3,250,000
Purpose: To provide jobs and job training opportunities for disabled
and other veterans through employer contacts, on-the-job training,
and apprenticeships.
Who May Apply: State Employment Security Agencies and small
businesses and individuals associated with these agencies.
Requirements: Variable by state.
Contact: J. Dale Madsen.
Application Information: Application required.
Initial Approach: Letter or phone.

Disabled Veterans Outreach Program
for Vermont $139,700–$9,500,000

Department of Labor – VETS
PO Box 603
Montpelier, VT 05602
(802) 828-4441

Field of Interest: Business Development – General
Average Amount Given: $1,200,000
Purpose: To provide jobs and job training opportunities for disabled and other veterans through employer contacts, on-the-job training, and apprenticeships.
Who May Apply: State Employment Security Agencies and small businesses and individuals associated with these agencies.
Requirements: Variable by state.
Contact: Ronald Benoit.
Application Information: Application required.
Initial Approach: Letter or phone.

Disabled Veterans Outreach Program
for Virginia $139,700–$9,500,000

Department of Labor – VETS
701 E. Franklin St., Suite 1409
Richmond, VA 23219
(804) 786-7269

Field of Interest: Business Development – General
Average Amount Given: $7,600,550
Purpose: To provide jobs and job training opportunities for disabled and other veterans through employer contacts, on-the-job training, and apprenticeships.
Who May Apply: State Employment Security Agencies and small businesses and individuals associated with these agencies.
Requirements: Variable by state.
Contact: Benjamin I. Trotter, Jr.
Application Information: Application required.
Initial Approach: Letter or phone.

Disabled Veterans Outreach Program
for Washington $139,700–$9,500,000

Department of Labor – VETS
1111 Third Ave., Suite 800
Seattle, WA 98101
(206) 442-4831

Field of Interest: Business Development – General
Average Amount Given: $5,888,600
Purpose: To provide jobs and job training opportunities for disabled and other veterans through employer contacts, on-the-job training, and apprenticeships.
Who May Apply: State Employment Security Agencies and small businesses and individuals associated with these agencies.
Requirements: Variable by state.
Contact: Joseph Molinari.
Application Information: Application required.
Initial Approach: Letter or phone.

Disabled Veterans Outreach Program
for West Virginia $139,700–$9,500,000

Department of Labor – VETS
112 California Ave., Room 212
Charleston, WV 25305
(304) 348-4001

Field of Interest: Business Development – General
Average Amount Given: $1,750,000
Purpose: To provide jobs and job training opportunities for disabled and other veterans through employer contacts, on-the-job training, and apprenticeships.
Who May Apply: State Employment Security Agencies and small businesses and individuals associated with these agencies.
Requirements: Variable by state.
Contact: David L. Bush.
Application Information: Application required.
Initial Approach: Letter or phone.

Disabled Veterans Outreach Program for Wisconsin $139,700–$9,500,000

Department of Labor – VETS
201 E. Washington Ave., Room 250
Madison, WI 53701
(608) 266-3110

Field of Interest: Business Development – General
Average Amount Given: $2,600,000
Purpose: To provide jobs and job training opportunities for disabled and other veterans through employer contacts, on-the-job training, and apprenticeships.
Who May Apply: State Employment Security Agencies and small businesses and individuals associated with these agencies.
Requirements: Variable by state.
Contact: James Gutowski.
Application Information: Application required.
Initial Approach: Letter or phone.

Disabled Veterans Outreach Program for Wyoming $139,700–$9,500,000

Department of Labor – VETS
100 West Midwest Ave.
Casper, WY 82602
(307) 235-3281

Field of Interest: Business Development – General
Average Amount Given: $700,500
Purpose: To provide jobs and job training opportunities for disabled and other veterans through employer contacts, on-the-job training, and apprenticeships.
Who May Apply: State Employment Security Agencies and small businesses and individuals associated with these agencies.
Requirements: Variable by state.
Contact: Ernest Fender.
Application Information: Application required.
Initial Approach: Letter or phone.

REGIONAL – EDUCATION

*Mathematics and Science Education in California $63,000–$1,340,000

Department of Education, Region IX
50 United Nations Plaza, Room 205
San Francisco, CA 94102
(415) 556-4920

Field of Interest: Education – Science and Math
Average Amount Given: $83,000
Purpose: To improve the skills of teachers and the quality of instruction in mathematics and science and to increase the accessibility of such instruction to all students.
Who May Apply: Entities associated with the state education agency, including those in Arizona, Nevada, Hawaii, and Guam.
Requirements: Variable by state.
Contact: Dr. John B. Tsu.
Application Information: Application required.
Initial Approach: Letter or phone.

*Mathematics and Science Education In Colorado $63,500–$1,340,000

Department of Education, Region VIII
1961 Stout Street, Room 380
Denver, CO 80294
(303) 837-3544

Field of Interest: Education – Science and Math
Average Amount Given: $65,000
Purpose: To improve the skills of teachers and the quality of instruction in mathematics and science and to increase the accessibility of such instruction to all students.
Who May Apply: Entities associated with the state education agency, including those in Montana, Wyoming, Utah, North Dakota, and South Dakota.
Requirements: Variable by state.
Contact: Tom Tancredo.
Application Information: Application required.
Initial Approach: Letter or phone.

*Mathematics and Science Education in Georgia $63,500–$1,340,000

Department of Education, Region IV
101 Marietta Tower, Room 2221
Atlanta, GA 30323
(404) 242-2502

Field of Interest: Education – Science and Math
Average Amount Given: $52,200
Purpose: To improve the skills of teachers and the quality of instruction in mathematics and science and to increase the accessibility of such instruction to all students.
Who May Apply: Entities associated with the state education agency, including those in Alabama, Florida, Mississippi, North Carolina, and South Carolina.
Requirements: Variable by state.
Contact: Dr. John F. Will.
Application Information: Application required.
Initial Approach: Letter or phone.

*Mathematics and Science Education in Illinois $63,500–$1,340,000

Department of Education, Region V
300 South Wacker Drive, 16th Floor
Chicago, IL 60606
(312) 353-5215

Field of Interest: Education – Science and Math
Average Amount Given: $111,000
Purpose: To improve the skills of teachers and the quality of instruction in mathematics and science and to increase the accessibility of such instruction to all students.
Who May Apply: Entities associated with the state education agency, including those in Indiana, Michigan, Ohio, and Wisconsin.
Requirements: Variable by state.
Contact: Brian E. Carey, Acting Secretary.
Application Information: Application required.
Initial Approach: Letter or phone.

*Mathematics and Science Education
in Massachusetts $63,500–$1,340,000

Department of Education, Region I
McCormack Post Office and Courthouse, Room 526
Boston, MA 02109
(617) 223-7500

Field of Interest: Education – Science and Math
Average Amount Given: $63,211
Purpose: To improve the skills of teachers and the quality of instruction in mathematics and science and to increase the accessibility of such instruction to all students.
Who May Apply: Entities associated with the state education agency, including those in Connecticut, Maine, New Hampshire, Vermont, and Rhode Island.
Requirements: Variable by state.
Contact: Dennis R. Smith.
Application Information: Application required.
Initial Approach: Letter or phone.

*Mathematics and Science Education
in Missouri $63,500–$1,340,000

Department of Education, Region VII
324 East 11th Street
Kansas City, MO 64106
(816) 374-2276

Field of Interest: Education – Science and Math
Average Amount Given: $29,770
Purpose: To improve the skills of teachers and the quality of instruction in mathematics and science and to increase the accessibility of such instruction to all students.
Who May Apply: Entities associated with the state education agency, including those in Kansas, Iowa, and Nebraska.
Requirements: Variable by state.
Contact: Cynthia A. Harris.
Application Information: Application required.
Initial Approach: Letter or phone.

*Mathematics and Science Education
in New York $63,500–$1,340,000

Department of Education, Region II
26 Federal Plaza, Room 3954
New York, NY 10278
(212) 264-7005

Field of Interest: Education – Science and Math
Average Amount Given: $121,100
Purpose: To improve the skills of teachers and the quality of instruction in mathematics and science and to increase the accessibility of such instruction to all students.
Who May Apply: Entities associated with the state education agency, including those in New Jersey and Delaware.
Requirements: Variable by state.
Contact: Dr. Roland Alum.
Application Information: Application required.
Initial Approach: Letter or phone.

*Mathematics and Science Education
in Pennsylvania $63,500–$1,340,000

Department of Education, Region III
3535 Market Street, Room 16350
Philadelphia, PA 19104
(215) 596-1001

Field of Interest: Education – Science and Math
Average Amount Given: $78,600
Purpose: To improve the skills of teachers and the quality of instruction in mathematics and science and to increase the accessibility of such instruction to all students.
Who May Apply: Entities associated with the state education agency, including those in Maryland, Virginia, and West Virginia.
Requirements: Variable by state.
Contact: Dr. D. Kay Wright.
Application Information: Application required.
Initial Approach: Letter or phone.

***Mathematics and Science Education
in Texas** $63,500–$1,340,000

Department of Education, Region VI
1200 Main Tower Building, Room 1460
Dallas, TX 75202
(214) 729-3626

Field of Interest: Education – Science and Math
Average Amount Given: $76,000
Purpose: To improve the skills of teachers and the quality of instruc-
tion in mathematics and science and to increase the accessibility of
such instruction to all students.
Who May Apply: Entities associated with the state education agency,
including those in Oklahoma, New Mexico, Arkansas, and Louisiana.
Requirements: Variable by state.
Contact: Dr. Sam P. Wilson.
Application Information: Application required.
Initial Approach: Letter or phone.

***Mathematics and Science Education
in Washington** $63,500–$1,340,000

Department of Education, Region X
3rd and Broad Building, 2901 3rd Ave., MS 108
Seattle, WA 98121
(206) 399-0460

Field of Interest: Education – Science and Math
Average Amount Given: $63,500
Purpose: To improve the skills of teachers and the quality of instruc-
tion in mathematics and science and to increase the accessibility of
such instruction to all students.
Who May Apply: Entities associated with the state education agency
including those in Alaska, Idaho, and Oregon.
Requirements: Variable by state.
Contact: Roberta May.
Application Information: Application required.
Initial Approach: Letter or phone.

REGIONAL – ENVIRONMENT

*Alaska Sport Fish and Wildlife Restoration
Formula Grant   **$2,700,000**

Fish and Wildlife Service
1101 E. Tudor Road
Anchorage, AK 99503
(907) 786-3542

Field of Interest: Environment – General
Average Amount Given: $499,300
Purpose: To support projects designed to restore and manage indigenous sport fish and wildlife populations.
Who May Apply: Public and nonprofit entities.
Requirements: Variable by state.
Contact: Walter Steiglitz.
Application Information: Application required.
Initial Approach: Letter.

*Colorado Sport Fish and Wildlife Restoration
Formula Grant   **$4,525,000**

Fish and Wildlife Service
PO Box 25486
Denver Federal Center
Denver, CO 80225
(303) 236-7920

Field of Interest: Environment – General
Average Amount Given: $511,000
Purpose: To support projects designed to restore and manage indigenous sport fish and wildlife populations.
Who May Apply: Public and nonprofit entities, including those in Kansas, Montana, Nebraska, North Dakota, South Dakota, Utah, and Wyoming.
Requirements: Variable by state.
Contact: Galen Buterbaugh.
Application Information: Application required.
Initial Approach: Letter.

*Georgia Sport Fish and Wildlife Restoration
Formula Grant   **$5,445,000**

Fish and Wildlife Service
75 Spring Street, SW
Atlanta, GA 30303
(404) 331-3588

Field of Interest: Environment – General
Average Amount Given: $640,700
Purpose: To support projects designed to restore and manage indigenous sport fish and wildlife populations.
Who May Apply: Public and nonprofit entities, including those in Alabama, Arkansas, Florida, Kentucky, Louisiana, Mississippi, North Carolina, South Carolina, and Tennessee.
Requirements: Variable by state.
Contact: James W. Pulliam, Jr.
Application Information: Application required.
Initial Approach: Letter.

*Massachusetts Sport Fish and Wildlife Restoration
Formula Grant   **$5,602,000**

Fish and Wildlife Service
One Gateway Center, Suite 700
Newton Corner, MA 02158
(617) 965-5100

Field of Interest: Environment – General
Average Amount Given: $478,000
Purpose: To support projects designed to restore and manage indigenous sport fish and wildlife populations.
Who May Apply: Public and nonprofit entities, including those in Connecticut, Delaware, Maine, Maryland, New Hampshire, New Jersey, New York, Pennsylvania, Rhode Island, Vermont, Virginia, and West Virginia.
Requirements: Variable by state.
Contact: Ronald E. Lambertson.
Application Information: Application required.
Initial Approach: Letter.

*Minnesota Sport Fish and Wildlife Restoration Formula Grant   **$7,650,000**

Fish and Wildlife Service
Federal Building, Fort Snelling
Twin Cities, MN 55111
(612) 725-3563

Field of Interest: Environment – General
Average Amount Given: $620,000
Purpose: To support projects designed to restore and manage indigenous sport fish and wildlife populations.
Who May Apply: Public and nonprofit entities, including those in Illinois, Indiana, Iowa, Michigan, Missouri, Ohio, and Wisconsin.
Requirements: Variable by state.
Contact: James C. Gritman.
Application Information: Application required.
Initial Approach: Letter.

---

*New Mexico Sport Fish and Wildlife Restoration Formula Grant   **$4,457,000**

Fish and Wildlife Service
PO Box 1306
500 Gold Ave., SW, Room 1306
Albuquerque, NM 87103
(505) 766-2321

Field of Interest: Environment – General
Average Amount Given: $540,000
Purpose: To support projects designed to restore and manage indigenous sport fish and wildlife populations.
Who May Apply: Public and nonprofit entities, including those in Arizona, Oklahoma, and Texas.
Requirements: Variable by state.
Contact: Michael J. Spear.
Application Information: Application required.
Initial Approach: Letter.

---

*Oregon Sport Fish and Wildlife Restoration Formula Grant   **$3,200,000**

Fish and Wildlife Service
500 NE Multnomah Street, Suite 1692
Portland, OR 97232
(503) 231-6118

Field of Interest: Environment – General
Average Amount Given: $750,000
Purpose: To support projects designed to restore and manage indigenous sport fish and wildlife populations.
Who May Apply: Public and nonprofit entities, including those in California, Hawaii, Idaho, Nevada, and Washington.
Requirements: Variable by state.
Contact: Marvin L. Plenert.
Application Information: Application required.
Initial Approach: Letter to local State Fish and Wildlife Agency.

REGIONAL – HEALTH CARE

Protection and Advocacy for the Mentally Ill in California $750,000

Department of Health and Human Services, Region IX
50 United Nations Plaza, Room 431
San Francisco, CA 94102
(415) 556-1961

Field of Interest: Health Care – Mental Health
Average Amount Given: $47,000
Purpose: To establish and administer a new state system to protect and advocate the rights of the mentally ill and to investigate incidents of their abuse and neglect.
Who May Apply: Qualified individuals and qualified public and private agencies in these additional states: Arizona, Hawaii, and Nevada.
Requirements: Variable by state.
Contact: Emery Lee.
Application Information: Application required.
Initial Approach: Letter or phone.

Protection and Advocacy for the Mentally Ill in Colorado $175,000

Department of Health and Human Services, Region VIII
Room 1185, Federal Bldg.
1961 Stout Street
Denver, CO 80294-3538
(303) 844-3372

Field of Interest: Health Care – Mental Health
Average Amount Given: $43,000
Purpose: To establish and administer a new state system to protect and advocate the rights of the mentally ill and to investigate incidents of their abuse and neglect.
Who May Apply: Qualified individuals and qualified public and private agencies in these additional states: Montana, North Dakota, South Dakota, Utah, and Wyoming.
Requirements: Variable by state.
Contact: Paul Denham.
Application Information: Application required.
Initial Approach: Letter or phone.

Protection and Advocacy for the Mentally Ill in Georgia $133,550

Department of Health and Human Services, Region IV
101 Marietta Tower, Suite 1515
Atlanta, GA 30323
(404) 331-2442

Field of Interest: Health Care – Mental Health
Average Amount Given: $37,000
Purpose: To establish and administer a new state system to protect and advocate the rights of the mentally ill and to investigate incidents of their abuse and neglect.
Who May Apply: Qualified individuals and qualified public and private agencies in these additional states: Alabama, Florida, Kentucky, Mississippi, North Carolina, South Carolina, and Tennessee.
Requirements: Variable by state.
Contact: Earl Forsythe.
Application Information: Application required.
Initial Approach: Letter or phone.

Protection and Advocacy for the Mentally Ill in Illinois $580,000

Department of Health and Human Services, Region V
105 West Adams, 23rd Floor
Chicago, IL 60603
(312) 353-5132

Field of Interest: Health Care – Mental Health
Average Amount Given: $52,000
Purpose: To establish and administer a new state system to protect and advocate the rights of the mentally ill and to investigate incidents of their abuse and neglect.
Who May Apply: Qualified individuals and qualified public and private agencies in these additional states: Indiana, Michigan, Minnesota, Ohio, and Wisconsin.
Requirements: Variable by state.
Contact: Hiroshi Kanno.
Application Information: Application required.
Initial Approach: Letter or phone.

**Protection and Advocacy for the Mentally Ill
in Massachusetts**   **$463,000**

Department of Health and Human Services, Region I
JFK Federal Bldg., Room 2411
Boston, MA 12203
(617) 565-1500

Field of Interest: Health Care – Mental Health
Average Amount Given: $42,000
Purpose: To establish and administer a new state system to protect
and advocate the rights of the mentally ill and to investigate incidents
of their abuse and neglect.
Who May Apply: Qualified individuals and qualified public and pri-
vate agencies in these additional states: Connecticut, Maine, New
Hampshire, Rhode Island, and Vermont.
Requirements: Variable by state.
Contact: Maureen Osolnik.
Application Information: Application required.
Initial Approach: Letter or phone.

**Protection and Advocacy for the Mentally Ill
in Missouri**   **$420,660**

Department of Health and Human Services, Region VI
601 East 12th Street, Room 210
Kansas City, MO 64106
(816) 426-2304

Field of Interest: Health Care – Mental Health
Average Amount Given: $29,000
Purpose: To establish and administer a new state system to protect
and advocate the rights of the mentally ill and to investigate incidents
of their abuse and neglect.
Who May Apply: Qualified individuals and qualified public and pri-
vate agencies in these additional states: Iowa, Kansas, and Nebraska.
Requirements: Variable by state.
Contact: Merle M. Schmidt.
Application Information: Application required.
Initial Approach: Letter or phone.

**Protection and Advocacy for the Mentally Ill
in New York**   **$201,700**

Department of Health and Human Services, Region II
26 Federal Plaza, Room 3835
New York, NY 10278
(212) 264-4600

Field of Interest: Health Care – Mental Health
Average Amount Given: $50,300
Purpose: To establish and administer a new state system to protect
and advocate the rights of the mentally ill and to investigate incidents
of their abuse and neglect.
Who May Apply: Qualified individuals and qualified public and pri-
vate agencies in New York and New Jersey.
Requirements: Variable by state.
Contact: Kathleen Harten.
Application Information: Application required.
Initial Approach: Letter or phone.

**Protection and Advocacy for the Mentally Ill
in Pennsylvania**   **$184,000**

Department of Health and Human Services, Region III
3535 Market Street, Room 11480
Philadelphia, PA 19104
(215) 596-6492

Field of Interest: Health Care – Mental Health
Average Amount Given: $20,500
Purpose: To establish and administer a new state system to protect
and advocate the rights of the mentally ill and to investigate incidents
of their abuse and neglect.
Who May Apply: Qualified individuals and qualified public and pri-
vate agencies in these additional states: Delaware, Maryland, Virginia,
and West Virginia.
Requirements: Variable by state.
Contact: James Mengel.
Application Information: Application required.
Initial Approach: Letter or phone.

**Protection and Advocacy for the Mentally Ill
in Texas**   **$300,300**
Department of Health and Human Services, Region VII
1200 Main Tower, Room 1100
Dallas, TX 75202
(214) 767-3301
Field of Interest: Health Care – Mental Health
Average Amount Given: $45,700
Purpose: To establish and administer a new state system to protect
and advocate the rights of the mentally ill and to investigate incidents
of their abuse and neglect.
Who May Apply: Qualified individuals and qualified public and pri-
vate agencies in these additional states: Arkansas, Louisiana, New
Mexico, and Oklahoma.
Requirements: Variable by state.
Contact: J.B. Keith.
Application Information: Application required.
Initial Approach: Letter or phone.

**Protection and Advocacy for the Mentally Ill
in Washington**   **$621,000**
Department of Health and Human Services, Region X
2901 Sixth Ave., RX–01
Seattle, WA 98121
(206) 442-0420
Field of Interest: Health Care – Mental Health
Average Amount Given: $36,850
Purpose: To establish and administer a new state system to protect
and advocate the rights of the mentally ill and to investigate incidents
of their abuse and neglect.
Who May Apply: Qualified individuals and qualified public and pri-
vate agencies in these additional states: Alaska, Idaho, and Oregon.
Requirements: Variable by state.
Contact: Elizabeth G. Healy.
Application Information: Application required.
Initial Approach: Letter or phone.

REGIONAL – MEDICAL RESEARCH

**Alcohol and Drug Abuse Research and Services
Block Grant to California** $25,099,500

Department of Health and Human Services, Region IX
50 United Nations Plaza, Room 431
San Francisco, CA 94102
(415) 556-1961

Field of Interest: Medical Research – Substance Abuse
Average Amount Given: $298,000
Purpose: To develop more effective treatments for drug and alcohol abuse.
Who May Apply: Qualified individuals in these additional states: Arizona, Hawaii, and Nevada.
Requirements: Variable by state.
Contact: Emory Lee.
Application Information: Application required.
Initial Approach: Letter or phone.

**Alcohol and Drug Abuse Research and Services
Block Grant to Colorado** $9,080,000

Department of Health and Human Services, Region VIII
1961 Stout Street, Room 1185
Denver, CO 80294-3538
(303) 844-3372

Field of Interest: Medical Research – Substance Abuse
Average Amount Given: $176,500
Purpose: To develop more effective treatments for drug and alcohol abuse.
Who May Apply: Qualified individuals in these additional states: Montana, North Dakota, South Dakota, Utah, and Wyoming.
Requirements: Variable by state.
Contact: Paul Denham.
Application Information: Application required.
Initial Approach: Letter or phone.

**Alcohol and Drug Abuse Research and Services
Block Grant to Georgia** $14,000,000

Department of Health and Human Services, Region IV
101 Marietta Tower, Suite 1515
Atlanta, GA 30323
(404) 331-2442

Field of Interest: Medical Research – Substance Abuse
Average Amount Given: $210,000
Purpose: To develop more effective treatments for drug and alcohol abuse.
Who May Apply: Qualified individuals in these additional states: Alabama, Florida, Kentucky, Mississippi, North Carolina, South Carolina, and Tennessee.
Requirements: Variable by state.
Contact: Earl Forsythe.
Application Information: Application required.

**Alcohol and Drug Abuse Research and Services
Block Grant to Illinois** $18,900,000

Department of Health and Human Services, Region V
105 West Adams, 23rd Floor
Chicago, IL 60603
(312) 353-5132

Field of Interest: Medical Research – Substance Abuse
Average Amount Given: $230,000
Purpose: To develop more effective treatments for drug and alcohol abuse.
Who May Apply: Qualified individuals in these additional states: Indiana, Michigan, Minnesota, Ohio, and Wisconsin.
Requirements: Variable by state.
Contact: Hiroshi Kanno.
Application Information: Application required.
Initial Approach: Letter or phone.

Alcohol and Drug Abuse Research and Services
Block Grant to Massachusetts   **$17,300,000**

Department of Health and Human Services, Region I
JFK Bldg., Room 2411
Boston, MA 02203
(617) 565-1500

Field of Interest: Medical Research – Substance Abuse
Average Amount Given: $175,320
Purpose: To develop more effective treatments for drug and alcohol abuse.
Who May Apply: Qualified individuals in these additional states: Connecticut, Maine, New Hampshire, Rhode Island, and Vermont.
Requirements: Variable by state.
Contact: Maureen Osolnik.
Application Information: Application required.
Initial Approach: Letter or phone.

Alcohol and Drug Abuse Research and Services
Block Grant to Missouri   **$14,077,000**

Department of Health and Human Services, Region VI
601 East 12th Street, Room 210
Kansas City, MO 64106
(816) 462-2304

Field of Interest: Medical Research – Substance Abuse
Average Amount Given: $127,773
Purpose: To develop more effective treatments for drug and alcohol abuse.
Who May Apply: Qualified individuals in these additional states: Iowa, Kansas, and Nebraska.
Requirements: Variable by state.
Contact: Merle M. Schmidt.
Application Information: Application required.
Initial Approach: Letter or phone.

Alcohol and Drug Abuse Research and Services
Block Grant to New York   **$22,000,000**

Department of Health and Human Services, Region II
26 Federal Plaza, Room 3835
New York, NY 10278
(212) 264-4600

Field of Interest: Medical Research – Substance Abuse
Average Amount Given: $239,000
Purpose: To develop more effective treatments for drug and alcohol abuse.
Who May Apply: Qualified individuals in New York and New Jersey.
Requirements: Variable by state.
Contact: Kathleen Harten.
Application Information: Application required.
Initial Approach: Letter or phone.

Alcohol and Drug Abuse Research and Services
Block Grant to Pennsylvania   **$17,500,000**

Department of Health and Human Services, Region III
3535 Market St., Room 11480
Philadelphia, PA 19104
(215) 596-6492

Field of Interest: Medical Research – Substance Abuse
Average Amount Given: $230,500
Purpose: To develop more effective treatments for drug and alcohol abuse.
Who May Apply: Qualified individuals in these additional states: Maryland, Virginia, and West Virginia.
Requirements: Variable by state.
Contact: James Mengel.
Application Information: Application required.
Initial Approach: Letter or phone.

Alcohol and Drug Abuse Research and Services Block Grant to Texas   **$19,459,000**

Department of Health and Human Services, Region VII
1200 Main Tower, Room 1100
Dallas, TX 75202

Field of Interest: Medical Research – Substance Abuse
Average Amount Given: $243,960
Purpose: To develop more effective treatments for drug and alcohol abuse.
Who May Apply: Qualified individuals in these additional states: Arkansas, Louisiana, New Mexico, and Oklahoma.
Requirements: Variable by state.
Contact: J.B. Keith.
Application Information: Application required.
Initial Approach: Letter or phone.

Alcohol and Drug Abuse Research and Services Block Grant to Washington   **$20,000,000**

Department of Health and Human Services, Region X
2901 Sixth Ave., RX–01
Seattle, WA 98121
(206) 442-0420

Field of Interest: Medical Research – Substance Abuse
Average Amount Given: $160,780
Purpose: To develop more effective treatments for drug and alcohol abuse.
Who May Apply: Qualified individuals in these additional states: Alaska, Idaho, and Oregon.
Requirements: Variable by state.
Contact: Elizabeth G. Healy.
Application Information: Application required.
Initial Approach: Letter or phone.

REGIONAL – SCIENCE RESEARCH

Clean Coal Scientific Research Technology Program for Alabama $6,000,000

Alabama Science and Technology Division
3465 Norman Bridge Road
Montgomery, AL 36105
(205) 284-8952

Field of Interest: Science Research – Energy
Average Amount Given: $240,000
Purpose: To create innovative, cost-effective, clean coal technologies capable of commercialization.
Who May Apply: States, small businesses, individuals, partnerships, and joint ventures.
Requirements: 50% matching funding required.
Contact: Dr. Munsell-McPhillips.
Application Information: Application required.
Initial Approach: Letter or phone.

Clean Coal Scientific Research Technology Program for Alaska $3,500,000

Department of Community and Regional Affairs
949 E. 36th Ave., Suite 400
Anchorage, AK 99508
(907) 563-1955

Field of Interest: Science Research – Energy
Average Amount Given: $120,000
Purpose: To create innovative, cost-effective, clean coal technologies capable of commercialization.
Who May Apply: States, small businesses, individuals, partnerships, and joint ventures.
Requirements: 50% matching funding required.
Contact: Michael C. Harper.
Application Information: Application required.
Initial Approach: Letter or phone.

Clean Coal Scientific Research Technology Program for Arizona $5,400,000

Arizona Energy Office
State Capitol Tower, 5th Floor
1700 West Washington
Phoenix, AZ 85007
(602) 255-4955

Field of Interest: Science Research – Energy
Average Amount Given: $310,000
Purpose: To create innovative, cost-effective, clean coal technologies capable of commercialization.
Who May Apply: States, small businesses, individuals, partnerships, and joint ventures.
Requirements: 50% matching funding required.
Contact: Mark Ginsberg.
Application Information: Application required.
Initial Approach: Letter or phone.

Clean Coal Scientific Research Technology Program for Arkansas $3,770,00

Arkansas Energy Office
One State Capitol Mall, Suite 4B
Little Rock, AR 72201
(501) 682-7315

Field of Interest: Science Research – Energy
Average Amount Given: $270,000
Purpose: To create innovative, cost-effective, clean coal technologies capable of commercialization.
Who May Apply: States, small businesses, individuals, partnerships, and joint ventures.
Requirements: 50% matching funding required.
Contact: Jim Blakley.
Application Information: Application required.
Initial Approach: Letter or phone.

Clean Coal Scientific Research Technology Program for California $7,650,00

Governor's Office of Planning and Research
1400 10th Street
Sacramento, CA 95814
(916) 322-2318

Field of Interest: Science Research – Energy
Average Amount Given: $670,000
Purpose: To create innovative, cost-effective, clean coal technologies capable of commercialization.
Who May Apply: States, small businesses, individuals, partnerships, and joint ventures.
Requirements: 50% matching funding required.
Contact: Robert P. Martinez.
Application Information: Application required.
Initial Approach: Letter or phone.

Clean Coal Scientific Research Technology Program for Colorado $4,500,000

Colorado Office of Energy Conservation
112 E. 14th Ave.
Denver, CO 80203
(303) 894-2144

Field of Interest: Science Research – Energy
Average Amount Given: $423,000
Purpose: To create innovative, cost-effective, clean coal technologies capable of commercialization.
Who May Apply: States, small businesses, individuals, partnerships, and joint ventures.
Requirements: 50% matching funding required.
Contact: Karen Reinertson.
Application Information: Application required.
Initial Approach: Letter or phone.

Clean Coal Scientific Research Technology Program for Connecticut $1,750,000

Secretary's Office for Energy Management
80 Washington St.
Hartford, CT 06106
(203) 566-2800

Field of Interest: Science Research – Energy
Average Amount Given: $167,000
Purpose: To create innovative, cost-effective, clean coal technologies capable of commercialization.
Who May Apply: States, small businesses, individuals, partnerships, and joint ventures.
Requirements: 50% matching funding required.
Contact: Bradford S. Chase.
Application Information: Application required.
Initial Approach: Letter or phone.

Clean Coal Scientific Research Technology Program for Delaware $1,113,000

Energy Office
PO Box 1401
Dover, DE 19901
(302) 736-5644

Field of Interest: Science Research – Energy
Average Amount Given: $99,800
Purpose: To create innovative, cost-effective, clean coal technologies capable of commercialization.
Who May Apply: States, small businesses, individuals, partnerships, and joint ventures.
Requirements: 50% matching funding required.
Contact: George P. Donnelly.
Application Information: Application required.
Initial Approach: Letter or phone.

Clean Coal Scientific Research Technology Program for Florida $3,760,000

Governor's Energy Office
214 S. Bronough
Tallahassee, FL 32399
(904) 488-6764

Field of Interest: Science Research – Energy
Average Amount Given: $332,700
Purpose: To create innovative, cost-effective, clean coal technologies capable of commercialization.
Who May Apply: States, small businesses, individuals, partnerships, and joint ventures.
Requirements: 50% matching funding required.
Contact: Gwendolyn F. Spencer.
Application Information: Application required.
Initial Approach: Letter or phone.

Clean Coal Scientific Research Technology Program for Georgia $2,820,000

Office of Energy Resources
270 Washington St., SW, Suite 615
Atlanta, GA 30334
(404) 656-5176

Field of Interest: Science Research – Energy
Average Amount Given: $171,000
Purpose: To create innovative, cost-effective, clean coal technologies capable of commercialization.
Who May Apply: States, small businesses, individuals, partnerships, and joint ventures.
Requirements: 50% matching funding required.
Contact: Paul Burks.
Application Information: Application required.
Initial Approach: Letter or phone.

Clean Coal Scientific Research Technology Program for Hawaii $1,343,000

State Energy Division
335 Merchant St., Room 110
Honolulu, HI 96813
(808) 548-2306

Field of Interest: Science Research – Energy
Average Amount Given: $116,200
Purpose: To create innovative, cost-effective, clean coal technologies capable of commercialization.
Who May Apply: States, small businesses, individuals, partnerships, and joint ventures.
Requirements: 50% matching funding required.
Contact: Maurice H. Kaya.
Application Information: Application required.
Initial Approach: Letter or phone.

Clean Coal Scientific Research Technology Program for Idaho $3,566,000

Idaho Department of Water Resources, Energy Division
1301 N. Orchard
State House Mail
Boise, ID 83720
(208) 334-3597

Field of Interest: Science Research – Energy
Average Amount Given: $367,000
Purpose: To create innovative, cost-effective, clean coal technologies capable of commercialization.
Who May Apply: States, small businesses, individuals, partnerships, and joint ventures.
Requirements: 50% matching funding required.
Contact: Robert Hoppie.
Application Information: Application required.
Initial Approach: Letter or phone.

Clean Coal Scientific Research Technology Program for Illinois   **$5,349,000**

Department of Energy and Natural Resources
325 West Adams St., Room 300
Springfield, IL 62706
(217) 785-2800

Field of Interest: Science Research – Energy
Average Amount Given: $416,500
Purpose: To create innovative, cost-effective, clean coal technologies capable of commercialization.
Who May Apply: States, small businesses, individuals, partnerships, and joint ventures.
Requirements: 50% matching funding required.
Contact: Karen Witter.
Application Information: Application required.
Initial Approach: Letter or phone.

Clean Coal Scientific Research Technology Program for Indiana   **$3,900,000**

Division of Energy Policy
One North Capitol, Suite 700
Indianapolis, IN 46204
(317) 232-8940

Field of Interest: Science Research – Energy
Average Amount Given: $378,250
Purpose: To create innovative, cost-effective, clean coal technologies capable of commercialization.
Who May Apply: States, small businesses, individuals, partnerships, and joint ventures.
Requirements: 50% matching funding required.
Contact: David Zweisler.
Application Information: Application required.
Initial Approach: Letter or phone.

Clean Coal Scientific Research Technology Program for Iowa   **$1,222,400**

Iowa Department of Natural Resources
Wallace State Office Bldg.
Des Moines, IA 50319
(515) 281-6682

Field of Interest: Science Research – Energy
Average Amount Given: $136,700
Purpose: To create innovative, cost-effective, clean coal technologies capable of commercialization.
Who May Apply: States, small businesses, individuals, partnerships, and joint ventures.
Requirements: 50% matching funding required.
Contact: Larry Bean.
Application Information: Application required.
Initial Approach: Letter or phone.

Clean Coal Scientific Research Technology Program for Kansas   **$1,216,000**

Kansas Corporation Commission
State Office Bldg., Fourth Floor
Topeka, KS 66612
(913) 296-3326

Field of Interest: Science Research – Energy
Average Amount Given: $119,000
Purpose: To create innovative, cost-effective, clean coal technologies capable of commercialization.
Who May Apply: States, small businesses, individuals, partnerships, and joint ventures.
Requirements: 50% matching funding required.
Contact: Judith McConnell.
Application Information: Application required.
Initial Approach: Letter or phone.

Clean Coal Scientific Research Technology Program for Kentucky $3,995,000

Department of Natural Resources, Division of Enenrgy
PO Box 3249
Frankfort, KY 40603
(502) 564-7192

Field of Interest: Science Research – Energy
Average Amount Given: $379,000
Purpose: To create innovative, cost-effective, clean coal technologies capable of commercialization.
Who May Apply: States, small businesses, individuals, partnerships, and joint ventures.
Requirements: 50% matching funding required.
Contact: Lana Rogers.
Application Information: Application required.
Initial Approach: Letter or phone.

Clean Coal Scientific Research Technology Program for Louisiana $2,225,500

Louisiana Department of Natural Resources
PO Box 44156
Baton Rouge, LA 70804
(504) 342-4534

Field of Interest: Science Research – Energy
Average Amount Given: $236,000
Purpose: To create innovative, cost-effective, clean coal technologies capable of commercialization.
Who May Apply: States, small businesses, individuals, partnerships, and joint ventures.
Requirements: 50% matching funding required.
Contact: Mary Mitchell.
Application Information: Application required.
Initial Approach: Letter or phone.

Clean Coal Scientific Research Technology Program for Maine $1,050,000

Office of Energy Resources
State House Station No. 130
Augusta, ME 04333
(207) 289-6000

Field of Interest: Science Research – Energy
Average Amount Given: $100,500
Purpose: To create innovative, cost-effective, clean coal technologies capable of commercialization.
Who May Apply: States, small businesses, individuals, partnerships, and joint ventures.
Requirements: 50% matching funding required.
Contact: Leonard A. Dow.
Application Information: Application required.
Initial Approach: Letter or phone.

Clean Coal Scientific Research Technology Program for Maryland $1,344,000

Maryland Energy Office
45 Calvert Street
Annapolis, MD 21401
(301) 974-3755

Field of Interest: Science Research – Energy
Average Amount Given: $105,500
Purpose: To create innovative, cost-effective, clean coal technologies capable of commercialization.
Who May Apply: States, small businesses, individuals, partnerships, and joint ventures.
Requirements: 50% matching funding required.
Contact: Dr. Donald E. Milsten.
Application Information: Application required.
Initial Approach: Letter or phone.

Clean Coal Scientific Research Technology Program for Massachusetts $1,233,900

Massachusetts Division of Energy Resources
100 Cambridge St., Room 1500
Boston, MA 02202
(617) 727-4732

Field of Interest: Science Research – Energy
Average Amount Given: $180,000
Purpose: To create innovative, cost-effective, clean coal technologies capable of commercialization.
Who May Apply: States, small businesses, individuals, partnerships, and joint ventures.
Requirements: 50% matching funding required.
Contact: Paul W. Gromer.
Application Information: Application required.
Initial Approach: Letter or phone.

Clean Coal Scientific Research Technology Program for Michigan $3,500,000

Michigan Public Service Commission
PO Box 30228
Lansing, MI 48909
(517) 334-6258

Field of Interest: Science Research – Energy
Average Amount Given: $333,750
Purpose: To create innovative, cost-effective, clean coal technologies capable of commercialization.
Who May Apply: States, small businesses, individuals, partnerships, and joint ventures.
Requirements: 50% matching funding required.
Contact: William E. Long.
Application Information: Application required.
Initial Approach: Letter or phone.

Clean Coal Scientific Research Technology Program for Minnesota $3,498,000

Department of Energy and Economic Development
900 American Center Bldg.
150 East Kellogg Blvd.
St. Paul, MN 55101
(612) 297-6424

Field of Interest: Science Research – Energy
Average Amount Given: $367,000
Purpose: To create innovative, cost-effective, clean coal technologies capable of commercialization.
Who May Apply: States, small businesses, individuals, partnerships, and joint ventures.
Requirements: 50% matching funding required.
Contact: Tony Perpich.
Application Information: Application required.
Initial Approach: Letter or phone.

Clean Coal Scientific Research Technology Program for Mississippi $2,350,000

Department of Energy and Transportation
Dickson Bldg., Suite 100
510 George St.
Jackson, MS 39202
(601) 961-4733

Field of Interest: Science Research – Energy
Average Amount Given: $167,500
Purpose: To create innovative, cost-effective, clean coal technologies capable of commercialization.
Who May Apply: States, small businesses, individuals, partnerships, and joint ventures.
Requirements: 50% matching funding required.
Contact: Andrew Jenkins.
Application Information: Application required.
Initial Approach: Letter or phone.

Clean Coal Scientific Research Technology Program for Missouri $2,950,500

Department of Natural Resources, Division of Energy
PO Box 176
Jefferson City, MO 65101
(314) 751-4000

Field of Interest: Science Research – Energy
Average Amount Given: $276,000
Purpose: To create innovative, cost-effective, clean coal technologies capable of commercialization.
Who May Apply: States, small businesses, individuals, partnerships, and joint ventures.
Requirements: 50% matching funding required.
Contact: Robert Jackson.
Application Information: Application required.
Initial Approach: Letter or phone.

Clean Coal Scientific Research Technology Program for Montana $3,920,200

Department of Natural Resources and Conservation
1520 East Sixth Ave.
Helena, MT 59620
(406) 444-6697

Field of Interest: Science Research – Energy
Average Amount Given: $375,600
Purpose: To create innovative, cost-effective, clean coal technologies capable of commercialization.
Who May Apply: States, small businesses, individuals, partnerships, and joint ventures.
Requirements: 50% matching funding required.
Contact: Van Jamison.
Application Information: Application required.
Initial Approach: Letter or phone.

Clean Coal Scientific Research Technology Program for Nebraska $2,430,700

Nebraska Energy Office
PO Box 95085
State Capitol Bldg., 9th Floor
Lincoln, NE 68509
(402) 471-2867

Field of Interest: Science Research – Energy
Average Amount Given: $190,000
Purpose: To create innovative, cost-effective, clean coal technologies capable of commercialization.
Who May Apply: States, small businesses, individuals, partnerships, and joint ventures.
Requirements: 50% matching funding required.
Contact: Gary L. Rex.
Application Information: Application required.
Initial Approach: Letter or phone.

Clean Coal Scientific Research Technology Program for Nevada $3,780,000

Nevada State Office of Community Services
Capitol Complex
Carson City, NV 89710
(702) 687-4990

Field of Interest: Science Research – Energy
Average Amount Given: $210,200
Purpose: To create innovative, cost-effective, clean coal technologies capable of commercialization.
Who May Apply: States, small businesses, individuals, partnerships, and joint ventures.
Requirements: 50% matching funding required.
Contact: Jim Hawke.
Application Information: Application required.
Initial Approach: Letter or phone.

Clean Coal Scientific Research Technology Program for New Hampshire $1,000,500

Governor's Energy Office
2 1/2 Beacon Street
Concord, NH 03301
(603) 271-2711

Field of Interest: Science Research – Energy
Average Amount Given: $120,000
Purpose: To create innovative, cost-effective, clean coal technologies capable of commercialization.
Who May Apply: States, small businesses, individuals, partnerships, and joint ventures.
Requirements: 50% matching funding required.
Contact: Jonathan S. Osgood.
Application Information: Application required.
Initial Approach: Letter or phone.

Clean Coal Scientific Research Technology Program for New Jersey $2,100,000

New Jersey Board of Public Utilities
2 Gateway Center
Newark, NJ 07102
(201) 648-2904

Field of Interest: Science Research – Energy
Average Amount Given: $195,000
Purpose: To create innovative, cost-effective, clean coal technologies capable of commercialization.
Who May Apply: States, small businesses, individuals, partnerships, and joint ventures.
Requirements: 50% matching funding required.
Contact: John V. Conti.
Application Information: Application required.
Initial Approach: Letter or phone.

Clean Coal Scientific Research Technology Program for New Mexico $4,100,000

Energy Conservation and Management Division
525 Camino de los Marquez
Santa Fe, NM 87501
(505) 827-5902

Field of Interest: Science Research – Energy
Average Amount Given: $311,600
Purpose: To create innovative, cost-effective, clean coal technologies capable of commercialization.
Who May Apply: States, small businesses, individuals, partnerships, and joint ventures.
Requirements: 50% matching funding required.
Contact: Kerry Boyd.
Application Information: Application required.
Initial Approach: Letter or phone.

Clean Coal Scientific Research Technology Program for New York $3,222,000

New York State Energy Office
2 Rockefeller Plaza
Albany, NY 12223
(518) 474-4376

Field of Interest: Science Research – Energy
Average Amount Given: $201,500
Purpose: To create innovative, cost-effective, clean coal technologies capable of commercialization.
Who May Apply: States, small businesses, individuals, partnerships, and joint ventures.
Requirements: 50% matching funding required.
Contact: William D. Cotter.
Application Information: Application required.
Initial Approach: Letter or phone.

Clean Coal Scientific Research Technology Program for North Carolina $2,905,200

Department of Commerce, Energy Division
4430 N. Salisbury St.
Raleigh, NC 27611
(919) 733-2230

Field of Interest: Science Research – Energy
Average Amount Given: $176,300
Purpose: To create innovative, cost-effective, clean coal technologies capable of commercialization.
Who May Apply: States, small businesses, individuals, partnerships, and joint ventures.
Requirements: 50% matching funding required.
Contact: Carson D. Culbreth, Jr.
Application Information: Application required.
Initial Approach: Letter or phone.

Clean Coal Scientific Research Technology Program for North Dakota $3,900,000

Office of Intergovernmental Assistance
State Capitol Bldg.
Bismarck, ND 58505
(701) 224-2094

Field of Interest: Science Research – Energy
Average Amount Given: $250,500
Purpose: To create innovative, cost-effective, clean coal technologies capable of commercialization.
Who May Apply: States, small businesses, individuals, partnerships, and joint ventures.
Requirements: 50% matching funding required.
Contact: Shirley R. Dykshoorn.
Application Information: Application required.
Initial Approach: Letter or phone.

Clean Coal Scientific Research Technology Program for Ohio $3,007,000

Ohio Department of Development
77 S. High Street, 4th Floor
Columbus, OH 43266
(614) 466-3465

Field of Interest: Science Research – Energy
Average Amount Given: $217,000
Purpose: To create innovative, cost-effective, clean coal technologies capable of commercialization.
Who May Apply: States, small businesses, individuals, partnerships, and joint ventures.
Requirements: 50% matching funding required.
Contact: David Baker.
Application Information: Application required.
Initial Approach: Letter or phone.

Clean Coal Scientific Research Technology Program for Oklahoma $3,700,000

Oklahoma Department of Commerce
6601 Broadway Extension, Suite 200
Oklahoma City, OK 73116
(405) 521-3501

Field of Interest: Science Research – Energy
Average Amount Given: $351,800
Purpose: To create innovative, cost-effective, clean coal technologies capable of commercialization.
Who May Apply: States, small businesses, individuals, partnerships, and joint ventures.
Requirements: 50% matching funding required.
Contact: Sherwood Washington.
Application Information: Application required.
Initial Approach: Letter or phone.

Clean Coal Scientific Research Technology Program for Oregon $3,450,000

Oregon Department of Energy
625 Marion St., NE
Salem, OR 97310
(503) 378-0404

Field of Interest: Science Research – Energy
Average Amount Given: $197,300
Purpose: To create innovative, cost-effective, clean coal technologies capable of commercialization.
Who May Apply: States, small businesses, individuals, partnerships, and joint ventures.
Requirements: 50% matching funding required.
Contact: David Yaden.
Application Information: Application required.
Initial Approach: Letter or phone.

Clean Coal Scientific Research Technology Program for Pennsylvania $5,700,000

Pennsylvania Energy Office
116 Pine St.
Harrisburg, PA 17101
(717) 783-9981

Field of Interest: Science Research – Energy
Average Amount Given: $521,400
Purpose: To create innovative, cost-effective, clean coal technologies capable of commercialization.
Who May Apply: States, small businesses, individuals, partnerships, and joint ventures.
Requirements: 50% matching funding required.
Contact: Jan H. Freeman.
Application Information: Application required.
Initial Approach: Letter or phone.

Clean Coal Scientific Research Technology Program for Rhode Island $1,262,000

Governor's Office of Housing and Energy
275 Westminster Mall
Providence, RI 02903
(401) 277-3370

Field of Interest: Science Research – Energy
Average Amount Given: $138,100
Purpose: To create innovative, cost-effective, clean coal technologies capable of commercialization.
Who May Apply: States, small businesses, individuals, partnerships, and joint ventures.
Requirements: 50% matching funding required.
Contact: Charles R. Mansollilo.
Application Information: Application required.
Initial Approach: Letter or phone.

Clean Coal Scientific Research Technology Program for South Carolina $2,391,000

Governor's Division of Energy and Natural Resources
1205 Pendleton St., Third Floor
Columbia, SC 29201
(803) 734-0445

Field of Interest: Science Research – Energy
Average Amount Given: $178,250
Purpose: To create innovative, cost-effective, clean coal technologies capable of commercialization.
Who May Apply: States, small businesses, individuals, partnerships, and joint ventures.
Requirements: 50% matching funding required.
Contact: John McMillan.
Application Information: Application required.
Initial Approach: Letter or phone.

Clean Coal Scientific Research Technology Program for South Dakota $2,900,000

Governor's Office of Energy Policy
217-1/2 West Missouri
Pierre, SD 57501
(605) 773-3603

Field of Interest: Science Research – Energy
Average Amount Given: $225,700
Purpose: To create innovative, cost-effective, clean coal technologies capable of commercialization.
Who May Apply: States, small businesses, individuals, partnerships, and joint ventures.
Requirements: 50% matching funding required.
Contact: Ron Reed.
Application Information: Application required.
Initial Approach: Letter or phone.

Clean Coal Scientific Research Technology Program for Tennessee $3,933,000

Department of Economic and Community Development
320 6th Ave North, 6th Floor
Nashville, TN 37219
(615) 741-2373

Field of Interest: Science Research – Energy
Average Amount Given: $321,900
Purpose: To create innovative, cost-effective, clean coal technologies capable of commercialization.
Who May Apply: States, small businesses, individuals, partnerships, and joint ventures.
Requirements: 50% matching funding required.
Contact: Carl Johnson.
Application Information: Application required.
Initial Approach: Letter or phone.

Clean Coal Scientific Research Technology Program for Texas $3,790,200

Energy Management Center
PO Box 12428, Capitol Station
Austin, TX 78711
(512) 463-1878

Field of Interest: Science Research – Energy
Average Amount Given: $256,100
Purpose: To create innovative, cost-effective, clean coal technologies capable of commercialization.
Who May Apply: States, small businesses, individuals, partnerships, and joint ventures.
Requirements: 50% matching funding required.
Contact: Carol Tombari.
Application Information: Application required.
Initial Approach: Letter or phone.

Clean Coal Scientific Research Technology Program for Utah $3,405,000

Utah Energy Office
355 West North Temple
3 Triad Center, Suite 450
Salt Lake City, UT 84180
(801) 538-5428

Field of Interest: Science Research – Energy
Average Amount Given: $283,600
Purpose: To create innovative, cost-effective, clean coal technologies capable of commercialization.
Who May Apply: States, small businesses, individuals, partnerships, and joint ventures.
Requirements: 50% matching funding required.
Contact: Richard M. Anderson.
Application Information: Application required.
Initial Approach: Letter or phone.

Clean Coal Scientific Research Technology Program for Vermont   **$1,112,000**

Department of Public Services
State Office Bldg.
Montpelier, VT 05602
(802) 828-2811

Field of Interest: Science Research – Energy
Average Amount Given: $142,300
Purpose: To create innovative, cost-effective, clean coal technologies capable of commercialization.
Who May Apply: States, small businesses, individuals, partnerships, and joint ventures.
Requirements: 50% matching funding required.
Contact: George J. Sterzinger.
Application Information: Application required.
Initial Approach: Letter or phone.

Clean Coal Scientific Research Technology Program for Virginia   **$3,002,900**

Department of Mines, Minerals and Energy
2201 W. Broad Street
Richmond, VA 23220
(804) 257-1310

Field of Interest: Science Research – Energy
Average Amount Given: $237,850
Purpose: To create innovative, cost-effective, clean coal technologies capable of commercialization.
Who May Apply: States, small businesses, individuals, partnerships, and joint ventures.
Requirements: 50% matching funding required.
Contact: Ronald J. DesRoches.
Application Information: Application required.
Initial Approach: Letter or phone.

Clean Coal Scientific Research Technology Program for Washington   **$3,100,000**

State Energy Office
809 Legion Way, SE
Olympia, WA 98504
(206) 506-6000

Field of Interest: Science Research – Energy
Average Amount Given: $206,000
Purpose: To create innovative, cost-effective, clean coal technologies capable of commercialization.
Who May Apply: States, small businesses, individuals, partnerships, and joint ventures.
Requirements: 50% matching funding required.
Contact: Richard Watson.
Application Information: Application required.
Initial Approach: Letter or phone.

Clean Coal Scientific Research Technology Program for West Virginia   **$4,830,000**

Fuel and Energy Office
1204 Kanawha Blvd. E., 2nd Floor
Charleston, WV 25301
(304) 348-8860

Field of Interest: Science Research – Energy
Average Amount Given: $346,000
Purpose: To create innovative, cost-effective, clean coal technologies capable of commercialization.
Who May Apply: States, small businesses, individuals, partnerships, and joint ventures.
Requirements: 50% matching funding required.
Contact: John F. Herholdt, Jr.
Application Information: Application required.
Initial Approach: Letter or phone.

**Clean Coal Scientific Research Technology Program
for Wisconsin** $3,213,600
Division of Energy
101 S. Webster St.
Madison, WI 53702
(608) 266-7257

Field of Interest: Science Research – Energy
Average Amount Given: $248,000
Purpose: To create innovative, cost-effective, clean coal technologies capable of commercialization.
Who May Apply: States, small businesses, individuals, partnerships, and joint ventures.
Requirements: 50% matching funding required.
Contact: John Bilotti.
Application Information: Application required.
Initial Approach: Letter or phone.

**Clean Coal Scientific Research Technology Program
for Wyoming** $4,940,000
Economic Development and Stabilization Board
Herschler Bldg., 3rd Floor, East Wing
Cheyenne, WY 82002
(307) 777-7284

Field of Interest: Science Research – Energy
Average Amount Given: $362,600
Purpose: To create innovative, cost-effective, clean coal technologies capable of commercialization.
Who May Apply: States, small businesses, individuals, partnerships, and joint ventures.
Requirements: 50% matching funding required.
Contact: Steven Schmitz.
Application Information: Application required.
Initial Approach: Letter or phone.

REGIONAL – SOCIAL SERVICES

Job Training Partnership for Alabama $2,550,000

Department of Labor
Berry Bldg., Suite 301
2015 N. Second Ave.
Birmingham, AL 35203
(205) 731-1305

Field of Interest: Social Services – General
Average Amount Given: $175,000
Purpose: To provide job training and related assistance to economically disadvantaged individuals through partnerships between the private sector and local and state government.
Who May Apply: Qualified profit and nonprofit agencies.
Requirements: None.
Contact: Lloyd Christopher.
Application Information: Application required.
Initial Approach: Letter or phone.

Job Training Partnership for Alaska $1,890,000

Department of Labor
909 First Ave., Room 4141
Seattle, WA 98174
(206) 442-1914

Field of Interest: Social Services – General
Average Amount Given: $167,000
Purpose: To provide job training and related assistance to economically disadvantaged individuals through partnerships between the private sector and local and state government.
Who May Apply: Qualified profit and nonprofit agencies.
Requirements: None.
Contact: Wilbur Olsen.
Application Information: Application required.
Initial Approach: Letter or phone.

Job Training Partnership for Arizona $3,500,700

Department of Labor
3221 N. 16th St., Suite 301
Phoenix, AZ 85016
(602) 241-2990

Field of Interest: Social Services – General
Average Amount Given: $310,000
Purpose: To provide job training and related assistance to economically disadvantaged individuals through partnerships between the private sector and local and state government.
Who May Apply: Qualified profit and nonprofit agencies.
Requirements: None.
Contact: John Breen.
Application Information: Application required.
Initial Approach: Letter or phone.

Job Training Partnership for Arkansas $2,350,000

Department of Labor
Capitol and Spring Streets, Suite 611
Little Rock, AR 72201
(501) 378-5292

Field of Interest: Social Services – General
Average Amount Given: $220,600
Purpose: To provide job training and related assistance to economically disadvantaged individuals through partnerships between the private sector and local and state government.
Who May Apply: Qualified profit and nonprofit agencies.
Requirements: None.
Contact: J. Dean Speer.
Application Information: Application required.
Initial Approach: Letter or phone.

Job Training Partnership for California $7,900,000

Department of Labor
2981 Fulton Ave.
Sacramento, CA 95821
(916) 978-4233

Field of Interest: Social Services – General
Average Amount Given: $350,000
Purpose: To provide job training and related assistance to economically disadvantaged individuals through partnerships between the private sector and local and state government.
Who May Apply: Qualified profit and nonprofit agencies.
Requirements: None.
Contact: Timothy Reardon.
Application Information: Application required.
Initial Approach: Letter or phone.

Job Training Partnership for Colorado $3,900,000

Department of Labor
721 19th Street, Room 228
Denver, CO 80202
(303) 844-4405

Field of Interest: Social Services – General
Average Amount Given: $265,000
Purpose: To provide job training and related assistance to economically disadvantaged individuals through partnerships between the private sector and local and state government.
Who May Apply: Qualified profit and nonprofit agencies.
Requirements: None.
Contact: Gerald H. Hill.
Application Information: Application required.
Initial Approach: Letter or phone.

Job Training Partnership for Connecticut $3,120,400

Department of Labor
135 High Street, Room 311
Hartford, CT 06103
(203) 240-4160

Field of Interest: Social Services – General
Average Amount Given: $235,000
Purpose: To provide job training and related assistance to economically disadvantaged individuals through partnerships between the private sector and local and state government.
Who May Apply: Qualified profit and nonprofit agencies.
Requirements: None.
Contact: John J. Reardon.
Application Information: Application required.
Initial Approach: Letter or phone.

Job Training Partnership for Delaware $2,138,770

Department of Labor
3535 Market Street, Room 15230
Philadelphia, PA 19104
(215) 596-1194

Field of Interest: Social Services – General
Average Amount Given: $176,000
Purpose: To provide job training and related assistance to economically disadvantaged individuals through partnerships between the private sector and local and state government.
Who May Apply: Qualified profit and nonprofit agencies.
Requirements: None.
Contact: James E. Sykes.
Application Information: Application required.
Initial Approach: Letter or phone.

Job Training Partnership for Florida $6,400,000

Department of Labor
1150 SW First St., Room 202
Miami, FL 33130
(305) 536-5767

Field of Interest: Social Services – General
Average Amount Given: $290,000
Purpose: To provide job training and related assistance to economically disadvantaged individuals through partnerships between the private sector and local and state government.
Who May Apply: Qualified profit and nonprofit agencies.
Requirements: None.
Contact: Robert Chauvin.
Application Information: Application required.
Initial Approach: Letter or phone.

Job Training Partnership for Georgia $2,333,300

Department of Labor
1375 Peachtree St., NE, Suite 673
Atlanta, GA 30367
(404) 347-4707

Field of Interest: Social Services – General
Average Amount Given: $199,500
Purpose: To provide job training and related assistance to economically disadvantaged individuals through partnerships between the private sector and local and state government.
Who May Apply: Qualified profit and nonprofit agencies.
Requirements: None.
Contact: Mary Fagen.
Application Information: Application required.
Initial Approach: Letter or phone.

Job Training Partnership for Hawaii $2,954,000

Department of Labor
71 Stevenson St., Suite 930
San Francisco, CA 94105
(415) 744-6625

Field of Interest: Social Services – General
Average Amount Given: $235,000
Purpose: To provide job training and related assistance to economically disadvantaged individuals through partnerships between the private sector and local and state government.
Who May Apply: Qualified profit and nonprofit agencies.
Requirements: None.
Contact: Herbert Goldstein.
Application Information: Application required.
Initial Approach: Letter or phone.

Job Training Partnership for Idaho $1,300,000

Department of Labor
212 Maple Park, PO Box 367
Olympia, WA 98504
(206) 753-5114

Field of Interest: Social Services – General
Average Amount Given: $165,400
Purpose: To provide job training and related assistance to economically disadvantaged individuals through partnerships between the private sector and local and state government.
Who May Apply: Qualified profit and nonprofit agencies.
Requirements: None.
Contact: Wes Charleton.
Application Information: Application required.
Initial Approach: Letter or phone.

Job Training Partnership for Illinois $7,400,000

Department of Labor
524 S. 2nd St., Room 630
Springfield, IL 62701
(217) 492-4060

Field of Interest: Social Services – General
Average Amount Given: $310,000
Purpose: To provide job training and related assistance to economically disadvantaged individuals through partnerships between the private sector and local and state government.
Who May Apply: Qualified profit and nonprofit agencies.
Requirements: None.
Contact: Henry Rodriguez.
Application Information: Application required.
Initial Approach: Letter or phone.

Job Training Partnership for Indiana $4,500,000

Department of Labor
501 E. Monroe, Suite 160
South Bend, IN 46601
(219) 236-8331

Field of Interest: Social Services – General
Average Amount Given: $260,000
Purpose: To provide job training and related assistance to economically disadvantaged individuals through partnerships between the private sector and local and state government.
Who May Apply: Qualified profit and nonprofit agencies.
Requirements: None.
Contact: Donald J. Laurent.
Application Information: Application required.
Initial Approach: Letter or phone.

Job Training Partnership for Iowa $1,900,000

Department of Labor
210 Walnut St., Room 643
Des Moines, IA 50309
(515) 284-4625

Field of Interest: Social Services – General
Average Amount Given: $145,800
Purpose: To provide job training and related assistance to economically disadvantaged individuals through partnerships between the private sector and local and state government.
Who May Apply: Qualified profit and nonprofit agencies.
Requirements: None.
Contact: Donald Chleborad.
Application Information: Application required.
Initial Approach: Letter or phone.

Job Training Partnership for Kansas $4,100,000

Department of Labor
911 Walnut St.
Kansas City, MO 64106
(816) 426-5721

Field of Interest: Social Services – General
Average Amount Given: $231,000
Purpose: To provide job training and related assistance to economically disadvantaged individuals through partnerships between the private sector and local and state government.
Who May Apply: Qualified profit and nonprofit agencies.
Requirements: None.
Contact: Terry L. Burger.
Application Information: Application required.
Initial Approach: Letter or phone.

Job Training Partnership for Kentucky $2,410,000

Department of Labor
600 Federal Place, Room 187–E
Louisville, KY 40202
(502) 582-5226

Field of Interest: Social Services – General
Average Amount Given: $210,000
Purpose: To provide job training and related assistance to economically disadvantaged individuals through partnerships between the private sector and local and state government.
Who May Apply: Qualified profit and nonprofit agencies.
Requirements: None.
Contact: John Traczewski.
Application Information: Application required.
Initial Approach: Letter or phone.

Job Training Partnership for Louisiana $1,850,000

Department of Labor
600 S. Maestri Pl., Room 703
New Orleans, LA 70130
(504) 589-6171

Field of Interest: Social Services – General
Average Amount Given: $176,000
Purpose: To provide job training and related assistance to economically disadvantaged individuals through partnerships between the private sector and local and state government.
Who May Apply: Qualified profit and nonprofit agencies.
Requirements: None.
Contact: Charles R. Beckwith.
Application Information: Application required.
Initial Approach: Letter or phone.

Job Training Partnership for Maine $1,300,000

Department of Labor
66 Pearl St., Room 211
Portland, ME 04101
(207) 780-3344

Field of Interest: Social Services – General
Average Amount Given: $167,000
Purpose: To provide job training and related assistance to economically disadvantaged individuals through partnerships between the private sector and local and state government.
Who May Apply: Qualified profit and nonprofit agencies.
Requirements: None.
Contact: Alfred F. Butler.
Application Information: Application required.
Initial Approach: Letter or phone.

Job Training Partnership for Maryland $2,400,000

Department of Labor
31 Hopkins Plaza, Room 913
Baltimore, MD 21201
(301) 962-2265

Field of Interest: Social Services – General
Average Amount Given: $ 235,000
Purpose: To provide job training and related assistance to economically disadvantaged individuals through partnerships between the private sector and local and state government.
Who May Apply: Qualified profit and nonprofit agencies.
Requirements: None.
Contact: Travis Campbell.
Application Information: Application required.
Initial Approach: Letter or phone.

Job Training Partnership for Massachusetts $5,300,000

Department of Labor
McCormack PO and Courthouse, Room 806
Boston, MA 02109
(617) 223-9970

Field of Interest: Social Services – General
Average Amount Given: $255,700
Purpose: To provide job training and related assistance to economically disadvantaged individuals through partnerships between the private sector and local and state government.
Who May Apply: Qualified profit and nonprofit agencies.
Requirements: None.
Contact: Corey Surett.
Application Information: Application required.
Initial Approach: Letter or phone.

Job Training Partnership for Michigan $5,900,000

Department of Labor
2920 Fuller Ave., NE, Suite 100
Grand Rapids, MI 49505
(616) 456-2183

Field of Interest: Social Services – General
Average Amount Given: $300,000
Purpose: To provide job training and related assistance to economically disadvantaged individuals through partnerships between the private sector and local and state government.
Who May Apply: Qualified profit and nonprofit agencies.
Requirements: None.
Contact: Daniel Ocharzak.
Application Information: Application required.
Initial Approach: Letter or phone.

Job Training Partnership for Minnesota $2,900,000

Department of Labor
220 S. 2nd St., Room 106
Minneapolis, MN 55401
(612) 370-3371

Field of Interest: Social Services – General
Average Amount Given: $250,000
Purpose: To provide job training and related assistance to economically disadvantaged individuals through partnerships between the private sector and local and state government.
Who May Apply: Qualified profit and nonprofit agencies.
Requirements: None.
Contact: Lawrence Peterson.
Application Information: Application required.
Initial Approach: Letter or phone.

Job Training Partnership for Mississippi $1,200,500

Department of Labor
100 West Capitol St., Suite 1414
Jackson, MS 39269
(601) 965-4347

Field of Interest: Social Services – General
Average Amount Given: $176,000
Purpose: To provide job training and related assistance to economically disadvantaged individuals through partnerships between the private sector and local and state government.
Who May Apply: Qualified profit and nonprofit agencies.
Requirements: None.
Contact: Robert M. Brock.
Application Information: Application required.
Initial Approach: Letter or phone.

Job Training Partnership for Missouri $3,540,000

Department of Labor
210 N. Tucker Blvd., Room 563
St. Louis, MO 63101
(314) 425-4706

Field of Interest: Social Services – General
Average Amount Given: $210,000
Purpose: To provide job training and related assistance to economically disadvantaged individuals through partnerships between the private sector and local and state government.
Who May Apply: Qualified profit and nonprofit agencies.
Requirements: None.
Contact: Kenneth M. Kelly.
Application Information: Application required.
Initial Approach: Letter or phone.

Job Training Partnership for Montana $1,070,000

Department of Labor
1961 Stout Street, Room 1490
Denver, CO 80294
(303) 844-4613

Field of Interest: Social Services – General
Average Amount Given: $125,000
Purpose: To provide job training and related assistance to economically disadvantaged individuals through partnerships between the private sector and local and state government.
Who May Apply: Qualified profit and nonprofit agencies.
Requirements: None.
Contact: Loren E. Gilbert.
Application Information: Application required.
Initial Approach: Letter or phone.

Job Training Partnership for Nebraska $2,100,000

Department of Labor
106 S. 15th St., Room 715
Omaha, NE 68102
(402) 221-4682

Field of Interest: Social Services – General
Average Amount Given: $195,500
Purpose: To provide job training and related assistance to economically disadvantaged individuals through partnerships between the private sector and local and state government.
Who May Apply: Qualified profit and nonprofit agencies.
Requirements: None.
Contact: James Skolaut.
Application Information: Application required.
Initial Approach: Letter or phone.

Job Training Partnership for Nevada $1,875,000

Department of Labor
500 E. 3rd St.
Carson City, NV 89713
(702) 885-4635

Field of Interest: Social Services – General
Average Amount Given: $136,000
Purpose: To provide job training and related assistance to economically disadvantaged individuals through partnerships between the private sector and local and state government.
Who May Apply: Qualified profit and nonprofit agencies.
Requirements: None.
Contact: John Fitch.
Application Information: Application required.
Initial Approach: Letter or phone.

Job Training Partnership
for New Hampshire $1,800,000

Department of Labor
32 S. Main St., Rm. 204
Concord, NH 03301
(603) 224-3311

Field of Interest: Social Services – General
Average Amount Given: $143,000
Purpose: To provide job training and related assistance to economically disadvantaged individuals through partnerships between the private sector and local and state government.
Who May Apply: Qualified profit and nonprofit agencies.
Requirements: None.
Contact: William L. Smith.
Application Information: Application required.
Initial Approach: Letter or phone.

Job Training Partnership for New Jersey $5,600,000

Department of Labor
970 Broad St., Room 836
Newark, NJ 07102
(201) 645-2279

Field of Interest: Social Services – General
Average Amount Given: $300,500
Purpose: To provide job training and related assistance to economically disadvantaged individuals through partnerships between the private sector and local and state government.
Who May Apply: Qualified profit and nonprofit agencies.
Requirements: None.
Contact: Thomas Davine.
Application Information: Application required.
Initial Approach: Letter or phone.

Job Training Partnership for New Mexico $2,100,000

Department of Labor
320 Central Ave., NW, Suite 12
Albuquerque, NM 87102
(505) 766-2477

Field of Interest: Social Services – General
Average Amount Given: $125,000
Purpose: To provide job training and related assistance to economically disadvantaged individuals through partnerships between the private sector and local and state government.
Who May Apply: Qualified profit and nonprofit agencies.
Requirements: None.
Contact: Michael J. Ward.
Application Information: Application required.
Initial Approach: Letter or phone.

Job Training Partnership for New York $8,500,000

Department of Labor
O'Brien Federal Bldg., Room 822
Albany, NY 12207
(518) 472-3596

Field of Interest: Social Services – General
Average Amount Given: $366,000
Purpose: To provide job training and related assistance to economically disadvantaged individuals through partnerships between the private sector and local and state government.
Who May Apply: Qualified profit and nonprofit agencies.
Requirements: None.
Contact: Samuel Weitman.
Application Information: Application required.
Initial Approach: Letter or phone.

Job Training Partnership for North Carolina $1,670,500
Department of Labor
800 Briar Creek Road, Suite CC–412
Charlotte, NC 28205
(704) 371-6120

Field of Interest: Social Services – General
Average Amount Given: $111,000
Purpose: To provide job training and related assistance to economically disadvantaged individuals through partnerships between the private sector and local and state government.
Who May Apply: Qualified profit and nonprofit agencies.
Requirements: None.
Contact: Gerald M. Parks.
Application Information: Application required.
Initial Approach: Letter or phone.

Job Training Partnership for North Dakota $900,500
Department of Labor
1000 E. Divide Ave., Box 1537
Bismarck, ND 58501
(701) 224-2836

Field of Interest: Social Services – General
Average Amount Given: $110,000
Purpose: To provide job training and related assistance to economically disadvantaged individuals through partnerships between the private sector and local and state government.
Who May Apply: Qualified profit and nonprofit agencies.
Requirements: None.
Contact: Brian Chadwick.
Application Information: Application required.
Initial Approach: Letter or phone.

Job Training Partnership for Ohio $7,300,000
Department of Labor
200 N. High Street, Room 646
Columbus, OH 43215
(614) 469-5677

Field of Interest: Social Services – General
Average Amount Given: $312,400
Purpose: To provide job training and related assistance to economically disadvantaged individuals through partnerships between the private sector and local and state government.
Who May Apply: Qualified profit and nonprofit agencies.
Requirements: None.
Contact: Richard Malloy.
Application Information: Application required.
Initial Approach: Letter or phone.

Job Training Partnership for Oklahoma $3,290,000
Department of Labor
440 S. Houston, Room 208
Tulsa, OK 74127
(918) 581-7695

Field of Interest: Social Services – General
Average Amount Given: $230,000
Purpose: To provide job training and related assistance to economically disadvantaged individuals through partnerships between the private sector and local and state government.
Who May Apply: Qualified profit and nonprofit agencies.
Requirements: None.
Contact: Bill Hamilton.
Application Information: Application required.
Initial Approach: Letter or phone.

Job Training Partnership for Oregon $2,459,000
Department of Labor
1220 SW 3rd Ave.
Portland, OR 97204
(503) 221-3052

Field of Interest: Social Services – General
Average Amount Given: $199,500
Purpose: To provide job training and related assistance to economi-
cally disadvantaged individuals through partnerships between the pri-
vate sector and local and state government.
Who May Apply: Qualified profit and nonprofit agencies.
Requirements: None.
Contact: Robert Providencio.
Application Information: Application required.
Initial Approach: Letter or phone.

Job Training Partnership for Pennsylvania $6,555,500
Department of Labor
1000 Liberty Ave., Room 1429
Pittsburgh, PA 15222
(412) 644-2996

Field of Interest: Social Services – General
Average Amount Given: $333,800
Purpose: To provide job training and related assistance to economi-
cally disadvantaged individuals through partnerships between the pri-
vate sector and local and state government.
Who May Apply: Qualified profit and nonprofit agencies.
Requirements: None.
Contact: Linda Burleson.
Application Information: Application required.
Initial Approach: Letter or phone.

Job Training Partnership for Rhode Island $1,420,000
Department of Labor
24 Weybosset St., Room 1429
Providence, RI 02903
(401) 528-5141

Field of Interest: Social Services – General
Average Amount Given: $175,000
Purpose: To provide job training and related assistance to economi-
cally disadvantaged individuals through partnerships between the pri-
vate sector and local and state government.
Who May Apply: Qualified profit and nonprofit agencies.
Requirements: None.
Contact: John McMahon.
Application Information: Application required.
Initial Approach: Letter or phone.

Job Training Partnership for South Carolina $1,470,000
Department of Labor
1835 Assembly St., Room 1072
Columbia, SC 29201

Field of Interest: Social Services – General
Average Amount Given: $127,000
Purpose: To provide job training and related assistance to economi-
cally disadvantaged individuals through partnerships between the pri-
vate sector and local and state government.
Who May Apply: Qualified profit and nonprofit agencies.
Requirements: None.
Contact: Jerry Stuckey.
Application Information: Application required.
Initial Approach: Letter or phone.

Job Training Partnership for South Dakota $1,070,000

Department of Labor
700 Governor's Drive
Pierre, SD 57501
(605) 773-3101

Field of Interest: Social Services – General
Average Amount Given: $120,000
Purpose: To provide job training and related assistance to economically disadvantaged individuals through partnerships between the private sector and local and state government.
Who May Apply: Qualified profit and nonprofit agencies.
Requirements: None.
Contact: Bill Olaf.
Application Information: Application required.
Initial Approach: Letter or phone.

Job Training Partnership for Tennessee $4,300,000

Department of Labor
460 Metroplex Dr., Suite 102
Nashville, TN 37203
(615) 736-5452

Field of Interest: Social Services – General
Average Amount Given: $283,000
Purpose: To provide job training and related assistance to economically disadvantaged individuals through partnerships between the private sector and local and state government.
Who May Apply: Qualified profit and nonprofit agencies.
Requirements: None.
Contact: Bennie L. Edwards.
Application Information: Application required.
Initial Approach: Letter or phone.

Job Training Partnership for Texas $7,300,000

Department of Labor
525 Griffin St., Room 828
Dallas, TX 75202
(214) 767-6294

Field of Interest: Social Services – General
Average Amount Given: $314,000
Purpose: To provide job training and related assistance to economically disadvantaged individuals through partnerships between the private sector and local and state government.
Who May Apply: Qualified profit and nonprofit agencies.
Requirements: None.
Contact: Curtis Poer.
Application Information: Application required.
Initial Approach: Letter or phone.

Job Training Partnership for Utah $1,950,000

Department of Labor
125 S. State St., Room 3420
Salt Lake City, UT 84138
(801) 524-5706

Field of Interest: Social Services – General
Average Amount Given: $162,000
Purpose: To provide job training and related assistance to economically disadvantaged individuals through partnerships between the private sector and local and state government.
Who May Apply: Qualified profit and nonprofit agencies.
Requirements: None.
Contact: Ruth M. Bauman.
Application Information: Application required.
Initial Approach: Letter or phone.

Job Training Partnership for Vermont $1,729,000

Department of Labor
5 Green Mountain Dr.
Montpelier, VT 05602
(802) 229-0311

Field of Interest: Social Services – General
Average Amount Given: $100,000
Purpose: To provide job training and related assistance to economically disadvantaged individuals through partnerships between the private sector and local and state government.
Who May Apply: Qualified profit and nonprofit agencies.
Requirements: None.
Contact: Brenda Joyce.
Application Information: Application required.
Initial Approach: Letter or phone.

Job Training Partnership for Virginia $5,581,000

Department of Labor
400 N. 8th St., Room 7000
Richmond, VA 23240
(804) 771-2995

Field of Interest: Social Services – General
Average Amount Given: $330,500
Purpose: To provide job training and related assistance to economically disadvantaged individuals through partnerships between the private sector and local and state government.
Who May Apply: Qualified profit and nonprofit agencies.
Requirements: None.
Contact: Gilbert C. Parker.
Application Information: Application required.
Initial Approach: Letter or phone.

Job Training Partnership for Washington $4,100,000

Department of Labor
909 First Ave., Room 1056
Seattle, WA 98174
(206) 442-4482

Field of Interest: Social Services – General
Average Amount Given: $272,000
Purpose: To provide job training and related assistance to economically disadvantaged individuals through partnerships between the private sector and local and state government.
Who May Apply: Qualified profit and nonprofit agencies.
Requirements: None.
Contact: Larry Wilson.
Application Information: Application required.
Initial Approach: Letter or phone.

Job Training Partnership for West Virginia $2,590,000

Department of Labor
2 Hale St., Suite 301
Charleston, WV 25301
(304) 347-5207

Field of Interest: Social Services – General
Average Amount Given: $211,000
Purpose: To provide job training and related assistance to economically disadvantaged individuals through partnerships between the private sector and local and state government.
Who May Apply: Qualified profit and nonprofit agencies.
Requirements: None.
Contact: Joseph Dixon.
Application Information: Application required.
Initial Approach: Letter or phone.

Job Training Partnership for Wisconsin   **$5,600,000**
Department of Labor
212 E. Washington Ave., Room 309
Madison, WI 53703
(608) 264-5221

Field of Interest: Social Services – General
Average Amount Given: $319,000
Purpose: To provide job training and related assistance to economically disadvantaged individuals through partnerships between the private sector and local and state government.
Who May Apply: Qualified profit and nonprofit agencies.
Requirements: None.
Contact: Jerome Estock.
Application Information: Application required.
Initial Approach: Letter or phone.

Job Training Partnership for Wyoming   **$ 1,544,000**
Department of Labor
Center and Midwest Streets
Casper, WY 82602
(307) 235-3650

Field of Interest: Social Services – General
Average Amount Given: $105,600
Purpose: To provide job training and related assistance to economically disadvantaged individuals through partnerships between the private sector and local and state government.
Who May Apply: Qualified profit and nonprofit agencies.
Requirements: None.
Contact: George Eccles.
Application Information: Application required.
Initial Approach: Letter or phone.

FISCAL SPONSORSHIP

Grants in this category, requiring fiscal sponsorship, are not made directly to individuals but instead to enterprises that are designated as charitable under section 501(c)(3) of the Internal Revenue Code. However, you as an individual can apply for these grants, working through a nonprofit sponsor. Affiliation can occur for a short period of time or for a longer term, depending on the nature of the project (many scientific projects, for example, take place over several years). Individuals can affiliate with nonprofit organizations in one of two ways:

1. Fiscal Sponsorship: An individual may enter into a relationship with an existing nonprofit organization which would receive monies from the granting agency to support the individual's work. The funds raised are contributed to the nonprofit organization with the understanding that they will be given to the individual. The nonprofit organizations must at all times assure that the individual uses the grant money appropriately and for the intended purpose.

2. Adoption: Adoption is a more encompassing relationship than fiscal sponsorship. Typically, an individual and his project would be adopted as a project by the nonprofit organization. Under this arrangement, the nonprofit organization assumes full financial responsibility for, and legal control of, the individual's project. The project is "housed" within the organizational structure of the nonprofit organization. As a result (and here's the critical point), the nonprofit organization has the power to get involved in the decision making and creation of the individual's project. Many scientific or multi-year projects are structured as adoption; if you have a shorter-time-period project, I suggest fiscal sponsorship.

What are the advantages and disadvantages of this arrangement? For the individual, you truly have nothing to lose and everything to gain. Depending on your fiscal affiliation, you have the name of a nonprofit organization that probably has had a good funding history. Your main concern as an individual arranging for a nonprofit sponsor is to work with someone you know or trust, as all grant monies will be paid to the sponsor who, in turn, will pay you (as an agent does his client). Though there is no obligation for you to pay any monies to the nonprofit, common practice is to donate to the nonprofit 3% to 7% of any monies raised to cover administrative and bookkeeping costs for acting as your fiscal sponsor. The nonprofit sponsor has a lot at stake, however. As it is the receiver of grant monies, it is accountable and liable for the proper spending of such monies. Its tax-exempt status and reputation are on the line. Therefore, to the greatest extent possible, the relationship between you and your nonprofit sponsor should be spelled out in a written agreement that denotes the terms of understanding between the two parties.

How do you go about finding a nonprofit conduit? First, remember that the best sponsors are organizations whose purpose and activities are compatible with your own. Check any local directories of nonprofit organizations that are available (your local library will usually have such directories in its collection, perhaps in a community services section). Contact local citywide consortium-styled associations that operate in your area of interest, such as the United Way, arts councils, health and welfare planning bodies, federations, and so on. Speak to their directors or public information officers and elicit their suggestions for possible sponsors. Also check national organizational reference books like the *Encyclopedia of Associations* for other potential candidates. Don't hesitate to include institutions you may consider too large or formidable. When deciding on a fiscal sponsor, consider the following:

1. Be sure the potential nonprofit sponsor has goals that are compatible with your project's mission.

2. Check out the potential nonprofit sponsor's administrative capabilities, especially in fiscal matters and grants management.

3. Be sure the nonprofit has a strong record of accomplishment in fundraising.

After deciding on a nonprofit sponsor, be sure to draw up a letter of agreement setting out your mutually-agreed-upon terms, to be signed by both parties. In the case of the nonprofit, this signature should come from the chair or president of the non- profit's board of directors as the board serves as the fiscal arm for any nonprofit organization.

In this agreement, certain terms and conditions must be spelled out: i.e., the exact percentage or amount you will be donating to the nonprofit sponsor to cover bookkeeping and administrative costs; when the nonprofit will deduct this sum from the overall award; the anticipated time frame for the pass–through of monies from the funder to the nonprofit to you; details regarding specifics on how the money will be received (i.e., directly into the nonprofit's bank account or a specially designated "new account"); and, how the money will be paid to you.

As part of this agreement, the sponsor should agree to provide any and all documents needed in order for you to make a successful grant application, including proof of their current nonprofit, tax–exempt status, a list of their board of directors, their mission statement, audited financial statements, and overall operating budget. If the sponsoring organization agrees to help you in other ways, such as having major supporters of their organization provide you with letters of support—this should be spelled out as part of your agreement, along with the fact that the nonprofit can collaborate with you directly on all application documents and has the right of approval on whatever you submit. As it is the nonprofit's responsibility to keep fiscal records according to the requirements of the federal funding program or agency, this must also be part of any agreement. Any additional responsibilities on your part must also be described in as much detail as possible, such as providing documentation of the success of your proposed project or endeavor, xeroxes of receipts for monies spent, and so forth.

In many states it is possible to have this agreement drawn up on a pro bono basis under the expert eye of a nonprofit attorney or attorneys. Check *Foundation Fundamentals* (published by The Foundation Center, New York) or other reference guides to find out about tracking down individual attorneys or consortiums of nonprofit attorneys providing pro bono assistance in you state and/or specific area.

HOW TO WRITE A PROPOSAL

Once you have identified which government departments are likely prospects for support, your next step is to contact them directly. Request any information that they make available to prospective applicants, including the application form and instruction booklet. (You may apply for more than one grant. However, as federal grants are much more complicated and labor-intensive than private foundation or corporate grants, I would not recommend applying for more than two or three grants.) In addition, try to identify the contact person at the funding program you are applying for. After you receive information about the program and determine that you are eligible for funding from this particular program, try to speak with the contact person, or if that is not possible, write to the contact person. Ask what the government official's agency is looking for in proposals or applications. Are there particular types of projects it wants? Don't hesitate to ask questions about completing the application. The government does not expect you to be totally knowledgeable in government grantsmanship.

Most government funding boards make available application forms or formats for proposals. The proposal or the application is a very important document, for it is your opportunity to demonstrate who you are, what you hope to accomplish, and how you are especially qualified to work toward the objectives that you have set forth. Again, if you have any questions that arise while you are preparing your written materials, speak or write to the government official you have previously contacted.

Begin your proposal with a title page. This should include:

—the amount requested
—the name of the funding agency
—the purpose of the grant
—a short descriptive title
—the time frame of the project

—your full name and affiliation, if any
—your address and phone number
—the date of submission
—the name of your institutional fiscal sponsor, if relevant.

The title page should be followed by a clear and precise statement of purpose. Your statement of purpose should answer the following three questions:

1. What do you hope to accomplish?

2. How do you plan to accomplish your goals? (What activities, programs, or services will you undertake to accomplish your goals? Would you characterize these efforts as service related, advocacy focused, or public education related?)

3. For whose benefit will your project function? (How specifically can you define your prime constituents by age, sex, geography, minority–group status, or income?)

The proposal should always include an evaluation section, briefly outlining how you intend to show that the proposed results were achieved.

The budget reflects the cost of the project in detail. It should be justified in relation to the tasks. Job descriptions of all staff should be presented, with a description of the overall organizational structure.

The budget section is followed by a section called the capability of the contractor. This section documents the reasons why you and, if appropriate, your fiscal sponsor are in a strong position to conduct this project. Your resume, resources, and letters of support should be included with this section.

Frequently government grant proposals are lengthier than foundation and corporate proposals, because of the detail required. Detail does not mean verbosity; rather, clarity and succinct prose are in order.

Be sure to observe grant deadlines. Like tax returns, they require close adherence.

The Yes

You have been awarded a grant. Congratulations! As you will be receiving public tax dollars, make sure you understand all the financial reporting requirements that accompany your award. You may also want to clarify when you will receive your funds. Given the red tape inherent in any bureaucracy, you may have to wait a number of months before you actually receive monies, so plan accordingly.

The No

Don't despair. Inquire why your proposal was rejected and, if possible, ask the contact person for a specific reason. Find out what were the strengths of your proposal and what were its weaknesses. Ask how you can submit an application the next time around that addresses the issues that have been raised during your discussion with the government official. You can always apply again. Persistence will be your best ally as long as any subsequent application demonstrates that you have dealt with the concerns that prompted the first rejection.

Be sure that you have been added to the mailing list of the targeted agency to receive future requests for proposals and any other information that they periodically make available to prospective applicants. Thank the official with whom you have been in touch for his or her time and help.

Remember, do not apply for government grants unless you are willing to play the game by the funders' rules. You must have a certain tolerance for frustration and a willingness to confront red tape. Patience is an absolute necessity to government grant seekers.

Successful Proposal Sample

Individual Grant Application
National Endowment for the Arts

Applications must be submitted in triplicate and mailed with other required materials to the address indicated under "Application Procedures" for your category.

Visual Arts Program
Category under which support is requested:
COLLABORATIVE PROJECTS

Name (last, first, middle initial)

Brown, Joseph

U.S. Citizenship
Yes X   No   Visa Number_____

Present mailing address/phone

123 Main Street
New York, N.Y. 12345

(212) 555–1111

Professional field or discipline
Artist, Preparator (see background)

Birth Date   **Place of Birth**
1–1–53   *Raleigh, N.C.*

Permanent mailing address/phone

123 Main Street
New York, N.Y. 12345

(212) 555–1111

Period of support requested

Starting   October 1, 1991
                  month day year

Ending   October 1, 1992
                  month day year

Career summary or background

Matthew Smith and Joseph Brown met while undergraduates at New York University in 1972. Their past collaborations include "REAPER–CUSSION," a musical performance for the Todd Ensemble at the Picasso Art Gallery in Rochester, N.Y., in June 1990, and, most recently, "Hyper–Space," a performance and installation at the Rosen–Fox Gallery in Buffalo, N.Y., in September 1990.

Matthew Smith is currently teaching drawing and painting at the State University of New York at Buffalo and is preparing for the "Albright–Knox Invitational" this March. Please see attached resume.

Joseph Brown is working as a full–time artist and is a preparator at the West Museum in New York City. Please see attached resume.

Amount requested from National Endowment for the Arts: $5,000.

Education

Name of institution	Major area of study	Inclusive dates	Degree
New York University	Drawing/printmaking	1972–1976	BFA
Yale University	Drawing/sculpture	1976–1978	MFA

Fellowships or grants previously awarded

Name of award	Area of study	Inclusive dates	Amount

Present employment

Employer	Position/Occupation	Total income last calendar year
West Museum	Preparator, installationist	$7200.00

Prizes/Honors received

Permanent collection–Missouri Art
  Center, 1977
Mural–World Trade Center–Observation
  Deck, 1979

Membership professional societies

Description of proposed activity

(Do not complete this section if you are applying for an Artists', Craftsmen's or Photographers' Fellowship)

The goal of our collaboration is to produce a lively and harmonious relationship between the organic and inorganic aspects of our natural world.

Matthew Smith has created a series of drawings and musical pieces that express the atomic structure of four elements taken from the Periodic Table of Elements (which is a mathematical inventory of the natural elements). The series is enhanced by the clean technical feel of the drawings and the "architectural" feel of the music, achieved by using a Moog synthesizer and an electric piano in the building and reduction of tones.

Conversely, Andrew Franklin's work projects the earthy textural resonance of animals as they interact among themselves.

The collaboration will involve the building of a scale environment (details are attached to the slide sheet). Through music, abstract depiction of animals will "interact" in the environment. The music will blend electronically synthesized sound with live recordings of animals, previously recorded on site in the Peruvian jungles. The drawings will be developed using the same methods as Matthew Smith's earlier works (using the Periodic Tables), by systematically scoring the pieces using the animals' spatial placement. The result will be a euphonious conversation between the living and non–living world.

The interdisciplinary focus of the proposed installation will be amplified through the use of drawings, sculpture and sound. The result will be a completely enveloping and engrossing environment.

Certification: I certify that the foregoing statements are true and complete to the best of my knowledge.

Signature of applicant _____ **Date**_____

Alphabetical Index

A

Abandoned Infants Project Grants 143

Adolescent Family Life Demonstration Project
Grants 143

Adolescent Family Life Research Grants 54

Adoption Opportunities Project Grants 143

Advanced Nurse Education 86

Advanced Technology Program Project Grants 22

Aging Research Career Development Awards 95

Aging Research Clinical Investigator Development Award
95

Aging Research National Service Awards 95

Aging Research Project Grants 74

Aging Research Small Business Innovation Research
Grants 9

Aging Research Small Instrumentation Grants 9

Agricultural Research Grant 43

AIDS Activity Project Grant 52

AIDS Education and Training Centers 52

Air Pollution Control Research 44

Airport Improvement Program 153

Alaska Sport Fish and Wildlife Restoration Formula
Grant 186

Alcohol and Drug Abuse Clinical Training Program
Grants 60

Alcohol and Drug Abuse Research and Services
Block Grant to California 191

Alcohol and Drug Abuse Research and Services
Block Grant to Colorado 191

Alcohol and Drug Abuse Research and Services
Block Grant to Georgia 191

Alcohol and Drug Abuse Research and Services
Block Grant to Illinois 191

Alcohol and Drug Abuse Research and Services
Block Grant to Massachusetts 192

Alcohol and Drug Abuse Research and Services
Block Grant to Missouri 192

Alcohol and Drug Abuse Research and Services
Block Grant to New York 192

Alcohol and Drug Abuse Research and Services
Block Grant to Pennsylvania 192

Alcohol and Drug Abuse Research and Services
Block Grant to Texas 193

Alcohol and Drug Abuse Research and Services
Block Grant to Washington 193

Alcohol National Research Service Awards for
Research Training 96

Alcohol Research Center Project Grants 75

Alcohol Research Programs 75

Alcohol Scientist Development Award for Clinicians . 96

Allergy, Immunology, and Transplantation Clinical
Investigator Development Award 96

Allergy, Immunology, and Transplantation National
Research Service Awards 97

Allergy, Immunology, and Transplantation Research .. 76

Allergy, Immunology, and Transplantation Research
Career Development Awards 96

Allergy, Immunology, and Transplantation Research
Small Business Innovation Research Grants 10

Allergy, Immunology, and Transplantation Research
Small Instrumentation Grants 10

Allied Health Project Grants 87

Anadromous Fish Conservation 48

Anadromous and Great Lake Fisheries Conservation
Project Grant 48

Animal Damage Control Project Grant 43

Anterior Segment Diseases Clinical Investigator
Development Award 97

Anterior Segment Diseases National Research
Service Awards 97

Anterior Segment Diseases Research 76

Anterior Segment Diseases Research Career
Development Awards 97

Anterior Segment Diseases Research Small Business
Innovation Research Grants 10

Anterior Segment Diseases Research Small
Instrumentation Grants 10

Appalachian Child Development 144

Appalachian Community Development Project
Grants 7

Appalachian Health Programs 55

*Indicates grants for which fiscal sponsorship is required.

Appalachian Housing Project Development Grants 7

Appalachian Local Access Roads 7

Applied Methods in Surveillance Projects 57

Applied Toxicological Research and Testing
Academic Awards 121

Applied Toxicological Research and Testing
Career Development Awards 122

Applied Toxicological Research and Testing
Mid-Career Development Awards 122

Applied Toxicological Research and Testing
Physician–Scientist Awards 122

Applied Toxicological Research and Testing
Research Grants 133

Applied Toxicological Research and Testing
Small Business Project Grants 133

Applied Toxicological Research and Testing
Small Instrumentation Grants 134

Arthritis, Musculoskeletal, and Skin Diseases
Clinical Investigator Development Award 98

Arthritis, Musculoskeletal, and Skin Diseases
National Research Service Awards 98

Arthritis, Musculoskeletal, and Skin Diseases
Research 76

Arthritis, Musculoskeletal, and Skin Diseases
Research Career Development Awards 98

Arthritis, Musculoskeletal, and Skin Diseases
Research Small Business Innovation Research
Grants 11

Arthritis, Musculoskeletal, and Skin Diseases
Research Small Instrumentation Grants 11

Arts Administration Fellows Program 86

Arts in Education Project Grants 26

Assistance Payments Research Project Grants 142

Atmospheric Sciences Project Grants 138

B

Behavioral Science Project Grants 137

Bicentennial Educational Grant Program 90

Bilingual Education 26

Bilingual Education Support Services 26

Bilingual Education Training Fellowships 91

Bilingual Education Training Grants 27

Bilingual Vocational Instructor Training 37

Bilingual Vocational Materials, Methods,
and Techniques 37

Bilingual Vocational Training 37

Biofuels and Municipal Waste Technology Project
Grants 50

Biological Basis Research in the Neurosciences 76

Biological Models and Material Resources 77

Biological Neurological Disorders Career
Development Awards 98

Biological Neurological Disorders Clinical
Investigator Development Awards 99

Biological Neurological Disorders National Research Service Awards 99

Biological Research Related to Deafness and
Communicative Disorders 77

Biological Response to Environmental Health
Hazards Academic Awards 122

Biological Response to Environmental Health
Hazards Mid–Career Development Awards 123

Biological Response to Environmental Health
Hazards Physician–Scientist Awards 123

Biological Response to Environmental Health
Hazards Research Career Development Awards ... 123

Biological Response to Environmental Health
Hazards Research Grants 73

Biological Response to Environmental Health
Hazards Small Business Project Grants 73

Biological Response to Environmental Health
Hazards Small Instrumentation Program 73

Biological Science Project Grants 138

Biomedical Research – Minority High School
Student Research Apprentice Grants 74

Biomedical Research – NIH Research Awards 99

Biomedical Research Support Grants 77

Biometry and Risk Estimation Academic Awards 134

Biometry and Risk Estimation Career Development
Awards 134

Biometry and Risk Estimation Mid–Career
Development Awards 134

Biometry and Risk Estimation Physician–
Scientist Awards 135

Biometry and Risk Estimation Research Grants 135

Biometry and Risk Estimation Small Business Project
Grants 137

Biometry and Risk Estimation Small Instrumentation
    Grants 135

Biophysics National Research Service Award 99

Biophysics and Physiological Sciences Project Grants .. 77

Biophysics Research Small Business Innovation
    Research Grant 11

Biophysics Small Instrumentation Grant 11

Black Lung Clinics Project Grants 62

Blood Diseases Career Development Awards 100

Blood Diseases Clinical Investigator Development
    Award 100

Blood Diseases National Research Service Awards ... 100

Blood Diseases Research – Small Business Innovation
    Research Grants 12

Blood Diseases Research – Small Instrumentation
    Grants 12

Blood Diseases and Resources Research 78

Boating Safety Financial Assistance 153

Business and International Education 27

C

Cancer Biology Research 78

Cancer Biology Research – Small Instrumentation
    Program 12

Cancer Biology – Small Business Innovation Research
    Grants 12

Cancer Cause and Prevention Research 78

Cancer Cause and Prevention – Small Business
    Innovation Research Grants 13

Cancer Centers Support – Small Instrumentation
    Program 13

Cancer Control 78

Cancer Control – Controlled Intervention 79

Cancer Control – Defined Populations Research 79

Cancer Control – Demonstration and Implementation
    Grants 79

Cancer Control – Methods Development and Testing . 13

Cancer Control – Small Instrumentation Program 13

Cancer Detection and Diagnosis Research 79

Cancer Detection and Diagnosis – Small Business
    Innovation Research Grants 14

Cancer Detection and Diagnosis – Small
    Instrumentation Program 14

Cancer Research Manpower – Cancer Education
    Grants 100

Cancer Research Manpower – Cancer Education
    Program for Short–Term Support 101

Cancer Research Manpower – NRSA Individual
    Fellowship Awards 101

Cancer Treatment Research 80

Cancer Treatment Research – Small Business
    Innovation Research Grants 14

Cancer Treatment Research – Small Instrumentation Pro-
    gram 14

Capital Assistance for Elderly and Handicapped
    Persons 141

Capital Construction Fund 23

Cellular and Molecular Basis for Disease
    Clinical Investigator Development Award 101

Cellular and Molecular Basis for Disease
    National Research Service Awards 102

Cellular and Molecular Basis for Disease Research ... 80

Cellular and Molecular Basis for Disease Research
    Career Development Awards 101

Cellular and Molecular Basis for Disease Research
    Small Business Innovation Research Grants 15

Cellular and Molecular Basis for Disease Research
    Small Instrumentation Grants 15

Centers for Disease Control – Research Program
    Grants 80

Centers for Independent Living 153

Centers for International Business Education 27

Challenge Grants in the Arts 5

Characterization of Environmental Health Hazards –
    Small Business Projects 45

Characterization of Environmental Health Hazards –
    New Research 46

Child Abuse and Neglect Discretionary Activities ... 144

Child Support Enforcement Research Project Grants 144

Child Welfare Research and Demonstration Project
    Grants 144

Child Welfare Services Training Grants 145

Christa McAuliffe Fellowships 126

Clearinghouses for the Handicapped Project Grants .. 28

Clean Coal Scientific Research Technology Program
for Alabama 194

Clean Coal Scientific Research Technology Program
for Alaska 194

Clean Coal Scientific Research Technology Program
for Arizona 194

Clean Coal Scientific Research Technology Program
for Arkansas 194

Clean Coal Scientific Research Technology Program
for California 195

Clean Coal Scientific Research Technology Program
for Colorado 195

Clean Coal Scientific Research Technology Program
for Connecticut 195

Clean Coal Scientific Research Technology Program
for Delaware 195

Clean Coal Scientific Research Technology Program
for Florida 196

Clean Coal Scientific Research Technology Program
for Georgia 196

Clean Coal Scientific Research Technology Program
for Hawaii 196

Clean Coal Scientific Research Technology Program
for Idaho 196

Clean Coal Scientific Research Technology Program
for Illinois 197

Clean Coal Scientific Research Technology Program
for Indiana 197

Clean Coal Scientific Research Technology Program
for Iowa 197

Clean Coal Scientific Research Technology Program
for Kansas 197

Clean Coal Scientific Research Technology Program
for Kentucky 198

Clean Coal Scientific Research Technology Program
for Louisiana 198

Clean Coal Scientific Research Technology Program
for Maine 198

Clean Coal Scientific Research Technology Program
for Maryland 198

Clean Coal Scientific Research Technology Program
for Massachusetts 199

Clean Coal Scientific Research Technology Program
for Michigan 199

Clean Coal Scientific Research Technology Program
for Minnesota 199

Clean Coal Scientific Research Technology Program
for Mississippi 199

Clean Coal Scientific Research Technology Program
for Missouri 200

Clean Coal Scientific Research Technology Program
for Montana 200

Clean Coal Scientific Research Technology Program
for Nebraska 200

Clean Coal Scientific Research Technology Program
for Nevada 200

Clean Coal Scientific Research Technology Program
for New Hampshire 201

Clean Coal Scientific Research Technology Program
for New Jersey 201

Clean Coal Scientific Research Technology Program
for New Mexico 201

Clean Coal Scientific Research Technology Program
for New York 201

Clean Coal Scientific Research Technology Program
for North Carolina 202

Clean Coal Scientific Research Technology Program
for North Dakota 202

Clean Coal Scientific Research Technology Program
for Ohio 202

Clean Coal Scientific Research Technology Program
for Oklahoma 202

Clean Coal Scientific Research Technology Program
for Oregon 203

Clean Coal Scientific Research Technology Program
for Pennsylvania 203

Clean Coal Scientific Research Technology Program
for Rhode Island 203

Clean Coal Scientific Research Technology Program
for South Carolina 203

Clean Coal Scientific Research Technology Program
for South Dakota 204

Clean Coal Scientific Research Technology Program
for Tennessee 204

Clean Coal Scientific Research Technology Program
for Texas 204

Clean Coal Scientific Research Technology Program
for Utah 204

Clean Coal Scientific Research Technology Program
for Vermont 205

Clean Coal Scientific Research Technology Program
for Virginia 205

Clean Coal Scientific Research Technology Program
for Washington 205

Clean Coal Scientific Research Technology Program
for West Virginia 205

Clean Coal Scientific Research Technology Program
for Wisconsin 206

Clean Coal Scientific Research Technology Program
for Wyoming 206

Climate and Atmospheric Research 44

Clinical Neurological Disorders National Service
Award 102

Clinical Neurological Disorders Research Career
Development Awards 102

Clinical Research Related to Neurological Disorders .. 80

College–Community Forums on the U.S. Constitution   71

College Library Technology Combination Grants 66

College Library Technology Networking Grants 66

College Library Technology Research and
Demonstration Grants 66

College Library Technology Services Grants 66

Colorado Sport Fish and Wildlife Restoration
Formula Grant 186

Communications Program Aimed Toward the
Prevention of Alcohol and Other Drug Problems ... 152

Community–Based Anti–Arson Program 153

Community–Based Injury Control Projects 58

Community Demonstration Grant Projects for
Alcohol and Drug Abuse – Treatment
of Homeless Individuals 55

Community Development Work–Study Program
Project Grants 125

Community Health Centers Project Grants 62

Competitive Agricultural Research Grants 43

Comprehensive Child Development Centers 145

Computer and Information Science
and Engineering 138

Conservation Research and Development 130

Construction Reserve Fund 23

Cooperative Agreements for Research
in Public Lands Management Project Grants 43

Cooperative Education Project Grants 39

Corrections Research, Evaluation, and Policy
Formation 150

Corrections – Technical Assistance Clearinghouse ... 151

Corrections Training and Staff Development 151

Crime Victim Assistance Discretionary Grants 146

Criminal Justice Discretionary Grant Program 126

Criminal Justice Research and Development
Fellowships 126

Cuban and Haitian Resettlement Program 154

D

Dance Project Grants 1

Dance Project Grants 1

Demonstration Centers for the Retraining
of Displaced Workers 33

Desegregation Assistance, Civil Rights Training,
and Advisory Services 34

Design Arts Project Grants 1

Design Arts Project Grants 1

Development Assistance Program Project Grants 8

Development and Promotion of Ports and Intermodal
Transportation 23

Developmental Disability Projects of National
Significance 57

Diabetes, Endocrinology, and Metabolism Clinical
Investigator Development Award 103

Diabetes, Endocrinology, and Metabolism National
Research Service Awards 103

Diabetes, Endocrinology, and Metabolism Research .. 81

Diabetes, Endocrinology, and Metabolism Research
Career Development Awards 102

Diabetes, Endocrinology, and Metabolism Research Small
Business Innovation Research Grants 15

Diabetes, Endocrinology, and Metabolism Research Small
Instrumentation Grants 15

Digestive Diseases and Nutrition Career
Development Awards 103

Digestive Diseases and Nutrition Clinical
Investigator Development Award 103

Digestive Diseases and Nutrition National Research
Service Awards 104

Digestive Diseases and Nutrition Research 81

Digestive Diseases and Nutrition Research Small
Business Innovation Research Grants 16

Digestive Diseases and Nutrition Research Small
Instrumentation Grants 16

Disabilities Prevention Project Grants 57

Disabled Veterans Outreach Program for Alabama . . 170

Disabled Veterans Outreach Program for Alaska 170

Disabled Veterans Outreach Program for Arizona . . . 170

Disabled Veterans Outreach Program for Arkansas . . 170

Disabled Veterans Outreach Program for California . 171

Disabled Veterans Outreach Program for Colorado . . 171

Disabled Veterans Outreach Program for Connect-
icut 171

Disabled Veterans Outreach Program for Delaware . . 171

Disabled Veterans Outreach Program for Florida 172

Disabled Veterans Outreach Program for Georgia . . . 172

Disabled Veterans Outreach Program for Hawaii 172

Disabled Veterans Outreach Program for Idaho 172

Disabled Veterans Outreach Program for Illinois 173

Disabled Veterans Outreach Program for Indiana 173

Disabled Veterans Outreach Program for Iowa 173

Disabled Veterans Outreach Program for Kansas 173

Disabled Veterans Outreach Program for Kentucky . . 174

Disabled Veterans Outreach Program for Louisiana . . 174

Disabled Veterans Outreach Program for Maine 174

Disabled Veterans Outreach Program for Maryland . . 174

Disabled Veterans Outreach Program for Massa-
chusetts 175

Disabled Veterans Outreach Program for Michigan . . 175

Disabled Veterans Outreach Program for Minnesota . 175

Disabled Veterans Outreach Program for Mississippi . 175

Disabled Veterans Outreach Program for Missouri . . . 176

Disabled Veterans Outreach Program for Montana . . 176

Disabled Veterans Outreach Program for Nebraska . . 176

Disabled Veterans Outreach Program for Nevada 176

Disabled Veterans Outreach Program for New
Hampshire 177

Disabled Veterans Outreach Program for New
Jersey 177

Disabled Veterans Outreach Program for New
Mexico 177

Disabled Veterans Outreach Program for New
York 177

Disabled Veterans Outreach Program for North
Carolina 178

Disabled Veterans Outreach Program for North
Dakota 178

Disabled Veterans Outreach Program for Ohio 178

Disabled Veterans Outreach Program for Oklahoma . 178

Disabled Veterans Outreach Program for Oregon . . . 179

Disabled Veterans Outreach Program for Penn-
sylvania 179

Disabled Veterans Outreach Program for Rhode
Island 179

Disabled Veterans Outreach Program for South
Carolina 179

Disabled Veterans Outreach Program for South
Dakota 180

Disabled Veterans Outreach Program for Tennessee . 180

Disabled Veterans Outreach Program for Texas 180

Disabled Veterans Outreach Program for Utah 180

Disabled Veterans Outreach Program for Vermont . . 181

Disabled Veterans Outreach Program for Virginia . . . 181

Disabled Veterans Outreach Program for Washington 181

Disabled Veterans Outreach Program for West
Virginia 181

Disabled Veterans Outreach Program for Wisconsin . 182

Disabled Veterans Outreach Program for Wyoming . . 182

Disaster Assistance Project Grants and Payments 154

Diseases of the Teeth and Supporting Tissue 81

Disorders of the Craniofacial Structure and
Function and Behavioral Aspects of Dentistry 81

Distinguished Designer Fellowships 86

Drug Abuse Clinician Development Award 104

Drug Abuse National Research Service Awards 104

Drug Abuse National Research Service Awards –
Institutional Grants 104

Drug Abuse National Research Service Awards –
Postdoctoral Stipends 105

Drug Abuse National Research Service Awards – Predoctoral Stipends 105

Drug Abuse Prevention and Education Relating to Youth Gangs 151

Drug Abuse Prevention and Education for Runaway and Homeless Youth 145

Drug Abuse Research Programs 75

Drug Abuse Research Scientist Award 105

Drug Abuse Scientist Development Award 105

Drug Abuse Treatment Waiting List Reduction Grants 60

Drug and Alcohol Abuse Prevention Project Grant ... 61

Drug Alliance Project Grants 152

Drug Control and System Improvement 152

Drug-Free Schools and Communities – Regional Centers 36

E

Early Education Program for the Handicapped 28

Earth Sciences Project Grants 139

Educational Leadership Development 39

Educational Opportunity Centers 25

Educational Partnerships 27

Educational Program for Severely Handicapped Children 28

Educational Research and Development 39

Elementary and Secondary Programs in the Humanities 64

Elementary and Secondary Programs in the Humanities Masterwork Study Grants 64

Emergency Management Institute 125

Employee Assistance Program for Drug and Alcohol Abuse 152

Employment Services and Job Training Pilot and Demonstration Programs 149

Employment and Training Research and Development Projects 150

Energy and Field Operations Research in Energy and Related Fields 130

Energy Policy, Planning, and Development Project Grants 130

Energy-Related Inventions Project Grants 131

Engineering Grants 139

English Literacy Program 25

Environmental Health Hazards Mid-Career Development Award 124

Environmental Health Hazards Physician-Scientist Award 124

Environmental Health Hazards Research Career Development Award 123

Environmental Protection Research Project Grants ... 46

Environmental Restoration Project Grants 46

Environmental Toxicology Project Grants 46

Even Start Local Education Project Grants 25

Expansion Arts Project Grants 3

F

Fair Housing Education Initiatives Program 147

Fair Housing Private Enforcement Initiative Program 148

Family Planning Services Project Grants 62

Family Violence Prevention and Services Discretionary Grants 154

Fellowships for College Teachers and Independent Scholars 91

Fellowships for Native Americans 117

Film, Radio, and Television Project Grants 2

Film, Radio, and Television Project Grants 2

Financial Assistance for Disadvantaged Health Professions Students 118

First Schools and Teachers Project Grants 39

Fisheries Research and Development Project Grants . 45

Folk Arts Project Grants 2

Folk Arts Project Grants 2

Follow-Through Project Grants 34

Food and Drug Administration Research Project Grant 62

Fossil Energy Research and Development Project Grants 131

Foster Grandparent Program Project Grants 141

Fulbright-Hays Doctoral Dissertation Research Abroad 93

Fulbright–Hays Faculty Research Abroad Training
  Grants 93

Fulbright–Hays Group Projects Abroad 94

Fulbright–Hays Seminars Abroad 32

Fund for the Improvement of Postsecondary
  Education 32

G

General Research and Technology Activity 154

Genetics Research Career Development Awards 106

Genetics Research Clinical Investigator Development
  Award 106

Genetics Research National Research Service
  Awards 106

Genetics Research Project Grants 82

Genetics Research Small Business Innovation
  Research Grants 16

Genetics Research Small Instrumentation Grants 16

Georgia Sport Fish and Wildlife Restoration
  Formula Grant 186

Geriatrics Health Professions Training Grant 87

Graduate Assistance in Areas of National Need 126

Graduate Programs in Health Administration 87

Graduate Research Fellowships 124

Graduate Student Educational Exchange 94

Grants for Faculty Development in Family Medicine . 106

Grants for Faculty Development in General Internal
  Medicine and/or Pediatrics 107

Grants for Faculty Training Projects in Geriatric
  Medicine and Dentistry 107

Grants for Graduate Training in Family Medicine 87

Grants for Mining and Mineral Resources 127

Grants for Residency Training in General Internal
  Medicine and/or General Pediatrics 88

H

Handicapped Regional Resource Centers 28

Handicapped Special Studies 29

Harry S. Truman Scholarship Program 127

Health Administration Graduate Traineeships 88

Health Care Financing Research Project Grants 142

Health Careers Opportunity Program 118

Health Services Delivery to Persons with AIDS
  Demonstration Grants 52

Health Services in the Pacific Basin 56

Health Services Research and Development Grants .. 52

Heart and Vascular Diseases Career Development
  Awards 107

Heart and Vascular Diseases Clinical Investigator
  Development Award 107

Heart and Vascular Diseases National Research
  Service Awards 108

Heart and Vascular Diseases Research 82

Heart and Vascular Diseases Research Small
  Business Innovation Research Grants 17

Heart and Vascular Diseases Research Small
  Instrumentation Grants 17

Higher Education in the Humanities 64

Historic Preservation Fund Grants–in–Aid 71

Housing Counseling Assistance Program Project
  Grants 148

Human Genome Research Project Grant 82

Human Resource Programs 8

Humanities Challenge Grants 71

Humanities Conference Project Grants 71

Humanities Preservation Project Grants 67

Humanities Projects in Libraries and Archives 67

Humanities Projects in Media 70

Humanities Projects in Museums and Historical
  Associations 67

Humanities Text and Publications Project Grants 70

I

Immunization Research Project Grants 82

Indian Health Service Educational Loan Repayment .. 88

Indian Health Service Health Promotion and Disease Prevention Demonstration Projects 56

Industrial Energy Conservation Project Grants 131

Injury Prevention and Control Research Projects 58

Injury Prevention Research Centers 58

Institute of Museum Services Conservation Projects . . 67

Integrated Community–Based Primary Care and
   Drug Abuse Treatment Services Project Grant 53

Inter–Arts Project Grants 6

Intergovernmental Climate Program Grant 45

International Affairs and Energy Emergencies 131

International Peace and Conflict Management 65

International Peace and Conflict Management
   Articles and Manuscripts 65

International Research Project Grants 65

International Research and Studies 33

Interpretive Research in the Humanities, Science,
   and Technology 72

Interpretive Research and Projects in the Humanities . 72

Intramural Research Training Award 108

J

Jacob K. Javits Fellowships 91

Jacob K. Javits Gifted and Talented Students Project
   Grants 31

Job Training Partnership for Alabama 207

Job Training Partnership for Alaska 207

Job Training Partnership for Arizona 207

Job Training Partnership for Arkansas 207

Job Training Partnership for California 208

Job Training Partnership for Colorado 208

Job Training Partnership for Connecticut 208

Job Training Partnership for Delaware 208

Job Training Partnership for Florida 209

Job Training Partnership for Georgia 209

Job Training Partnership for Hawaii 209

Job Training Partnership for Idaho 209

Job Training Partnership for Illinois 210

Job Training Partnership for Indiana 210

Job Training Partnership for Iowa 210

Job Training Partnership for Kansas 210

Job Training Partnership for Kentucky 211

Job Training Partnership for Louisiana 211

Job Training Partnership for Maine 211

Job Training Partnership for Maryland 211

Job Training Partnership for Massachusetts 212

Job Training Partnership for Michigan 212

Job Training Partnership for Minnesota 212

Job Training Partnership for Mississippi 212

Job Training Partnership for Missouri 213

Job Training Partnership for Montana 213

Job Training Partnership for Nebraska 213

Job Training Partnership for Nevada 213

Job Training Partnership for New Hampshire 214

Job Training Partnership for New Jersey 214

Job Training Partnership for New Mexico 214

Job Training Partnership for New York 214

Job Training Partnership for North Carolina 215

Job Training Partnership for North Dakota 215

Job Training Partnership for Ohio 215

Job Training Partnership for Oklahoma 215

Job Training Partnership for Oregon 216

Job Training Partnership for Pennsylvania 216

Job Training Partnership for Rhode Island 216

Job Training Partnership for South Carolina 216

Job Training Partnership for South Dakota 217

Job Training Partnership for Tennessee 217

Job Training Partnership for Texas 217

Job Training Partnership for Utah 217

Job Training Partnership for Vermont 218

Job Training Partnership for Virginia 218

Job Training Partnership for Washington 218

Job Training Partnership for West Virginia 218

Job Training Partnership for Wisconsin 219

Job Training Partnership for Wyoming 219

Justice Research and Development Project Grants . . 146

Juvenile Gangs and Drug Abuse and Drug
   Trafficking 147

Juvenile Justice and Delinquency Prevention
   Project Grants 147

K

Kidney Diseases, Urology, and Hematology Clinical Investigator Development Award 108

Kidney Diseases, Urology, and Hematology National Research Service Awards 109

Kidney Diseases, Urology, and Hematology Research . 83

Kidney Diseases, Urology, and Hematology Research Career Development Awards 108

Kidney Diseases, Urology, and Hematology Research Small Business Innovation Research Grants 17

Kidney Diseases, Urology, and Hematology Research Small Instrumentation Grants 17

L

Labor and Management Cooperation Project Grants . . 23

Laboratory Animal and Primate Research Fellowships 109

Laboratory Animal Sciences Project Grants 83

Language Resource Centers Project Grants 40

Law–Related Education 40

Law School Clinical Experience Program 32

Legal Training for the Disadvantaged 118

Library Career Fellowships 91

Library Career Training 92

Library Research and Demonstration Project Grants . . 68

Literature Fellowships 86

Literature Project Grants 3

Literature Project Grants 3

Long–Term Care Facilities Project Grant 53

Lower Income Housing Assistance Program 148

Lung Diseases Clinical Investigator Development Award 109

Lung Diseases National Research Service Awards . . . 110

Lung Diseases Research 83

Lung Diseases Research Career Development Awards 109

Lung Diseases Research Small Business Innovation Research Grants 18

Lung Diseases Research Small Instrumentation Grants 18

M

Maritime Operations Differential Subsidies 24

Massachusetts Sport Fish and Wildlife Restoration Formula Grant 186

Materials Development, Research, and Informal Science Education 35

Maternal Child and Health Federal Consolidated Programs Project Grant 54

Mathematical and Physical Sciences Research Grants 139

Mathematics and Science Education in California . . . 183

Mathematics and Science Education in Colorado 183

Mathematics and Science Education in Georgia 183

Mathematics and Science Education in Illinois 183

Mathematics and Science Education in Massachusetts 184

Mathematics and Science Education in Missouri 184

Mathematics and Science Education in New York . . . 184

Mathematics and Science Education in Pennsylvania . 184

Mathematics and Science Education in Texas 185

Mathematics and Science Education in Washington . . 185

Media Materials for the Handicapped 29

Medical Library Assistance Project Grants 75

Medical Library Assistance Scientific Publication Grants 74

Medical Treatment Effectiveness Research 83

Mental Health National Research Service Awards . . . 110

Mental Health National Research Service Awards for Research Training 110

Mental Health National Research Service Postdoctoral Stipends 111

Mental Health National Research Service Predoctoral Stipends 110

Mental Health Research Clinician Development Award 111

Mental Health Research Faculty Fellowships 111

Mental Health Research Scientist Development Award 111

Microbiology and Infectious Diseases Clinical Investigator Development Award 112

Lung Diseases Research Small Instrumentation Grants 18

Microbiology and Infectious Diseases National
Research Service Awards 112

Microbiology and Infectious Diseases Research 84

Microbiology and Infectious Diseases Research
Career Development Awards 112

Microbiology and Infectious Diseases Research
Small Business Innovation Research Grants 18

Microbiology and Infectious Diseases Research
Small Instrumentation Grants 18

Mid–Career Teacher Training 33

Migrant Education College Assistance Program 118

Migrant Education High School Equivalency
Program 34

Migrant Health Centers Grants 56

Migrant and Seasonal Farmworkers Project Grant ... 150

Minigrant Program 155

Minnesota Sport Fish and Wildlife Restoration
Formula Grant 187

Minority Access to Research Careers 119

Minority AIDS Education Prevention Grants 53

Minority Biomedical Research Support 74

Minority Business Development Centers 8

Minority Community Health Demonstration Projects –
AIDS 53

Minority Community Health Demonstration Projects –
Cancer 58

Minority Community Health Demonstration Projects –
Cardiovascular Disease and Stroke 59

Minority Community Health Demonstration Projects –
Diabetes 59

Minority Community Health Demonstration Projects –
Homicide, Suicide, and Injury 59

Minority Community Health Demonstration Projects –
Infant Mortality 55

Minority Community Health Demonstration Projects –
Substance Abuse 61

Minority Educational Institution Assistance 135

Minority Educational Institution Research Travel
Fund 132

Minority Honors Training and Industrial Assistance
Program 119

Minority Participation in Graduate Education 119

Minority Research and Teaching Program Grants 119

Minority Science Improvement 120

Missing Children's Assistance 145

Model Substance Abuse Prevention Projects
for Pregnant and Postpartum Women
and their Infants 61

Museum Project Grants 68

Museum Project Grants 68

Music Project Grants 3

Music Project Grants 4

N

National Adult Education Research 25

National Diffusion Network Development Grants 40

National Diffusion Network Dissemination Processes
Project Grant 40

National Diffusion Network Private School Facilitator
Project Grant 41

National Diffusion Network State Facilitators Project
Grants 41

National Estuary Program Project Grants 49

National Fire Academy Educational Program 125

National Fire Academy Training Assistance 125

National Health Promotion 63

National Health Service Corps Loan Repayment
Project Grant 88

National Health Service Corps Scholarship Program .. 89

National Historical Publications and Records Project
Grants 68

National Institute on Disability and Rehabilitation
Research Fellowships 127

National Institute on Disability and Rehabilitation
Research Project Grants 29

National Institute of Justice Visiting Fellowships 127

National Institute for Juvenile Justice
and Delinquency Prevention 147

National Program for Mathematics and Science
Education 41

National Research Service Awards 63

National Research Services Awards 112

National Resource Centers for Language and
International Studies 33

National Resource Fellowships for Language
   and International Studies 94

National School Volunteer Program 41

National Vocational Education Research 37

National Vocational Education Research 38

National Water Resources Research Program 49

NEH/Reader's Digest Teacher–Scholar Program 64

Nehemiah Housing Opportunity Grant Program 148

Neurological Disorders Biological Research Small
   Business Innovation Research Grants 19

Neurological Disorders Biological Research Small
   Instrumentation Grants 19

Neurological Disorders Clinical Investigator
   Development Awards 113

Neurological Disorders Clinical Research Small
   Business Innovation Research Grants 19

Neurological Disorders Clinical Research Small
   Instrumentation Grants 19

New Mexico Sport Fish and Wildlife Restoration
   Formula Grant 187

NIEHS Superfund Hazardous Substances
   Research and Education 47

Non–Acute Care Intermediate Facilities Project
   Grant 54

Nuclear Energy Policy, Planning, and Development . . 132

Nuclear Energy Process and Safety Information
   Project Grants 132

Nurse Practitioner and Nurse Midwife Education
   and Traineeships 89

Nurse Training Improvement Special Project Grants . . 89

Nursing Education Opportunities for Individuals
   from Disadvantaged Backgrounds 117

Nursing Education Opportunities for Individuals
   from Disadvantaged Backgrounds 120

Nursing Research Project Grants 63

O

Occupational Health and Safety Project Grants 155

Occupational Safety and Health Research Project
   Grants 59

Occupational Safety and Health Training Grants 60

Ocean Sciences Project Grants 139

Opera and Musical Theater Project Grants 4

Opera and Musical Theater Project Grants 4

Oregon Sport Fish and Wildlife Restoration
   Formula Grant 187

P

Patricia Roberts Harris Fellowships 120

Pediatric AIDS Health Care Demonstration
   Program 55

Pell Grant Program 128

Pesticides Control Research 47

Pharmacological Sciences Clinical Investigator
   Development Award 113

Pharmacological Sciences National Research Service
   Awards 114

Pharmacological Sciences Project Grants 84

Pharmacological Sciences Research Career
   Development Awards 113

Pharmacological Sciences Research Small Business
   Innovation Research Grants 20

Pharmacological Sciences Research Small
   Instrumentation Grants 20

Physician's Assistant Training Program Grants 89

Physiological Sciences National Research Service
   Award 114

Physiological Sciences Project Grants 84

Physiological Sciences Small Business Innovation
   Research Grant 20

Physiological Sciences Small Instrumentation Grant . . 20

Polar Programs Project Grants 140

Population Research 137

Population Research Career Development Awards . . 114

Population Research Clinical Investigator
   Development Award 114

Population Research National Research Service
   Awards 115

Population Research Small Business Innovation
   Research Grants 21

Population Research Small Instrumentation Grants . . . 21

Post–Baccalaureate Faculty Fellowships 113

Postsecondary Education for the Handicapped 29

Pre–Freshman Enrichment Project Grants 120

Primate Research Project Grants 84

Prison Capacity Discretionary Project Grants 151

Professional Nurse Traineeships 90

Project Grants for Health Services to the Homeless ... 56

Promotion of the Arts in Alabama 157

Promotion of the Arts in Alaska 157

Promotion of the Arts in Arizona 157

Promotion of the Arts in Arkansas 157

Promotion of the Arts in California 158

Promotion of the Arts in Colorado 158

Promotion of the Arts in Connecticut 158

Promotion of the Arts in Delaware 158

Promotion of the Arts in Florida 159

Promotion of the Arts in Georgia 159

Promotion of the Arts in Hawaii 159

Promotion of the Arts in Idaho 159

Promotion of the Arts in Illinois 160

Promotion of the Arts in Indiana 160

Promotion of the Arts in Iowa 160

Promotion of the Arts in Kansas 160

Promotion of the Arts in Kentucky 161

Promotion of the Arts in Louisiana 161

Promotion of the Arts in Maine 161

Promotion of the Arts in Maryland 161

Promotion of the Arts in Massachusetts 162

Promotion of the Arts in Michigan 162

Promotion of the Arts in Minnesota 162

Promotion of the Arts in Mississippi 162

Promotion of the Arts in Missouri 163

Promotion of the Arts in Montana 163

Promotion of the Arts in Nebraska 163

Promotion of the Arts in Nevada 163

Promotion of the Arts in New Hampshire 164

Promotion of the Arts in New Jersey 164

Promotion of the Arts in New Mexico 164

Promotion of the Arts in New York 164

Promotion of the Arts in North Carolina 165

Promotion of the Arts in North Dakota 165

Promotion of the Arts in Ohio 165

Promotion of the Arts in Oklahoma 165

Promotion of the Arts in Oregon 166

Promotion of the Arts in Pennsylvania 166

Promotion of the Arts in Rhode Island 166

Promotion of the Arts in South Carolina 166

Promotion of the Arts in South Dakota 167

Promotion of the Arts in Tennessee 167

Promotion of the Arts in Texas 167

Promotion of the Arts in Utah 167

Promotion of the Arts in Vermont 168

Promotion of the Arts in Virginia 168

Promotion of the Arts in Washington 168

Promotion of the Arts in West Virginia 168

Promotion of the Arts in Wisconsin 169

Promotion of the Arts in Wyoming 169

Protection and Advocacy for the Mentally Ill
in California 188

Protection and Advocacy for the Mentally Ill
in Colorado 188

Protection and Advocacy for the Mentally Ill
in Georgia 188

Protection and Advocacy for the Mentally Ill
in Illinois 188

Protection and Advocacy for the Mentally Ill
in Massachusetts 189

Protection and Advocacy for the Mentally Ill
in Missouri 189

Protection and Advocacy for the Mentally Ill
in New York 189

Protection and Advocacy for the Mentally Ill
in Pennsylvania 189

Protection and Advocacy for the Mentally Ill
in Texas 190

Protection and Advocacy for the Mentally Ill
in Washington 190

Public Health Traineeships 90

Public Humanities Project Grants 65

R

Reference Materials/Access Project Grants 69

Reference Materials/Tools Project Grants 69

Rehabilitation Mortgage Insurance 149

Rehabilitation Service Projects 30

Rehabilitation Training 38

Renewable Energy Research and Development 132

Research in Education for the Handicapped 30

Research and Evaluation Project Grant 8

Research Initiation and Improvement 136

Research for Mothers and Children 73

Research for Mothers and Children Clinical
   Investigator Development Award 115

Research for Mothers and Children National
   Research Service Awards 115

Research for Mothers and Children Research
   Career Development Awards 115

Research for Mothers and Children Small Business
   Innovation Research Grants 21

Research for Mothers and Children Small
   Instrumentation Grants 21

Research Scientist Development Award for
   Clinicians 116

Resource and Manpower Development in
   the Environmental Health Sciences 60

Retinal and Choroidal Diseases Clinical Investigator
   Development Award 116

Retinal and Choroidal Diseases National Research
   Service Awards 116

Retinal and Choroidal Diseases Research 85

Retinal and Choroidal Diseases Research Career
   Development Awards 116

Retinal and Choroidal Diseases Research Small
   Business Innovation Research Grants 22

Retinal and Choroidal Diseases Research Small
   Instrumentation Grants 22

Retired Senior Volunteer Program 141

Ronald E. McNair Post–Baccalaureate Achievement
   Awards 121

Runaway and Homeless Youth Project Grants 146

Rural Health Resource Centers 57

S

Safe Drinking Water Research and Demonstration
   Project Grant 49

Scholarships for Students of Exceptional Financial
   Need 121

Scholarships for the Undergraduate Education
   of Professional Nurses 90

School Dropout Demonstration Assistance 42

School Personnel Training 36

Science and Engineering Research Semester 124

Scientific, Technological, and International Affairs .. 130

Sea Grant Support 49

Secondary Education and Transitional Services for
   Handicapped Youth 30

The Secretary's Fund for Innovation in Education 42

Selected Areas of Humanities Promotion 72

Senior Community Service Employment Program ... 141

Senior Companion Program 142

Senior Environmental Employment Program 45

Senior International Fellowships 117

Service Corps of Retired Executives (SCORE)
   Project Grants 24

Services for Deaf–Blind Children and Youth 30

Services Delivery Improvement Research Grants
   for Family Planning 155

Sexually Transmitted Diseases Research Grants 54

Small Business Innovation Research 7

Small Business Innovation Research Project Grant 9

Social Sciences Project Grants 137

Social Security Research and Demonstration Project
   Grants 143

Social Services Research and Demonstration Project
   Grants 155

Socioeconomic and Demographic Research Project
   Grants 138

Solid Waste Disposal Research Project Grants 50

Solid Waste Management Assistance Project Grants .. 51

Special Agricultural Research Grants 44

Special International Postdoctoral Research
   Program in AIDS 117

Special Programs for the Aging 142

Star Schools Program 42

State Marine Schools 128

Strabismus, Amblyopia, and Visual Processing 85

Strabismus, Amblyopia, and Visual Processing
  Research Small Instrumentation Grants 22

Strengthening Research Library Resources 69

Student Community Service Program 156

Student Literacy Corps Project Grants 42

Studies and Program Assessment Project Grants 36

Substance Abuse Conference Grant 61

Summer Seminars for College Teachers 92

Summer Seminars for School Teachers 92

Summer Stipend Project Grants 92

Superfund Innovative Technology Evaluation
  Program 47

Superfund Technical Assistance Grants for Citizens
  at Priority Sites 47

Supplemental Assistance for Facilities to Assist
  the Homeless 149

Supplemental Educational Opportunity Grants 121

Supportive Housing Demonstration Program Project
  Grants 149

T

Talent Search 34

Teacher Preparation and Enhancement Project
  Grants 36

Technical Assistance Program 156

Technology Assistance for Disabled Individuals
  Demonstration Grants 31

Technology, Educational Media, and Materials
  for the Handicapped 31

Text/Editions Project Grants 70

Text/Translations Project Grants 70

Theater Project Grants 4

Theater Project Grants 5

Toxic Substances Research 48

Toxic Substances Research Project Grants 48

Trade Adjustment Assistance Project Grant 24

Training Interpreters for Deaf Individuals 31

Training and Special Programs for Leadership
  Personnel 35

Transitional Living for Runaway and Homeless
  Youth Project Grants 146

Travel to Collections in the Humanities 69

U

Undergraduate Foreign Language Programs 93

Undergraduate International Studies Programs 94

Undergraduate Science, Mathematics,
  and Engineering Career Access Opportunities 136

Undergraduate Science, Mathematics,
  and Engineering Instrumentation and Laboratory
  Improvement 140

Undergraduate Science, Mathematics,
  and Engineering Model Projects 136

Undergraduate Science, Mathematics,
  and Engineering Undergraduate Faculty
  Enhancement 140

Undersea Research Project Grant 50

U.S. Merchant Marine Academy 128

University Coal Research 133

University–Laboratory Cooperative Program 133

University Professors and Research Scholars
  Educational Exchange 95

Upward Bound 32

Urban Mass Transportation Training Grants 128

V

Veterans Education Outreach Program 129

Veterans Employment Program 150

Veterans Entrepreneurial Training Assistance 24

Visual Arts Project Grants 5

Visual Arts Project Grants 5

Vocational Education Cooperative Demonstration
  Technology Grants 38

Vocational Education Cooperative Dropout
  Prevention Grants 38

Volunteer Demonstration Program Project Grants ... 156

W

Water Bank Program 44

Water Pollution Control Research and Development Project Grants 50

Women's Business Ownership Assistance Project Grants 9

Women's Educational Equity Grants 35

Women's Educational Equity Project Contracts 35

Workplace Literacy Project Grants 26

Y

Young Scholars Project Grants 136

Younger Scholars Project Grants 93

Regional Index

A

Alaska Sport Fish and Wildlife Restoration
  Formula Grant 186

Alcohol and Drug Abuse Research and Services
  Block Grant to California 191

Alcohol and Drug Abuse Research and Services
  Block Grant to Colorado 191

Alcohol and Drug Abuse Research and Services
  Block Grant to Georgia 191

Alcohol and Drug Abuse Research and Services
  Block Grant to Illinois 191

Alcohol and Drug Abuse Research and Services
  Block Grant to Massachusetts 192

Alcohol and Drug Abuse Research and Services
  Block Grant to Missouri 192

Alcohol and Drug Abuse Research and Services
  Block Grant to New York 192

Alcohol and Drug Abuse Research and Services
  Block Grant to Pennsylvania 192

Alcohol and Drug Abuse Research and Services
  Block Grant to Texas 193

Alcohol and Drug Abuse Research and Services
  Block Grant to Washington 193

C

Clean Coal Scientific Research Technology Program
  for Alabama 194

Clean Coal Scientific Research Technology Program
  for Alaska 194

Clean Coal Scientific Research Technology Program
  for Arizona 194

Clean Coal Scientific Research Technology Program
  for Arkansas 194

Clean Coal Scientific Research Technology Program
  for California 195

Clean Coal Scientific Research Technology Program
  for Colorado 195

Clean Coal Scientific Research Technology Program
  for Connecticut 195

Clean Coal Scientific Research Technology Program
  for Delaware 195

Clean Coal Scientific Research Technology Program
  for Florida 196

Clean Coal Scientific Research Technology Program
  for Georgia 196

Clean Coal Scientific Research Technology Program
  for Hawaii 196

Clean Coal Scientific Research Technology Program
  for Idaho 196

Clean Coal Scientific Research Technology Program
  for Illinois 197

Clean Coal Scientific Research Technology Program
  for Indiana 197

Clean Coal Scientific Research Technology Program
  for Iowa 197

Clean Coal Scientific Research Technology Program
  for Kansas 197

Clean Coal Scientific Research Technology Program
  for Kentucky 198

Clean Coal Scientific Research Technology Program
  for Louisiana 198

Clean Coal Scientific Research Technology Program
  for Maine 198

Clean Coal Scientific Research Technology Program
  for Maryland 198

Clean Coal Scientific Research Technology Program
  for Massachusetts 199

Clean Coal Scientific Research Technology Program
  for Michigan 199

Clean Coal Scientific Research Technology Program
  for Minnesota 199

Clean Coal Scientific Research Technology Program
  for Mississippi 199

Clean Coal Scientific Research Technology Program
  for Missouri 200

Clean Coal Scientific Research Technology Program
  for Montana 200

Clean Coal Scientific Research Technology Program
  for Nebraska 200

Clean Coal Scientific Research Technology Program
  for Nevada 200

Clean Coal Scientific Research Technology Program
  for New Hampshire 201

Clean Coal Scientific Research Technology Program
  for New Jersey 201

Clean Coal Scientific Research Technology Program
  for New Mexico 201

Clean Coal Scientific Research Technology Program
  for New York 201

Clean Coal Scientific Research Technology Program
  for North Carolina 202

Clean Coal Scientific Research Technology Program
  for North Dakota 202

Clean Coal Scientific Research Technology Program
  for Ohio 202

Clean Coal Scientific Research Technology Program
  for Oklahoma 202

*Indicates grants for which fiscal sponsorship is required.

Clean Coal Scientific Research Technology Program
  for Oregon 203
Clean Coal Scientific Research Technology Program
  for Pennsylvania 203
Clean Coal Scientific Research Technology Program
  for Rhode Island 203
Clean Coal Scientific Research Technology Program
  for South Carolina 203
Clean Coal Scientific Research Technology Program
  for South Dakota 204
Clean Coal Scientific Research Technology Program
  for Tennessee 204
Clean Coal Scientific Research Technology Program
  for Texas 204
Clean Coal Scientific Research Technology Program
  for Utah 204
Clean Coal Scientific Research Technology Program
  for Vermont 205
Clean Coal Scientific Research Technology Program
  for Virginia 205
Clean Coal Scientific Research Technology Program for
  Washington 205
Clean Coal Scientific Research Technology Program
  for West Virginia 205
Clean Coal Scientific Research Technology Program
  for Wisconsin 206
Clean Coal Scientific Research Technology Program
  for Wyoming 206
Colorado Sport Fish and Wildlife Restoration
  Formula Grant 186

D

Disabled Veterans Outreach Program
  for Alabama 170
Disabled Veterans Outreach Program
  for Alaska 170
Disabled Veterans Outreach Program
  for Arizona 170
Disabled Veterans Outreach Program
  for Arkansas 170
Disabled Veterans Outreach Program
  for California 171
Disabled Veterans Outreach Program
  for Colorado 171
Disabled Veterans Outreach Program
  for Connecticut 171
Disabled Veterans Outreach Program
  for Delaware 171
Disabled Veterans Outreach Program
  for Florida 172

Disabled Veterans Outreach Program
  for Georgia 172
Disabled Veterans Outreach Program
  for Hawaii 172
Disabled Veterans Outreach Program
  for Idaho 172
Disabled Veterans Outreach Program
  for Illinois 173
Disabled Veterans Outreach Program
  for Indiana 173
Disabled Veterans Outreach Program
  for Iowa 173
Disabled Veterans Outreach Program
  for Kansas 173
Disabled Veterans Outreach Program
  for Kentucky 174
Disabled Veterans Outreach Program
  for Louisiana 174
Disabled Veterans Outreach Program
  for Maine 174
Disabled Veterans Outreach Program
  for Maryland 174
Disabled Veterans Outreach Program
  for Massachusetts 175
Disabled Veterans Outreach Program
  for Michigan 175
Disabled Veterans Outreach Program
  for Minnesota 175
Disabled Veterans Outreach Program
  for Mississippi 175
Disabled Veterans Outreach Program
  for Missouri 176
Disabled Veterans Outreach Program
  for Montana 176
Disabled Veterans Outreach Program
  for Nebraska 176
Disabled Veterans Outreach Program
  for Nevada 176
Disabled Veterans Outreach Program
  for New Hampshire 177
Disabled Veterans Outreach Program
  for New Jersey 177
Disabled Veterans Outreach Program
  for New Mexico 177
Disabled Veterans Outreach Program
  for New York 177
Disabled Veterans Outreach Program
  for North Carolina 178
Disabled Veterans Outreach Program
  for North Dakota 178
Disabled Veterans Outreach Program
  for Ohio 178

Disabled Veterans Outreach Program
  for Oklahoma 178
Disabled Veterans Outreach Program
  for Oregon 179
Disabled Veterans Outreach Program
  for Pennsylvania 179
Disabled Veterans Outreach Program
  for Rhode Island 179
Disabled Veterans Outreach Program
  for South Carolina 179
Disabled Veterans Outreach Program
  for South Dakota 180
Disabled Veterans Outreach Program
  for Tennessee 180
Disabled Veterans Outreach Program
  for Texas 180
Disabled Veterans Outreach Program
  for Utah 180
Disabled Veterans Outreach Program
  for Vermont 181
Disabled Veterans Outreach Program
  for Virginia 181
Disabled Veterans Outreach Program
  for Washington 181
Disabled Veterans Outreach Program
  for West Virginia 181
Disabled Veterans Outreach Program
  for Wisconsin 182
Disabled Veterans Outreach Program
  for Wyoming 182

G

Georgia Sport Fish and Wildlife Restoration
  Formula Grant 186

J

Job Training Partnership for Alabama 207
Job Training Partnership for Alaska 207
Job Training Partnership for Arizona 207
Job Training Partnership for Arkansas 207
Job Training Partnership for California 208
Job Training Partnership for Colorado 208
Job Training Partnership for Connecticut 208
Job Training Partnership for Delaware 208
Job Training Partnership for Florida 209
Job Training Partnership for Georgia 209
Job Training Partnership for Hawaii 209
Job Training Partnership for Idaho 209

Job Training Partnership for Illinois 210
Job Training Partnership for Indiana 210
Job Training Partnership for Iowa 210
Job Training Partnership for Kansas 210
Job Training Partnership for Kentucky 211
Job Training Partnership for Louisiana 211
Job Training Partnership for Maine 211
Job Training Partnership for Maryland 211
Job Training Partnership for Massachusetts 212
Job Training Partnership for Michigan 212
Job Training Partnership for Minnesota 212
Job Training Partnership for Mississippi 212
Job Training Partnership for Missouri 213
Job Training Partnership for Montana 213
Job Training Partnership for Nebraska 213
Job Training Partnership for Nevada 213
Job Training Partnershipfor New Hampshire 214
Job Training Partnership for New Jersey 214
Job Training Partnership for New Mexico 214
Job Training Partnership for New York 214
Job Training Partnership for North Carolina 215
Job Training Partnership for North Dakota 215
Job Training Partnership for Ohio 215
Job Training Partnership for Oklahoma 215
Job Training Partnership for Oregon 216
Job Training Partnership for Pennsylvania 216
Job Training Partnership for Rhode Island 216
Job Training Partnership for South Carolina 216
Job Training Partnership for South Dakota 217
Job Training Partnership for Tennessee 217
Job Training Partnership for Texas 217
Job Training Partnership for Utah 217
Job Training Partnership for Vermont 218
Job Training Partnership for Virginia 218
Job Training Partnership for Washington 218
Job Training Partnership for West Virginia 218
Job Training Partnership for Wisconsin 219
Job Training Partnership for Wyoming 219

M

Massachusetts Sport Fish and Wildlife Restoration
  Formula Grant 186
Mathematics and Science Education
  in California 183
Mathematics and Science Education
  in Colorado 183
Mathematics and Science Education
  in Georgia 183

Mathematics and Science Education
in Illinois 183
Mathematics and Science Education
in Massachusetts 184
Mathematics and Science Education
in Missouri 184
Mathematics and Science Education
in New York 184
Mathematics and Science Education
in Pennsylvania 184
Mathematics and Science Education
in Texas 185
Mathematics and Science Education
in Washington 185
Minnesota Sport Fish and Wildlife Restoration
Formula Grant 187

N

New Mexico Sport Fish and Wildlife Restoration
Formula Grant 187

O

Oregon Sport Fish and Wildlife Restoration
Formula Grant 187

P

Promotion of the Arts in Alabama 157
Promotion of the Arts in Alaska 157
Promotion of the Arts in Arizona 157
Promotion of the Arts in Arkansas 157
Promotion of the Arts in California 158
Promotion of the Arts in Colorado 158
Promotion of the Arts in Connecticut 158
Promotion of the Arts in Delaware 158
Promotion of the Arts in Florida 159
Promotion of the Arts in Georgia 159
Promotion of the Arts in Hawaii 159
Promotion of the Arts in Idaho 159
Promotion of the Arts in Illinois 160
Promotion of the Arts in Indiana 160
Promotion of the Arts in Iowa 160
Promotion of the Arts in Kansas 160
Promotion of the Arts in Kentucky 161
Promotion of the Arts in Louisiana 161
Promotion of the Arts in Maine 161
Promotion of the Arts in Maryland 161
Promotion of the Arts in Massachusetts 162

Promotion of the Arts in Michigan 162
Promotion of the Arts in Minnesota 162
Promotion of the Arts in Mississippi 162
Promotion of the Arts in Missouri 163
Promotion of the Arts in Montana 163
Promotion of the Arts in Nebraska 163
Promotion of the Arts in Nevada 163
Promotion of the Arts in New Hampshire 164
Promotion of the Arts in New Jersey 164
Promotion of the Arts in New Mexico 164
Promotion of the Arts in New York 164
Promotion of the Arts in North Carolina 165
Promotion of the Arts in North Dakota 165
Promotion of the Arts in Ohio 165
Promotion of the Arts in Oklahoma 165
Promotion of the Arts in Oregon 166
Promotion of the Arts in Pennsylvania 166
Promotion of the Arts in Rhode Island 166
Promotion of the Arts in South Carolina 166
Promotion of the Arts in South Dakota 167
Promotion of the Arts in Tennessee 167
Promotion of the Arts in Texas 167
Promotion of the Arts in Utah 167
Promotion of the Arts in Vermont 168
Promotion of the Arts in Virginia 168
Promotion of the Arts in Washington 168
Promotion of the Arts in West Virginia 168
Promotion of the Arts in Wisconsin 169
Promotion of the Arts in Wyoming 169
Protection and Advocacy for the Mentally Ill
in California 188
Protection and Advocacy for the Mentally Ill
in Colorado 188
Protection and Advocacy for the Mentally Ill
in Georgia 188
Protection and Advocacy for the Mentally Ill
in Illinois 188
Protection and Advocacy for the Mentally Ill
in Massachusetts 189
Protection and Advocacy for the Mentally Ill
in Missouri 189
Protection and Advocacy for the Mentally Ill
in New York 189
Protection and Advocacy for the Mentally Ill
in Pennsylvania 189
Protection and Advocacy for the Mentally Ill
in Texas 190
Protection and Advocacy for the Mentally Ill
in Washington 190

Protection and Advocacy for the Mentally Ill
  in West Virginia 189
Protection and Advocacy for the Mentally Ill
  in Wyoming 188

R

*Rhode Island Sport Fish and Wildlife Restoration
  Formula Grant 186

S

*South Carolina Sport Fish and Wildlife Restoration
  Formula Grant 186
*South Dakota Sport Fish and Wildlife Restoration
  Formula Grant 186

T

*Tennessee Sport Fish and Wildlife Restoration Formula
  Grant 186
*Texas Sport Fish and Wildlife Restoration Formula
  Grant 187

U

*Utah Sport Fish and Wildlife Restoration
  Formula Grant 186

V

*Vermont Sport Fish and Wildlife Restoration Formula
  Grant 186
*Virginia Sport Fish and Wildlife Restoration Formula
  Grant 186

W

*Washington Sport Fish and Wildlife Restoration
  Formula Grant 187
*West Virginia Sport Fish and Wildlife Restoration
  Formula Grant 186
*Wisconsin Sport Fish and Wildlife Restoration
  Formula Grant 187
*Wyoming Sport Fish and Wildlife Restoration
  Formula Grant 186

Index of Grants by Field/Interest

ARTS AND LITERATURE

Dance

Dance Project Grants 1

*Dance Project Grants 1

Design

Design Arts Project Grants 1

*Design Arts Project Grants 1

Media

*Film, Radio and Television Project Grants 2

Film, Radio and Television Project Grants 2

Folk Arts

*Folk Arts Project Grants 2

Folk Arts Project Grants 2

Literature

Literature Project Grants 3

*Literature Project Grants 3

Minority Development

*Expansion Arts Project Grants 3

Music

Music Project Grants 3

*Music Project Grants 4

Opera

Opera and Musical Theater Project Grants 4

*Opera and Musical Theater Project Grants 4

Theater Arts

Theater Project Grants 4

*Theater Arts Project Grants 5

Visual Arts

Visual Arts Project Grants 5

*Visual Arts Project Grants 5

General

*Challenge Grants in the Arts 5

*Inter-Arts Project Grants 6

Promotion of the Arts in Alabama 157

Promotion of the Arts in Alaska 157

Promotion of the Arts in Arizona 157

Promotion of the Arts in Arkansas 157

Promotion of the Arts in California 158

Promotion of the Arts in Colorado 158

Promotion of the Arts in Connecticut 158

Promotion of the Arts in Delaware 158

Promotion of the Arts in Florida 159

Promotion of the Arts in Georgia 159

Promotion of the Arts in Hawaii 159

Promotion of the Arts in Idaho 159

Promotion of the Arts in Illinois 160

Promotion of the Arts in Indiana 160

Promotion of the Arts in Iowa 160

Promotion of the Arts in Kansa 160

Promotion of the Arts in Kentucky 161

Promotion of the Arts in Louisiana 161

Promotion of the Arts in Maine 161

Promotion of the Arts in Maryland 161

Promotion of the Arts in Massachusetts 162

Promotion of the Arts in Michigan 162

Promotion of the Arts in Minnesota 162

Promotion of the Arts in Mississippi 162

*Indicates grants for which fiscal sponsorship is required.

Promotion of the Arts in Missouri 163

Promotion of the Arts in Montana 163

Promotion of the Arts Nebraska 163

Promotion of the Arts in Nevada 163

Promotion of the Arts New Hampshire 164

Promotion of the Arts in New Mexico 164

Promotion of the Arts in New York 164

Promotion of the Arts in North Carolina 165

Promotion of the Arts in North Dakota 165

Promotion of the Arts in Ohio 165

Promotion of the Arts in Oklahoma 165

Promotion of the Arts in Oregon 166

Promotion of the Arts in Pennsylvania 166

Promotion of the Arts in Rhode Island 166

Promotion of the Arts South Carolina 166

Promotion of the Arts in South Dakota 167

Promotion of the Arts in Tennessee 167

Promotion of the Arts in Texas 167

Promotion of the Arts in Utah 167

Promotion of the Arts in Vermont 168

Promotion of the Arts in Virginia 168

Promotion of the Arts in Washington 168

Promotion of the Arts in West Virginia 168

Promotion of the Arts in Wisconsin 169

Promotion of the Arts in Wyoming 169

BUSINESS DEVELOPMENT

Health Care

Small Business Innovation Research 9

Minority and Disadvantaged

*Appalachian Community Development
   Project Grants 7

Appalachian Housing Project
   Development Grants 7

Appalachian Local Access Roads 7

Development Assistance Program Project Grants 8

Human Resource Programs 8

Minority Business Development Centers 8

Research and Evaluation Project Grant 9

Small Business Innovation Research Project Grant 9

Women's Business Ownership Assistance Project Grants 9

Science and Medicine

Aging Research Small Business Innovation
   Research Grants 9

Aging Research Small Instrumentation Grants 9

Allergy, Immunology, and Transplantation Research
   Small Business Innovation Research Grants 10

Allergy, Immunology, and Transplantation Research
   Small Instrumentation Grants 10

Anterior Segment Diseases Research Small Business
   Innovation Research Grants 10

Anterior Segment Diseases Research Small
   Instrumentation Grants 10

Arthritis, Musculoskeletal, and Skin Diseases Research
   Small Business Innovation Research Grants 11

Arthritis, Musculoskeletal, and Skin Diseases Research
   Small Instrumentation Grants 11

Biophysics Research Small Business Innovation
   Research Grant 11

Biophysics Small Instrumentation Grant 11

Blood Diseases Research – Small Business Innovation
   research Grants 12

Blood Diseases Research – Small Instrumentation
   Grants 12

Cancer Biology Research Grants 78

Cancer Biology – Small Business Innovation
   Research Grants 12

Cancer Cause and Prevention – Small Business
   Innovation Research Grants 13

Cancer Centers Support – Small Instrumentation
Program 13

Cancer Control – Methods, Development, and Testing . 13

Cancer Control – Small Instrumentation Program 13

Cancer Detection and Diagnosis – Small Business
Innovation Research Grants 14

Cancer Detection and Diagnosis – Small
Instrumentation Program 14

Cancer Treatment Research – Small Business
Innovation Research Grants 14

Cancer Treatment Research – Small Instrumentation
Program 14

Cellular and Molecular Basis for Disease Research
Small Business Innovation Research Grants 15

Cellular and Molecular Basis for Disease Research
Small Instrumentation Grants 15

Diabetes, Endocrinology, and Metabolism Research
Small Business Innovation Research Grants 15

Diabetes, Endocrinology, and Metabolism Research
Small Instrumentation Grants 15

Digestive Diseases and Nutrition Research Small
Business Innovation Research Grants 16

Digestive Diseases and Nutrition Research Small
Instrumentation Research Grants 16

Genetics Research Small Business Innovation
Research Grants 16

Genetics Research Small Instrumentation Grants 16

Heart and Vascular Diseases Research Small
Business Innovation Research Grants 17

Heart and Vascular Diseases Research Small
Instrumentation Grants 17

Kidney Diseases, Urology, and Hematology Research
Small Instrumentation Grants 17

Lung Diseases Research Small Business Innovation
Research Grants 18

Lung Diseases Research Small Instrumentation Grants 18

Microbiology and Infectious Diseases Research Small
Business Innovation Research Grants 18

Microbiology and Infectious Diseases Research Small
Instrumentation Grants 18

Neurological Disorders Biological Research Small
Business Innovation Research Grants 19

Neurological Disorders Biological Research Small
Instrumentation Grants 19

Neurological Disorders Clinical Research Small
Business Innovation Research Grants 19

Neurological Disorders Clinical Research Small
Instrumentation Grants 19

Pharmacological Sciences Research Small Business
Innovation Research Grants 20

Pharmacological Sciences Research Small
Instrumentation Grants 20

Physiological Sciences Small Business Innovation
Research Grant 20

Physiological Sciences Small Instrumentation Grant ... 20

Population Research Small Business Innovation
Research Grants 21

Population Research Small Instrumentation Grants ... 21

Research for Mothers and Children Small Business
Innovation Research Grants 21

Research for Mothers and Children Small
Instrumentation Grants 21

Retinal and Choroidal Diseases Research Small
Business Innovation Research Grants 22

Retinal and Choroidal Diseases Research Small
Instrumentation Grants 22

Strabismus, Amblyopia and Visual Processing Research
Small Instrumentation Grants 22

General

Advanced Technology Program Project Grants 22

Capital Construction Fund 23

Construction Reserve Fund 23

Development and Promotion of Ports and Intermodal
   Transportation 23

Disabled Veterans Outreach Program for Alabama 170

Disabled Veterans Outreach Program for Alaska 170

Disabled Veterans Outreach Program for Arizona 170

Disabled Veterans Outreach Program for Arkansas 170

Disabled Veterans Outreach Program for California . . . 171

Disabled Veterans Outreach Program for Colorado 171

Disabled Veterans Outreach Program for Connecticut . 171

Disabled Veterans Outreach Program for Delaware . . . 171

Disabled Veterans Outreach Program for Florida 172

Disabled Veterans Outreach Program for Georgia 172

Disabled Veterans Outreach Program for Hawaii 172

Disabled Veterans Outreach Program for Idaho 172

Disabled Veterans Outreach Program for Illinois 173

Disabled Veterans Outreach Program for Indiana 173

Disabled Veterans Outreach Program for Iowa 173

Disabled Veterans Outreach Program for Kansas 173

Disabled Veterans Outreach Program for Kentucky . . . 174

Disabled Veterans Outreach Program for Louisiana . . . 174

Disabled Veterans Outreach Program for Maine 174

Disabled Veterans Outreach Program for Maryland . . . 174

Disabled Veterans Outreach Program for Massachusetts 175

Disabled Veterans Outreach Program for Michigan 175

Disabled Veterans Outreach Program for Minnesota . . 175

Disabled Veterans Outreach Program for Mississippi . . 175

Disabled Veterans Outreach Program for Missouri 176

Disabled Veterans Outreach Program for Montana 176

Disabled Veterans Outreach Program for Nebraska 176

Disabled Veterans Outreach Program for Nevada 176

Disabled Veterans Outreach Program
   for New Hampshire 177

Disabled Veterans Outreach Program for New Jersey . . 177

Disabled Veterans Outreach Program for New Mexico . 177

Disabled Veterans Outreach Program for New York . . . 177

Disabled Veterans Outreach Program
   for North Carolina 178

Disabled Veterans Outreach Program for North Dakota 178

Disabled Veterans Outreach Program for Ohio 178

Disabled Veterans Outreach Program for Oklahoma . . . 178

Disabled Veterans Outreach Program for Oregon 179

Disabled Veterans Outreach Program for Pennsylvania 179

Disabled Veterans Outreach Program for Rhode Island 179

Disabled Veterans Outreach Program
   for South Carolina 179

Disabled Veterans Outreach Program for South Dakota 180

Disabled Veterans Outreach Program for Tennessee . . . 180

Disabled Veterans Outreach Program for Texas 180

Disabled Veterans Outreach Program for Utah 180

Disabled Veterans Outreach Program for Vermont 181

Disabled Veterans Outreach Program for Virginia 181

Disabled Veterans Outreach Program for Washington . . 181

Disabled Veterans Outreach Program for West Virginia 181

Disabled Veterans Outreach Program for Wisconsin . . . 182

Disabled Veterans Outreach Program for Wyoming 182

Labor and Management Cooperation Project Grants . . . 23

Maritime Operations Differential Subsidies 24

Service Corps of Retired Executives (SCORE)
   Project Grants 24

Trade Adjustment Assistance Project Grant 24

Veterans Entrepreneurial Training Assistance 24

EDUCATION

Adult

Educational Opportunity Centers 25

English Literacy Program 25

Even Start Local Education Project Grants 25

National Adult Education Research 25

Workplace Literacy Project Grants 26

Arts

Arts in Education Project Grants 26

Bilingual

Bilingual Education 26

Bilingual Education Support Services 26

Bilingual Education Training Grants 27

Business

Business and International Education 27

Centers for International Business Education 27

Educational Partnerships 27

Disabled

Clearinghouses for the Handicapped Project Grants ... 28

Early Education Program for the Handicapped 28

*Educational Program for Severely
   Handicapped Children 28

*Handicapped Regional Resource Centers 28

Handicapped Special Studies 29

Media Materials for the Handicapped 29

*National Institute on Disability and Rehabilitation
   Research Project Grants 29

*Postsecondary Education for the Handicapped 29

*Rehabilitation Service Projects 30

*Research in Education for the Handicapped 30

*Secondary Education and Transitional Services
   for Handicapped Youth 30

*Services for Deaf–Blind Children and Youth 30

Technology Assistance for Disabled Individuals
   Demonstration Grants 31

*Technology, Educational Media, and Materials
   for the Handicapped 31

Training Interpreters for Deaf Individuals 31

Gifted

Jacob K. Javits Gifted and Talented Students
   Project Grants 31

Higher Education

*Fund for the Improvement of Postsecondary
   Education 32

Law School Clinical Experience Program 32

Upward Bound 32

Fulbright–Hays Seminars Abroad 32

International Research and Studies 33

National Resource Centers for Language and
   International Studies 33

Job Retraining and Development

Demonstration Centers for the Retraining of
   Displaced Workers 33

Mid–Career Teacher Training 33

Minority Development

*Desegregation Assistance, Civil Rights Training
   and Advisory Services 34

*Migrant Education High School Equivalency
   Program 34

Talent Search 34

Training and Special Programs for Leadership
   Personnel 35

Women's Educational Equity Grants 35

Women's Educational Equity Project Contracts 35

Science and Math

Materials Development, Research, and Informal
   Science Education 35

*Mathematics and Science Education in Alabama 183

*Mathematics and Science Education in Alaska 185

*Mathematics and Science Education in Arizona 183

*Mathematics and Science Education in Arkansas 185

*Mathematics and Science Education in California 183

*Mathematics and Science Education in Colorado 183

*Mathematics and Science Education in Connecticut .. 184

*Mathematics and Science Education in Delaware 184

*Mathematics and Science Education in Florida 183

*Mathematics and Science Education in Georgia 183

*Mathematics and Science Education in Hawaii 183

*Mathematics and Science Education in Idaho 185

*Mathematics and Science Education in Illinois 183

*Mathematics and Science Education in Indiana 183

*Mathematics and Science Education in Iowa 184

*Mathematics and Science Education in Kansas 184

*Mathematics and Science Education in Louisiana 185

*Mathematics and Science Education in Maine 184

*Mathematics and Science Education in Maryland 184

*Mathematics and Science Education in Massachusetts 184

*Mathematics and Science Education in Michigan 183

*Mathematics and Science Education in Mississippi ... 183

*Mathematics and Science Education in Missouri 184

*Mathematics and Science Education in Montana 183

*Mathematics and Science Education in Nebraska 184

*Mathematics and Science Education in Nevada 183

*Mathematics and Science Education
  in New Hampshire 184

*Mathematics and Science Education in New Jersey ... 184

*Mathematics and Science Education in New Mexico .. 185

*Mathematics and Science Education in New York 184

*Mathematics and Science Education in North Carolina 183

*Mathematics and Science Education in North Dakota . 183

*Mathematics and Science Education in Ohio 183

*Mathematics and Science Education in Oklahoma 185

*Mathematics and Science Education in Oregon 185

*Mathematics and Science Education in Pennsylvania .. 184

*Mathematics and Science Education in Rhode Island . 184

*Mathematics and Science Education in South Carolina 183

*Mathematics and Science Education in South Dakota . 183

*Mathematics and Science Education in Texas 185

*Mathematics and Science Education in Utah 183

*Mathematics and Science Education in Vermont 184

*Mathematics and Science Educaiton in Virginia 184

*Mathematics and Science Education in Washington ... 185

*Mathematics and Science Education in West Virginia . 184

*Mathematics and Science Education in Wisconsin 183

*Mathematics and Science Education in Wyoming 183

National Program for Mathematics and Science
  Education 41

Studies and Program Assessment Project Grants 36

Teacher Preparation and Enhancement Project Grants .. 36

Substance Abuse

Drug–Free Schools and Communities – Regional
  Centers 36

School Personnel Training 36

Vocational

Bilingual Vocational Instructor Training 37

Bilingual Vocational Materials, Methods,
  and Techniques 37

Bilingual Vocational Training 37

National Vocational Education Research 37

*National Vocational Education Research 38

*Rehabilitation Training 38

Vocational Education Cooperative Dropout
  Prevention Grants 38

Vocational Education Cooperative Demonstration
  Technology Grants 38

General

Cooperative Education Project Grants 39

*Educational Leadership Development 39

Educational Research and Development 39

First Schools and Teachers Project Grants 39

Language Resource Centers Project Grants 40

*Law–Related Education 40

National Diffusion Network Development Grants 40

National Diffusion Network Dissemination Processes
Project Grant 40

National Diffusion Network Private School Facilitator
Project Grant 41

National Diffusion Network State Facilitators
Project Grants 41

National School Volunteer Program 41

The Secretary's Fund for Innovation in Education 42

Student Literacy Corps Project Grants 42

School Dropout Demonstration Assistance 42

Star Schools Program 42

ENVIRONMENT

Agriculture

*Agricultural Research Grant 43

Animal Damage Control Project Grant 43

Competitive Agricultural Research Grants 43

Cooperative Agreements for Research in Public
Lands Management Project Grants 43

Special Agricultural Research Grants 44

Water Bank Program 44

Air

Air Pollution Control Research 44

Climate and Atmospheric Research 44

Intergovernmental Climate Program Grant 45

Business Development

Characterization of Environmental Health Hazards –
Small Business Projects 45

Fisheries Research and Development Project Grants .. 45

Senior Environmental Employment Program 45

Toxics

Characterization of Environmental Health Hazards –
New Research 46

Environmental Toxicology Project Grants 46

Environmental Protection Research Project Grants 46

Environmental Restoration Project Grants 46

NIEHS Superfund Hazardous Substances Research
and Education 47

Pesticides Control Research 47

Superfund Innovative Technology Evaluation Program . 47

Superfund Technical Assistance Grants for Citizens
at Priority Sites 47

Toxic Substances Research 48

Toxic Substances Research Project Grants 48

Water

Anadromous Fish Conservation 48

Anadromous and Great Lake Fisheries Conservation
Project Grant 48

National Estuary Program Project Grants 49

National Water Resources Research Program 49

Safe Drinking Water Research and Demonstration
Project Grant 49

Sea Grant Support 49

Undersea Research Project Grant 50

Water Pollution Control Research and Development
Project Grants 50

Waste Management

Biofuels and Municipal Waste Technology Project
  Grants 50

Solid Waste Disposal Research Project Grants 50

*Solid Waste Management Assistance Project Grants .. 50

General

*Alabama Sport Fish and Wildlife Restoration
  Formula Grant 186

*Alaska Sport Fish and Wildlife Restoration
  Formula Grant 186

*Arizona Sport Fish and Wildlife Restoration
  Formula Grant 187

*Arkansas Sport Fish and Wildlife Restoration
  Formula Grant 186

*California Sport Fish and Wildlife Restoration
  Formula Grant 187

*Colorado Sport Fish and Wildlife Restoration
  Formula Grant 186

*Connecticut Sport Fish and Wildlife Restoration
  Formula Grant 186

*Delaware Sport Fish and Wildlife Restoration
  Formula Grant 186

*Florida Sport Fish and Wildlife Restoration
  Formula Grant 186

*Georgia Sport Fish and Wildlife Restoration
  Formula Grant 186

*Hawaii Sport Fish and Wildlife Restoration
  Formula Grant 187

*Idaho Sport Fish and Wildlife Restoration
  Formula Grant 187

*Illinois Sport Fish and Wildlife Restoration
  Formula Grant 187

*Indiana Sport Fish and Wildlife Restoration
  Formula Grant 187

*Iowa Sport Fish and Wildlife Restoration
  Formula Grant 187

*Kansas Sport Fish and Wildlife Restoration
  Formula Grant 186

*Kentucky Sport Fish and Wildlife Restoration
  Formula Grant 186

*Louisiana Sport Fish and Wildlife Restoration
  Formula Grant 186

*Maine Sport Fish and Wildlife Restoration
  Formula Grant 186

*Maryland Sport Fish and Wildlife Restoration
  Formula Grant 186

*Massachusetts Sport Fish and Wildlife Restoration
  Formula Grant 186

*Michigan Sport Fish and Wildlife Restoration
  Formula Grant 187

*Minnesota Sport Fish and Wildlife Restoration
  Formula Grant 187

*Mississippi Sport Fish and Wildlife Restoration
  Formula Grant 186

*Missouri Sport Fish and Wildlife Restoration
  Formula Grant 187

*Montana Sport Fish and Wildlife Restoration
  Formula Grant 186

*Nebraska Sport Fish and Wildlife Restoration
  Formula Grant 186

*Nevada Sport Fish and Wildlife Restoration
  Formula Grant 187

*New Hampshire Sport Fish and Wildlife Restoration
  Formula Grant 186

*New Jersey Sport Fish and Wildlife Restoration
  Formula Grant 186

*New Mexico Sport Fish and Wildlife Restoration
  Formula Grant 187

*New York Sport Fish and Wildlife Restoration
  Formula Grant 186

*North Carolina Sport Fish and Wildlife Restoration
  Formula Grant 186

*North Dakota Sport Fish and Wildlife Restoration
  Formula Grant 186

*Ohio Sport Fish and Wildlife Restoration
  Formula Grant 187

*Oklahoma Sport Fish and Wildlife Restoration
  Formula Grant 187

*Oregon Sport Fish and Wildlife Restoration
  Formula Grant 187

*Pennsylvania Sport Fish and Wildlife Restoration
  Formula Grant 186

*Rhode Island Sport Fish and Wildlife Restoration
  Formula Grant 186

*South Carolina Sport Fish and Wildlife Restoration
  Formula Grant 186

*South Dakota Sport Fish and Wildlife Restoration
  Formula Grant 186

*Tennessee Sport Fish and Wildlife Restoration
  Formula Grant 186

*Texas Sport Fish and Wildlife Restoration
  Formula Grant 187

*Utah Sport Fish and Wildlife Restoration
  Formula Grant 186

*Vermont Sport Fish and Wildlife Restoration
  Formula Grant 186

*Virginia Sport Fish and Wildlife Restoration
  Formula Grant 186

*Washington Sport Fish and Wildlife Restoration
  Formula Grant 187

*West Virginia Sport Fish and Wildlife Restoration
  Formula Grant 186

*Wisconsin Sport Fish and Wildlife Restoration
  Formula Grant 187

*Wyoming Sport Fish and Wildlife Restoration
  Formula Grant 186

HEALTH CARE

AIDS

AIDS Activity Project Grant 52

AIDS Education and Training Centers 52

Health Services Delivery to Persons with AIDS
  Demonstration Grants 52

Health Services Research and Development Grants ... 52

Integrated Community–Based Primary Care and Drug
  Abuse Treatment Services Project Grant 53

*Long–Term Care Facilities Project Grant 53

Minority AIDS Education Prevention Grants 53

Minority Community Health Demonstration
  Projects – AIDS 53

*Non–Acute Care Intermediate Facilities
  Project Grant 54

*Sexually Transmitted Diseases Research Grants 54

Children

Adolescent Family Life Research Grants 54

Maternal Child and Health Federal Consolidated
  Programs Project Grant 54

Minority Community Health Demonstration
  Projects – Infant Mortality 55

Pediatric AIDS Health Care Demonstration Program
  55

Disadvantaged

*Appalachian Health Programs 55

Community Demonstration Grant Projects for Alcohol
  and Drug Abuse Treatment of Homeless Individuals . 55

Health Services in the Pacific Basin 56

Indian Health Service Health Promotion and Disease
  Prevention Demonstration Projects 56

Migrant Health Centers Grants 56

Project Grants for Health Services to the Homeless ... 56

Rural Health Resource Centers 57

Disabilities

Developmental Disability Projects of National
  Significance 57

Disabilities Prevention Project Grants 57

Mental Health

Protection and Advocacy for the Mentally Ill
in Alabama 188

Protection and Advocacy for the Mentally Ill
in Alaska 190

Protection and Advocacy for the Mentally Ill
in Arizona 188

Protection and Advocacy for the Mentally Ill
in Arkansas 190

Protection and Advocacy for the Mentally Ill
in Colorado 188

Protection and Advocacy for the Mentally Ill
in Connecticut 189

Protection and Advocacy for the Mentally Ill
in Delaware 189

Protection and Advocacy for the Mentally Ill
in Florida 188

Protection and Advocacy for the Mentally Ill
in Georgia 188

Protection and Advocacy for the Mentally Ill
in Hawaii 188

Protection and Advocacy for the Mentally Ill
in Idaho 190

Protection and Advocacy for the Mentally Ill
in Illinois 188

Protection and Advocacy for the Mentally Ill
in Indiana 188

Protection and Advocacy for the Mentally Ill
in Iowa 189

Protection and Advocacy for the Mentally Ill
in Kansas 189

Protection and Advocacy for the Mentally Ill
in Kentucky 188

Protection and Advocacy for the Mentally Ill
in Louisiana 190

Protection and Advocacy for the Mentally Ill
in Maine 189

Protection and Advocacy for the Mentally Ill
in Maryland 189

Protection and Advocacy for the Mentally Ill
in Massachusetts 189

Protection and Advocacy for the Mentally Ill
in Michigan 188

Protection and Advocacy for the Mentally Ill
in Minnesota 188

Protection and Advocacy for the Mentally Ill
in Mississippi 188

Protection and Advocacy for the Mentally Ill
in Missouri 189

Protection and Advocacy for the Mentally Ill
in Montana 188

Protection and Advocacy for the Mentally Ill
in Nebraska 189

Protection and Advocacy for the Mentally Ill
in Nevada 188

Protection and Advocacy for the Mentally Ill
in New Hampshire 189

Protection and Advocacy for the Mentally Ill
in New Jersey 189

Protection and Advocacy for the Mentally Ill
in New Mexico 190

Protection and Advocacy for the Mentally Ill
in New York 189

Protection and Advocacy for the Mentally Ill
in North Carolina 188

Protection and Advocacy for the Mentally Ill
in North Dakota 188

Protection and Advocacy for the Mentally Ill
in Ohio 188

Protection and Advocacy for the Mentally Ill
in Oklahoma 190

Protection and Advocacy for the Mentally Ill
in Oregon 190

Protection and Advocacy for the Mentally Ill
in Pennsylvania 189

Protection and Advocacy for the Mentally Ill
in Rhode Island 189

Protection and Advocacy for the Mentally Ill
in South Carolina 188

Protection and Advocacy for the Mentally Ill
in South Dakota 188

Protection and Advocacy for the Mentally Ill
in Tennessee 188

Protection and Advocacy for the Mentally Ill
in Texas 190

Protection and Advocacy for the Mentally Ill
in Utah 188

Protection and Advocacy for the Mentally Ill
in Vermont 189

Protection and Advocacy for the Mentally Ill
in Virginia 189

Protection and Advocacy for the Mentally Ill
in Washington 190

Protection and Advocacy for the Mentally Ill
in West Virginia 189

Protection and Advocacy for the Mentally Ill
in Wisconsin 188

Protection and Advocacy for the Mentally Ill
in Wyoming 188

Prevention

Applied Methods in Surveillance Projects 57

Community–Based Injury Control Projects 58

Injury Prevention and Control Research Projects 58

Injury Prevention Research Centers 58

Minority Community Health Demonstration
Projects – Cancer 58

Minority Community Health Demonstration Projects –
Cardiovascular Disease and Stroke 59

Minority Community Health Demonstration
Projects – Diabetes 59

Minority Community Health Demonstration
Projects – Homicide, Suicide and Injury 59

Occupational Safety and Health Research
Project Grants 59

Occupational Safety and Health Training Grants 60

Resource and Manpower Development in the
Environmental Health Sciences 60

Substance Abuse

Alcohol and Drug Abuse Clinical Training
Program Grants 60

Drug Abuse Treatment Waiting List Reduction Grants .. 60

Drug and Alcohol Abuse Prevention Project Grant 61

Minority Community Health Demonstration
Projects – Substance Abuse 61

Model Substance Abuse Prevention Projects for
Pregnant and Postpartum Women and their Infants ... 61

Substance Abuse Conference Grant 61

General

*Black Lung Clinics Project Grants 62

Community Health Centers Project Grants 62

Family Planning Services Project Grants 62

Food and Drug Administration Research Project Grant . 62

National Research Service Awards 63

*National Health Promotion 63

Nursing Research Project Grants 63

HUMANITIES

Education

*Elementary and Secondary Programs
in the Humanities 64

Elementary And Secondary Programs
in the Humanities 64

Masterwork Study Grants 64

*Higher Education in the Humanities 64

NEH/Reader's Digest Teacher–Scholar Program 64

*Public Humanities Project Grants 65

International Understanding

International Peace and Conflict Management 65

International Peace and Conflict Management
   Articles and Manuscripts 65

*International Research Project Grants 65

Libraries and Museums

College Library Technology Research
   and Demonstration Grants 66

College Library Technology Combination Grants 66

College Library Technology Networking Grants 66

College Library Technology Services Grants 66

Humanities Preservation Project Grants 67

*Humanities Projects in Libraries and Archives 67

*Humanities Projects in Museums
   and Historical Associations 67

*Institute of Museum Services Conservation Projects .. 67

Library Research and Demonstration Project Grants .. 68

*Museum Project Grants 68

Museum Project Grants 68

National Historical Publications and Records
   Project Grants 68

Reference Materials/Access Project Grants 69

Reference Materials/Tools Project Grants 69

*Strengthening Research Library Resources 69

Travel to Collections in the Humanities 69

Publications

Humanities Text and Publications Project Grants 70

Text/Editions Project Grants 70

Text/Translations Project Grants 70

Urban Development

Historic Preservation Fund Grants–in–Aid 71

General

*College–Community Forums on the U.S. Constitution 71

*Humanities Challenge Grants 71

Humanities Conference Project Grants 71

Interpretive Research and Projects in the Humanities .. 72

Interpretive Research in the Humanities, Science
   and Technology 72

Selected Areas of Humanities Promotion 72

MEDICAL RESEARCH

Business Development

Biological Response to Environmental Health Hazards
   Small Business Project Grants 73

Research for Mothers and Children 73

Environment

Biological Response to Environmental Health Hazards
   Research Grants 73

Biological Response to Environmental Health Hazards
   Small Instrumentation Program 73

Gerontology

Aging Research Project Grants 74

Minority Development

Minority Biomedical Research Support 74

Biomedical Research – Minority High School Student
   Research Apprentice Grants 74

Publications

Medical Library Assistance Scientific Publication
   Grants 74

Substance Abuse

Alcohol and Drug Abuse Research and Services
   Block Grant to Alabama 191

Alcohol and Drug Abuse Research and Services
Block Grant to Alaska 193

Alcohol and Drug Abuse Research and Services
Block Grant to Arizona 191

Alcohol and Drug Abuse Research and Services
Block Grant to Arkansas......................... 193

Alcohol and Drug Abuse Research and Services
Block Grant to California 191

Alcohol and Drug Abuse Research and Services
Block Grant to Colorado 191

Alcohol and Drug Abuse Research and Services
Block Grant to Connecticut 192

Alcohol and Drug Abuse Research and Services
Block Grant to Florida 191

Alcohol and Drug Abuse Research and Services
Block Grant to Georgia.......................... 191

Alcohol and Drug Abuse Research and Services
Block Grant to Hawaii........................... 191

Alcohol and Drug Abuse Research and Services
Block Grant to Idaho 193

Alcohol and Drug Abuse Research and Services
Block Grant to Illinois.......................... 191

Alcohol and Drug Abuse Research and Services
Block Grant to Indiana 191

Alcohol and Drug Abuse Research and Services
Block Grant to Iowa 192

Alcohol and Drug Abuse Research and Services
Block Grant to Kansas 192

Alcohol and Drug Abuse Research and Services
Block Grant to Kentucky 191

Alcohol and Drug Abuse Research and Services
Block Grant to Louisiana 193

Alcohol and Drug Abuse Research and Services
Block Grant to Maine 192

Alcohol and Drug Abuse Research and Services
Block Grant to Maryland 192

Alcohol and Drug Abuse Research and Services
Block Grant to Massachusetts 192

Alcohol and Drug Abuse Research and Services
Block Grant to Michigan 191

Alcohol and Drug Abuse Research and Services
Block Grant to Minnesota 191

Alcohol and Drug Abuse Research and Services
Block Grant to Mississippi 191

Alcohol and Drug Abuse Research and Services
Block Grant to Missouri 192

Alcohol and Drug Abuse Research and Services
Block Grant to Montana 191

Alcohol and Drug Abuse Research and Services
Block Grant to Nebraska 192

Alcohol and Drug Abuse Research and Services
Block Grant to Nevada 191

Alcohol and Drug Abuse Research and Services
Block Grant to New Hampshire 192

Alcohol and Drug Abuse Research and Services
Block Grant to New Jersey....................... 192

Alcohol and Drug Abuse Research and Services
Block Grant to New Mexico 193

Alcohol and Drug Abuse Research and Services
Block Grant to New York 192

Alcohol and Drug Abuse Research and Services
Block Grant to North Carolina 191

Alcohol and Drug Abuse Research and Services
Block Grant to North Dakota 191

Alcohol and Drug Abuse Research and Services
Block Grant to Ohio 191

Alcohol and Drug Abuse Research and Services
Block Grant to Oklahoma 193

Alcohol and Drug Abuse Research and Services
Block Grant to Oregon 193

Alcohol and Drug Abuse Research and Services
Block Grant to Pennsylvania 192

Alcohol and Drug Abuse Research and Services
Block Grant to Rhode Island 192

Alcohol and Drug Abuse Research and Services
   Block Grant to South Carolina 191

Alcohol and Drug Abuse Research and Services
   Block Grant to South Dakota 191

Alcohol and Drug Abuse Research and Services
   Block Grant to Tennessee 191

Alcohol and Drug Abuse Research and Services
   Block Grant to Texas 193

Alcohol and Drug Abuse Research and Services
   Block Grant to Utah 191

Alcohol and Drug Abuse Research and Services
   Block Grant to Vermont 192

Alcohol and Drug Abuse Research and Services
   Block Grant to Virginia 192

Alcohol and Drug Abuse Research and Services
   Block Grant to Washington 193

Alcohol and Drug Abuse Research and Services
   Block Grant to West Virginia 192

Alcohol and Drug Abuse Research and Services
   Block Grant to Wisconsin 191

Alcohol and Drug Abuse Research and Services
   Block Grant to Wyoming 191

Alcohol Research Center Project Grants 75

Alcohol Research Programs 75

Drug Abuse Research Programs 75

General

Allergy, Immunology, and Transplantation Research 76

Anterior Segment Diseases Research 76

Arthritis, Musculoskeletal, and Skin Diseases Research . 76

Biological Models and Material Resources 76

Biological Research Related to Deafness and
   Communicative Disorders 77

Biomedical Research Support Grants 77

Biophysics and Physiological Sciences Project Grants ... 77

Blood Diseases and Resources Research 78

Cancer Biology Research 78

Cancer Cause and Prevention Research 78

Cancer Control 78

Cancer Control – Controlled Intervention 79

Cancer Control – Defined Populations Research 79

Cancer Control – Demonstration and Implementation
   Grants 79

Cancer Detection and Diagnosis Research 79

Cancer Treatment Research 80

Cellular and Molecular Basis of Disease Research 80

Centers for Disease Control – Research Program
   Grants 80

Clinical Research Related to Neurological Disorders .. 80

Diabetes, Endocrinology, and Metabolism Research ... 81

Digestive Diseases and Nutrition Research 81

Diseases of the Teeth and Supporting Tissue 81

Disorders of the Craniofacial Structure and Function
   and Behavioral Aspects of Dentistry 81

Genetics Research Project Grants 82

Heart and Vascular Diseases Research 82

Human Genome Research Project Grant 82

Immunization Research Project Grants 82

Kidney Diseases, Urology, and Hematology Research .. 83

Laboratory Animal Sciences Project Grants 83

Lung Diseases Research 83

Medical Treatment Effectiveness Research 83

Microbiology and Infectious Diseases Research 84

Pharmacological Sciences Project Grants 84

Physiological Sciences Project Grants 84

Primate Research Project Grants 84

Retinal and Choroidal Diseases Research 85

Strabismus, Amblyopia and Visual Processing 85

SCHOLARSHIPS, FELLOWSHIPS, AND GRANTS

Arts and Literature

Arts Administration Fellows Program 86

Distinguished Designer Fellowships 86

Literature Fellowships 86

Health Professions

Advanced Nurse Education 86

Allied Health Project Grants 87

Geriatrics Health Professions Training Grant 87

Graduate Programs in Health Administration 87

Grants for Graduate Training in Family Medicine 87

Grants for Residency Training in General Intern
   Medicine and/or General Pediatrics 88

Health Administration Graduate Traineeships 88

Indian Health Service Educational Loan Repayment .. 88

National Health Service Corps Loan Repayment
   Project Grant 88

National Health Service Corps Scholarship Program ... 89

Nurse Practitioner and Nurse Midwife Education
   and Traineeships 89

Nurse Training Improvement – Special Project Grants . 89

*Physician's Assistant Training Program Grants 89

Professional Nurse Traineeships 90

Public Health Traineeships 90

Scholarships for the Undergraduate Education of
   Professional Nurses 90

Humanities

Bicentennial Educational Grant Program 90

Bilingual Education Training Fellowships 91

Jacob K. Javits Fellowships 91

Library Career Fellowships 91

Library Career Training 92

Summer Seminars for College Teachers 92

Summer Seminars for School Teachers 92

Summer Stipend Project Grants 92

Undergraduate Foreign Language Programs 93

Younger Scholars Project Grants 93

International Understanding

Fulbright–Hays Doctoral Dissertation Research
   Abroad 93

Fulbright–Hays Faculty Research Abroad Training
   Grants 93

Fulbright–Hays Group Projects Abroad 94

Graduate Student Educational Exchange 94

National Resource Fellowships for Language
   and International Studies 94

Undergraduate International Studies Programs 94

University Professors and Research Scholars
   Educational Exchange 95

Medical Research

Aging Research Career Development Awards 95

Aging Research Clinical Investigator Development
   Award 95

Aging Research National Service Awards 95

Alcohol National Research Service Awards for
   Research Training 96

Alcohol Scientist Development Award for Clinicians .. 96

Allergy, Immunology, and Transplantation Research
   Career Development Awards 96

Allergy, Immunology, and Transplantation Clinical
   Investigator Development Award 96

Allergy, Immunology, and Transplantation National
   Research Service Awards 97

Anterior Segment Diseases Research Career
   Development Awards 97

Anterior Segment Diseases Clinical Investigator
   Development Award 97

Anterior Segment Diseases National Research
Service Awards 97

Arthritis, Musculoskeletal, and Skin Diseases Research
Career Development Awards 98

Arthritis, Musculoskeletal, and Skin Diseases Clinical
Investigator Development Award 98

Arthritis, Musculoskeletal, and Skin Diseases National
Research Service Awards 98

Biological Neurological Disorders Career
Development Awards 98

Biological Neurological Disorders Clinical Investigator
Development Awards 99

Biological Neurological Disorders National Research
Service Awards 99

Biomedical Research – NIH Research Awards 99

Biophysics National Research Service Award 99

Blood Diseases Career Development Awards 100

Blood Diseases Clinical Investigator Development
Awards 100

Blood Diseases National Research Service Awards 100

Cancer Research Manpower – Cancer Education Grants 100

Cancer Research Manpower – NRSA Individual
Fellowship Awards 101

Cancer Research Manpower – Cancer Education
Program for Short–Term Support 101

Cellular and Molecular Basis for Disease Research
Career Development Awards 101

Cellular and Molecular Basis for Disease Clinical
Investigator Development Award 101

Cellular and Molecular Basis for Disease National
Research Service Awards 102

Clinical Neurological Disorders Research Career
Development Awards 102

Clinical Neurological Disorders National Service Award 102

Diabetes, Endocrinology, and Metabolism Research
Career Development Awards 102

Diabetes, Endocrinology, and Metabolism Clinical
Investigator Development Award 103

Diabetes, Endocrinology, and Metabolism National
Research Service Awards 103

Digestive Diseases and Nutrition Career Development
Awards 103

Digestive Diseases and Nutrition Clinical Investigator
Development Award 103

Digestive Diseases and Nutrition National Research
Service Awards 104

Drug Abuse Clinician Development Award 104

Drug Abuse National Research Service Awards 104

Drug Abuse National Research Service Awards –
Institutional Grants 104

Drug Abuse National Research Service Awards –
Predoctoral Stipends 105

Drug Abuse National Research Service Awards –
Postdoctoral Stipends 105

Drug Abuse Research Scientist Award 105

Drug Abuse Scientist Development Award 105

Genetics Research Career Development Awards 106

Genetics Research Clinical Investigator
Development Award 106

Genetics Research National Research
Service Awards 106

Grants for Faculty Development in Family Medicine ... 106

Grants for Faculty Development in General Internal
Medicine and/or Pediatrics 107

Heart and Vascular Diseases Career
Development Awards 107

Heart and Vascular Diseases Clinical Investigator
Development Award 107

Heart and Vascular Diseases National Research
Service Awards 108

Intramural Research Training Award 108

Kidney Diseases, Urology, and Hematology Research
Career Development Awards 108

Kidney Diseases, Urology, and Hematology Clinical Investigator Development Award 108

Kidney Diseases, Urology, and Hematology National Research Service Awards 109

Laboratory Animal and Primate Research Fellowships . 109

Lung Diseases Research Career Development Awards . 109

Lung Diseases Clinical Investigator Development Awards 109

Lung Diseases National Research Service Awards 110

Mental Health National Research Service Awards 110

Mental Health National Research Service Awards for Research Training 110

Mental Health National Research Service Predoctoral Stipends 110

Mental Health National Research Service Postdoctoral Stipends 111

Mental Health Research Clinician Development Award 111

Mental Health Research Faculty Fellowships 111

Mental Health Research Scientist Development Award 111

Microbiology and Infectious Diseases Research Career Development Awards 112

Microbiology and Infectious Diseases Clinical Investigator Development Award 112

Microbiology and Infectious Diseases National Research Service Awards 112

National Research Services Awards 112

Neurological Disorders Clinical Investigator Development Awards 113

Post–Baccalaureate Faculty Fellowships 113

Pharmacological Sciences Research Career Development Awards 113

Pharmacological Sciences Clinical Investigator Development Award 113

Pharmacological Sciences National Research Service Awards 114

Physiological Sciences National Research Service Award 114

Population Research Career Development Awards 114

Population Research Clinical Investigator Development Award 114

Population Research National Research Service Awards 115

Research for Mothers and Children Clinical Investigator Development Award 115

Research for Mothers and Children National Research Service Awards 115

Retinal and Choroidal Diseases National Research Service Awards 116

Retinal and Choroidal Diseases Research Career Development Awards 116

Retinal and Choroidal Diseases Clinical Investigator Development Award 116

Research Scientist Development Award for Clinicians . 116

Senior International Fellowships 117

Special International Postdoctoral Research Program in AIDS 117

Minority and Disadvantaged

Fellowships for Native Americans 117

Financial Assistance for Disadvantaged Health Professions Students 118

Health Careers Opportunity Program 118

Legal Training for the Disadvantaged 118

*Migrant Education College Assistance Program 118

Minority Access to Research Careers 119

Minority Honors Training and Industrial Assistance Programs 119

Minority Participation in Graduate Education 119

Minority Research and Teaching Program Grants 119

Minority Science Improvement 120

Nursing Education Opportunities for Individuals
from Disadvantaged Backgrounds 117

Patricia Roberts Harris Fellowships 120

Pre-Freshman Enrichment Project Grants 120

Ronald E. McNair Post-Baccalaureate Achievement
Awards 121

Scholarships for Students of Exceptional
Financial Need 121

Supplemental Educational Opportunity Grants 121

Science Research

Applied Toxicological Research and Testing –
Academic Awards 121

Applied Toxicological Research and Testing Career
Development Awards 122

Applied Toxicological Research and Testing Mid-Career
Development Awards 122

Applied Toxicological Research and Testing Physician –
Scientist Awards 122

Biological Response to Environmental Health Hazards
Academic Awards 122

Biological Response to Environmental Health Hazards
Research Career Development Awards 123

Biological Response to Environmental Health Hazards
Mid-Career Development Awards 123

Biological Response to Environmental Health Hazards
Physician-Scientist Awards 123

Environmental Health Hazards Research Career
Development Award 123

Environmental Health Hazards Mid-Career
Development Award 124

Environmental Health Hazards Physician-Scientist
Awards 124

Graduate Research Fellowships 124

Science and Engineering Research Semester 124

Social Services

Community Development Work-Study Program
Project Grants 125

Emergency Management Institute 125

National Fire Academy Training Assistance 125

National Fire Academy Educational Program 125

General

Christa McAuliffe Fellowships 126

*Criminal Justice Discretionary Grant Program 126

Criminal Justice Research and Development
Fellowships 126

Graduate Assistance in Areas of National Need 126

Grants for Mining and Mineral Resources 127

Harry S. Truman Scholarship Program 127

National Institute on Disability and Rehabilitation
Research Fellowships 127

National Institute of Justice Visiting Fellowships 127

Pell Grant Program 128

State Marine Schools 128

U.S. Merchant Marine Academy 128

Urban Mass Transportation Training Grants 128

Veterans Education Outreach Program 129

SCIENCE RESEARCH

Energy

Applied Toxicological Research and Testing Research Grants 133

Applied Toxicological Research and Testing Small Business Project Grants 133

Applied Toxicological Research and Testing Small Instrumentation Grants 134

Biometry and Risk Estimation Academic Awards 134

Biometry and Risk Estimation Career Development Awards 134

Biometry and Risk Estimation Mid–Career Development Awards 134

Biometry and Risk Estimation Physician–Scientist Awards 135

Biometry and Risk Estimation Research Grants 135

Biometry and Risk Estimation Small Instrumentation Grants 135

Clean Coal Scientific Research Technology Program for Alabama 194

Clean Coal Scientific Research Technology Program for Alaska 194

Clean Coal Scientific Research Technology Program for Arizona 194

Clean Coal Scientific Research Technology Program for Arkansas 194

Clean Coal Scientific Research Technology Program for California 195

Clean Coal Scientific Research Technology Program for Colorado 195

Clean Coal Scientific Research Technology Program for Connecticut 195

Clean Coal Scientific Research Technology Program for Delaware 195

Clean Coal Scientific Research Technology Program for Florida 196

Clean Coal Scientific Research Technology Program for Georgia 196

Clean Coal Scientific Research Technology Program for Hawaii 196

Clean Coal Scientific Research Technology Program for Idaho 196

Clean Coal Scientific Research Technology Program for Illinois 197

Clean Coal Scientific Research Technology Program for Indiana 197

Clean Coal Scientific Research Technology Program for Iowa 197

Clean Coal Scientific Research Technology Program for Kansas 197

Clean Coal Scientific Research Technology Program for Kentucky 198

Clean Coal Scientific Research Technology Program for Louisiana 198

Clean Coal Scientific Research Technology Program for Maine 198

Clean Coal Scientific Research Technology Program for Maryland 198

Clean Coal Scientific Research Technology Program for Massachusetts 199

Clean Coal Scientific Research Technology Program for Michigan 199

Clean Coal Scientific Research Technology Program for Minnesota 199

Clean Coal Scientific Research Technology Program for Mississippi 199

Clean Coal Scientific Research Technology Program for Missouri 200

Clean Coal Scientific Research Technology Program for Montana 200

Clean Coal Scientific Research Technology Program for Nebraska 200

Clean Coal Scientific Research Technology Program for Nevada 200

Clean Coal Scientific Research Technology Program
for New Hampshire 201

Clean Coal Scientific Research Technology Program
for New Jersey 201

Clean Coal Scienctific Research Technology Program
for New Mexico 201

Clean Coal Scientific Research Technology Program
for New York 201

Clean Coal Scientific Research Technology Program
for North Carolina 202

Clean Coal Scientific Research Technology Program
for North Dakota 202

Clean Coal Scientific Research Technology Program
for Ohio 202

Clean Coal Scientific Research Technology Program
for Oklahoma 202

Clean Coal Scientific Research Technology Program
for Oregon 203

Clean Coal Scientific Research Technology Program
for Pennsylvania 203

Clean Coal Scientific Research Technology Program
for Rhode Island 203

Clean Coal Scientific Research Technology Program
for South Carolina 203

Clean Coal Scientific Research Technology Program
for South Dakota 204

Clean Coal Scientific Research Technology Program
for Tennessee 204

Clean Coal Scientific Research Technology Program
for Texas 204

Clean Coal Scientific Research Technology Program
for Utah 204

Clean Coal Scientific Research Technology Program
for Vermont 205

Clean Coal Scientific Research Technology Program
for Virginia 205

Clean Coal Scientific Research Technology Program
for Washington 205

Clean Coal Scientific Research Technology Program
for West Virginia 205

Clean Coal Scientific Research Technology Program
for Wisconsin 206

Clean Coal Scientific Research Technology Program
for Wyoming 206

Conservation Research and Development 130

Energy and Field Operations Research in Energy and
Related Fields 130

*Energy Policy, Planning, and Development
Project Grants 130

Energy–Related Inventions Project Grants 131

Fossil Energy Research and Development
Project Grants 131

Industrial Energy Conservation Project Grants 131

International Affairs and Energy Emergencies 131

Minority Educational Institution Research Travel Fund   132

*Nuclear Energy Policy, Planning, and Development .. 132

*Nuclear Energy Process and Safety Information
Project Grants 132

Renewable Energy Research and Development 132

University Coal Research 133

University–Laboratory Cooperative Program 133

Minority Development

Minority Educational Institution Assistance 135

Research Initiation and Improvement 136

Undergraduate Science, Mathematics, and Engineering
Career Access Opportunities 136

Undergraduate Science, Mathematics, and Engineering
Model Projects 136

Young Scholars Project Grants 136

Social Sciences

Behavioral Science Project Grants 137

Biometry and Risk Estimation Small Business
Project Grants 137

Population Research 137

Social Sciences Project Grants 137

Socioeconomic and Demographic Research
Project Grants 138

General

Atmospheric Sciences Project Grants 138

Biological Science Project Grants 138

Computer and Information Science and Engineering .. 138

Earth Sciences Project Grants 139

Engineering Grants 139

Mathematical and Physical Sciences Research Grants .. 139

Ocean Sciences Project Grants 139

Polar Programs Project Grants 140

Undergraduate Science, Mathematics, and
Engineering Undergraduate Faculty Enhancement ... 140

Undergraduate Science, Mathematics, and Engineering
Instrumentation And Laboratory Improvement 140

SOCIAL SERVICES

Aged

Capital Assistance for Elderly and Handicapped Persons 141

*Foster Grandparent Program Project Grants 141

*Retired Senior Volunteer Program 141

*Senior Community Service Employment Program 141

*Senior Companion Program 142

*Special Programs for the Aging 142

Business Development

Assistance Payments Research Project Grants 142

Health Care Financing Research Project Grants 142

Social Security Research and Demonstration
Project Grants 143

Children

Abandoned Infants Project Grants 143

*Adolescent Family Life Demonstration Project Grants 143

Adoption Opportunities Project Grants 143

*Appalachian Child Development 144

*Child Abuse and Neglect Discretionary Activities 144

Child Support Enforcement Research Project Grants .. 144

Child Welfare Research and Demonstration
Project Grants 144

Child Welfare Services Training Grants 145

*Comprehensive Child Development Centers 145

Drug Abuse Prevention and Education for Runaway
and Homeless Youth 145

Missing Children's Assistance 145

Runaway and Homeless Youth Project Grants 146

Transitional Living for Runaway and Homeless
Youth Project Grants 146

Crime

*Crime Victim Assistance Discretionary Grants 146

Justice Research and Development Project Grants 146

Juvenile Gangs and Drug Abuse and Drug Trafficking . 147

Juvenile Justice and Delinquency Prevention
Project Grants 147

National Institute for Juvenile Justice and Delinquency
Prevention 147

Housing

*Fair Housing Education Initiatives Program 147

*Fair Housing Private Enforcement Initiative Program . 148

Housing Counseling Assistance Program Project
Grants 148

Lower Income Housing Assistance Program 148

*Nehemiah Housing Opportunity Grant Program 148

Rehabilitation Mortgage Insurance 149

*Supplemental Assistance for Facilities to Assist the
Homeless 149

*Supportive Housing Demonstration Program
Project Grants 149

Employment Services and Job Training Pilot
and Demonstration Programs 149

Employment and Training Research and Development
Projects 150

*Migrant and Seasonal Farmworkers Project Grant 150

*Veterans Employment Program 150

Prisons

Corrections Research, Evaluation and Policy
Formation 150

Corrections – Technical Assistance Clearinghouse 151

Corrections Training and Staff Development 151

*Prison Capacity Discretionary Project Grants 151

Substance Abuse

Drug Abuse Prevention and Education Relating
to Youth Gangs 151

*Drug Alliance Project Grants 152

Communications Program Aimed Toward the
Prevention of Alcohol And Other Drug Problems ... 152

*Drug Control and System Improvement 152

*Employee Assistance Program for Drug
and Alcohol Abuse 152

General

Airport Improvement Program 153

*Boating Safety Financial Assistance 153

*Centers for Independent Living 153

*Community–Based Anti–Arson Program 153

Cuban and Haitian Resettlement Program 154

Disaster Assistance Project Grants and Payments 154

*Family Violence Prevention and Services
Discretionary Grants 154

General Research and Technology Activity 154

Job Training Partnership for Alabama 207

Job Training Partnership for Alaska 207

Job Training Partnership for Arizona 207

Job Training Partnership for Arkansas 207

Job Training Partnership for California 208

Job Training Partnership for Colorado 208

Job Training Partnership for Connecticut 208

Job Training Partnership for Delaware 208

Job Training Partnership for Florida 209

Job Training Partnership for Georgia 209

Job Training Partnership for Hawaii 209

Job Training Partnership for Idaho 209

Job Training Partnership for Illinois 210

Job Training Partnership for Indiana 210

Job Training Partnership for Iowa 210

Job Training Partnership for Kansas 210

Job Training Partnership for Kentucky 211

Job Training Partnership for Louisiana 211

Job Training Partnership for Maine 211

Job Training Partnership for Maryland 211

Job Training Partnership for Massachusetts 212

Job Training Partnership for Michigan 212

Job Training Partnership for Minnesota 212

Job Training Partnership for Mississippi 212

Job Training Partnership for Missouri 213

Job Training Partnership for Montana 213

Job Training Partnership for Nebraska 213

Job Training Partnership for Nevada 213

Job Training Partnership for New Hampshire 214

Job Training Partnership for New Jersey 214

Job Training Partnership for New Mexico 214

Job Training Partnership for New York 214

Job Training Partnership for North Carolina 215

Job Training Partnership for North Dakota 215

Job Training Partnership for Ohio 215

Job Training Partnership for Oklahoma 215

Job Training Partnership for Oregon 216

Job Training Partnership for Pennsylvania 216

Job Training Partnership for Rhode Island 216

Job Training Partnership for South Carolina 216

Job Training Partnership for South Dakota 217

Job Training Partnership for Tennessee 217

Job Training Partnership for Texas 217

Job Training Partnership for Utah 217

Job Training Partnership for Vermont 218

Job Training Partnership for Virginia 218

Job Training Partnership for Washington 218

Job Training Partnership for West Virginia 218

Job Training Partnership for Wisconsin 219

Job Training Partnership for Wyoming 219

*Minigrant Program 155

Occupational Health and Safety Project Grants 155

Services Delivery Improvement Research Grants for
    Family Planning 155

Social Services Research and Demonstration
    Project Grants 155

*Student Community Service Program 156

*Technical Assistance Program 156

*Volunter Demonstration Program Project Grants 156

Bibliography

Annual Register of Grant Support: A Directory of Funding Sources, 23rd edition, 1990, Wilmette, Illinois: National Register Publishing Co., Macmillan Directory Division, 1989.

Catalog of Federal Domestic Assistance, Washington, D.C., Government Printing Office, annual with supplementary updates; order from Superintendent of Documents, Washington, D.C. 20402.

Commerce Business Daily, five times a week, Washington, D.C., U.S. Government Printing Office order from Superintendent of Documents, Washington, D.C. 20402.

Federal Register, five times a week, Washington, D.C., U.S. Government Printing Office; order from Superintendent of Documents, Washington D.C. 20402.

Lesko, Matthew, *Getting Yours: The Complete Guide to Government Money*, 3rd edition, New York, Penguin Books, 1978.

Federal Grants & Contracts Weekly, once a week; order from Capital Publications, Alexandria, Virginia 22313.